What's the Worst Thing You

Can Do to Shakespeare?

D1467794

WHAT'S THE WORST THING YOU CAN DO TO SHAKESPEARE?

Richard Burt / Julian Yates

September 2013

Dear Kathy,

Bits of this are actually not bad! Thanks for a bit of advice at the beginning.

Hope all is well.

As ever,

Julian

palgrave
macmillan

An earlier version of Chapter 1 appeared as "What's the Worst Thing You Can Do to Shakespeare," *Renaissance Drama*, vol. 40, ed. William N. West (Evanston: Northwestern University Press, 2012), 71–89.

First published in 2013 by PALGRAVE MACMILLAN® in the United States—a division of St. Martin's Press LLC, 175 Fifth Avenue, New York, NY 10010.

Where this book is distributed in the UK, Europe and the rest of the world, this is by Palgrave Macmillan, a division of Macmillan Publishers Limited, registered in England, company number 785998, of Houndmills, Basingstoke, Hampshire RG21 6XS.

Palgrave Macmillan is the global academic imprint of the above companies and has companies and representatives throughout the world.

Palgrave® and Macmillan® are registered trademarks in the United States, the United Kingdom, Europe and other countries.

ISBN: 978-1-137-27048-1 (hc)
ISBN: 978-1-137-27049-8 (pbk)

Library of Congress Cataloging-in-Publication Data

Burt, Richard, 1954-
    What's the worst thing you can do to Shakespeare? / by Richard Burt and Julian Yates.
      pages cm.
    ISBN 978–1–137–27048–1 (hardback)
    1. Shakespeare, William, 1564–1616—Criticism and interpretation. 2. Deconstruction. 3. Shakespeare, William, 1564–1616—Influence. 4. Culture and globalization. I. Yates, Julian. II. Title.

    PR2976.B795 2013
    822.3'3—dc23   2013002511

A catalogue record of the book is available from the British Library.

Design by Scribe Inc.

First edition: July 2013

10 9 8 7 6 5 4 3 2 1

From Richard to Elizabeth and Wiley

From Julian to David and Hilary

Contents

ILLUSTRATIONS

ACKNOWLEDGMENTS[1]

If acknowledgments had titles, this coauthor would call these acknowledgments "Disclosure Acts." Not full disclosure, mind you, because the very notion of there being such a thing as "full" disclosure is a notion that both coauthors would call into question. "Disclosure Acts," then, because collaboration may offer, and in our case has offered, the possibility of creating a wonderfully messy intellectual commons within the enclosures of intellectual property rights established by our proper names and the legalities of copyright. Witness the paratexts of this book in your hands that refer to contracts we signed and countersigned. Reading paratexts is a threshold experience, of course, and as such serves as a borderless border, irreducible to any geopolitical residency or transatlantic migrations from the United Kingdom to California and from California to the East Coast of the United States. This coauthor, who shall remain anonymous, should like to thank his coauthor for providing an amazing, unprecedented experience of thinking at distances of uncertain proximity.

Having met only once in person, the coauthors began talking on the telephone about writings one or both had found to be worth discussing. They have been doing so for some three years. About a year and a half before the manuscript of this book was delivered to Palgrave Macmillan, the coauthors began cowriting an essay at what may only be characterized as telepathic speed. They realized that they had a book to cowrite, and so they did, by telephone, answering machines, email, and once in person just two months before the manuscript was finished. This anonymous coauthor feels compelled to write that he felt new kinds of growth pains arising from resistances from an unidentifiable unconscious that arose in the process—do you even own your own unconscious? "That part you wrote." "Yeah?" "I see why you/I needed to write it, but now I hope you see that

---

1. In the course of composing these acknowledgments, the coauthor of this book sent his fellow coauthor a draft of the words that appear here. After reading them with the usual care I reserve for such missives, it seemed to me that my substantial revisions would arrive too late to be included and so should be condensed and appended instead in the form of a footnote. I wish to declare a paratextual state of exception to the tone of much that appears in these acknowledgments. Indeed, I feel obliged to write that I revised the text but that those revisions have not been included. I shall not say how extensively I did so. I shall not say whether this note was revised or if it even was actually written by me, as my coauthor will have been the last to lay eyes on it. (To be sure, neither of us will know for certain that we will have had the last word.) All credit for anything worthy in this book should, of course, be credited to both authors. However, I think it is only fair to say, in dis/closing, that blame for any remaining errors or other faults in the book should be assigned exclusively to my coauthor, as he shall have had the very last word, at least as far as I know. Thank you.

it has to be cut." "Ok. Maybe some of it can go in a note." If growth pains are usually intense, this coauthor has always had a surgeon there capable of operating without the need for an anesthesiologist. Indeed, this coauthor has felt on numerous occasions that the surgeon was also a pharmacist, a dispenser of writing drugs of the highest order, totally uncut. Thanks to his coauthor/doctor's careful supervision, this coauthor was able to maintain the manic highs of writing experienced when you make a new connection, which were only multiplied, intensified, and extended by the always unexpected, surprising, and spirited exchanges we had. I confess I still have no idea how this could possibly have happened. But it did, again and again.

Although this publication is the most "emergent" work this coauthor has ever cowritten, he still feels compelled to acknowledge and disclose to you that one crucially important part of the book was his coauthor's idea. He came up with the brilliant title of the book. The title is his. It is not mine. Truly. Let me say it again. It is his title and his alone. My modest contribution was merely to persuade our editor, the wonderful Brigitte Shull, to have Palgrave Macmillan allow us to use the title of the book. I salute my coauthor. It has been a joy and an honor to talk/write a book that we both wrote entirely together (except for the title).

Both coauthors wish to thank the Medieval and Renaissance Center at NYU, the Graduate Student Colloquium of Tufts University, and the Japanese Shakespeare Forum for providing stimulating audiences for us to present parts of the book to (in person and in spirit). Thanks, hugs, and kisses are due to our two anonymous readers for Palgrave Macmillan; William N. West; John Archer; Claire Burt; Edward Larkin; Judith Haber; Kate Mesler; Martha Rust; Malini Schueler; Minami, Ryuta; Yoshihara, Yukari; Lei, Bi-qi Beatrice; Yang, Lingui Gary; Robert Ray; Stephen Booth; Al Braunmuller; and Susan Goodman.

Lastly we would each like to thank our wife or partner and our families for their love, patience, forbearance, and support.

CHAPTER 1

WHAT'S THE WORST THING YOU CAN DO TO SHAKESPEARE?

It is yours to reade him. And there we hope, to your divers capacities, you will finde enough, both to draw, and hold you: for his wit can no more lie hid, then it could be lost. Reade him, therefore; and againe, and againe: And if then you doe not like him, surely you are in some manifest danger, not to vnderstand him. And so we leaue you to other of his Friends, whom if you need, can bee your guides: if you neede them not, you can leade your selues, and others. And such Readers we wish him.

—John Heminge and Henrie Condell

To the great Variety of Readers

—The First Folio (1623)[1]

BEFORE, OR PERHAPS AFTER, ALL, THE WORST thing you can do to Shakespeare is not to read him. Here, at the *envoi cum* media launch that was the First Folio, John Heminge and Henrie Condell offer an economy of reading that threatens the putative reader/buyer with the "manifest danger" that "unreadability" might conjure. This rhetorical unreadability that reflects on you stands surety against a literal, prosaic nonreading of the book that would render it a media nonevent. Against this eventuality, Heminge and Condell recruit the "great variety of read-ers," "from the most able" "to him that can but spell." For it is upon our "capaci-ties" (heads and purses) that the "fate of Bookes depends." As "readers," then, we are recruited to become the biocultural "wetware," the life-in-death preservers, that this book and the defunct "Shakespeare" require to prosper, to go mobile, to survive, to *sur-vivre*—living on, in, with, and through our successive acts.[2] We become, in effect, the biosemiotic motor that enables "Shakespeare" to go viral, and thereby we make it possible for certain kinds of critical operations to count institutionally as doing something (worth doing).

Our aim in this book is to open a space to think the unreadability Heminge and Condell deploy as a phenomenon, a specter, that has been haunting Renaissance and Shakespeare studies for some time now—and that has been conscripted to do all sorts of work, as the Folio attests. We would like to pick up their modeling of readers as "wetware," the living component to media platforms, and think about what the labor of (not) reading entails.[3] Their sales pitch discloses the linkages between text, media, and reader that constitute the phenomenon that was, is, and will be "Shakespeare," reorienting us from the sense that a "play" or "plays" exist in the world as some self-identical entity, to the plays as a mobile, conflicting, conflicted, and partially time-bound set of practices. What happens then, we ask, if we proceed on the assumption that historical fields of study such as "Shakespeare" or "Renaissance drama" as well as school curricula, professional Shakespeare theaters, the film industry, and media libraries (on and offline) refer not to a series of agreed-upon texts or performances but instead, as Heminge and Condell imply, a series of differently distributed fetish communities, each of which tunes itself to the shifting auratics of its chosen ritual objects as they are variously mediated—from manuscript to quarto to folio, on and off and back to the stage, the movie theater, and the home entertainment system—the ontology of the thing we study waxing and waning, constantly picking up and dropping actants as it goes?[4] The distribution of readers into different fields of study (performance, theater history, criticism, theater production, and so on) comes to constitute not a happy holism but a series of discontinuous and only sometimes intersecting conversations or crowds that converge on variously mediatized forms of Shakespearean texts. The "Shakespeare industry," so it turns out, refers not merely to an elaborated infrastructure but to the industry of so very many readers and purveyors, whose vital juices the Bard requires to keep on flowing.

In this model, the labor of all such fetishists (ourselves included) stands in reciprocal relation to the past labors of reading, living, and dying that our work posits as "past." It is by our labors that readings and texts continue to circulate and continue also to recruit readers or readers become scrollers or whatever word issues forth from the latest medium in order to designate the activity of its users.[5] So what, we ask, would it mean to deactivate this reciprocity and dwell within the figural or stunt unreadability that Heminge and Condell deploy in order to fund their own launch of the First Folio as a facsimile of an archive, a Shakespearean impression that, dear reader, it is for us to recognize? What would it entail to opt out and do no "work" today but instead to allow the machine to idle and to allow the specter of not reading, of unreadability, to ramify?

By posing unreadability as a question we seek to interrupt the prevailing economies for managing the relation between reading and not reading in our various critical acts and so impede a return to business as usual. The structure of a question pertains for unreadability does not exist per se as a positivity but only as a shifting, partial effect of the process of reading itself. It might be said to unfold at the junctures or limits, as they are drawn, between reaction and response, the dead and the living, the automaticity of the machine and the immanence of the organism, and to resist the ontologizing of those limits. We regard unreadability as the uninvited guest to the surplus of "life" certain texts and authors are granted by their translation to successive media platforms and their sponsorship by such a great variety of readers. In this sense, the proliferation of textual aids that offer to pull you back up the "cliff" or "spark" life in some dead text constitutes a community of friendly readers become textual backups to see off the specter of literal not reading.

In this first chapter, we begin by offering a stenographic rendering of what we take to be some of the most brilliant contributions to the "New Textualism" and "history of the book," drawing attention to their sometimes delirious use of the rhetoric of unreadability. We then rewind the clock to 1983, as the soon-to-end Cold War raised increasingly apocalyptic tones in literary theory and "nuclear criticism," to stare the "manifest danger" of Shakespeare's irrelevance and unreadability in the face. Along the way we develop a model of how unreadability functions as a crux or crossroads between text and media, concluding with an air raid warning that calls for us all to leave our shelters, and with them the oddly regular announcements of critical apocalypse, and attempt to think unreadability. The book that follows can hardly be said to meet these burdens or to exhaust the endeavor. And we offer its chapters to you as invitations to play out the questions we pose according to your particular interests, skills, and requirements. Please think of this book as an attempt to open the question.

CAUTION! "MEDIA SPECIFICITY" DETECTED. "YOUR READING" WILL ABORT IN THREE, TWO, ONE . . .

In the First Folio, Heminge and Condell's rhetorical conversion of literal non-reading into rhetorical unreadability posits a conversion that keys unreadability to the success or failure of different media platforms. That is to say, competing models for managing, sorting, and organizing different iterations of texts, by which their anteriority and referentiality are produced, tend to rely on the specter of a breakdown to reading, a stalling or interruption. Media manifests in order to interrupt the process. The scene in which most of us encounter this order of stunt or figural unreadability might be the association of approaches to Renaissance drama that corral themselves within the "history of the book." Typically, they deploy media specificity to interrupt a reading process that they take to be routinized or reductive. Conjuring the book's presence as *thing*, "unediting" exposes your reading to the vast array of other *historical*—which is to say nothing more than *media-specific*—versions, inducing vertigo to a reading that detaches readers from their textual moorings. The salutary effect of this media interruption tends to be that every aspect of the book becomes readable, including page layout, fonts, lettering, paper, binding, bibliographic codes, marginalia, paratexts, wormholes, animal hairs and animal remains (paper), plant remains (paper), mineral remains (ink), the printer's urine, et cetera. What gives us pause, however, is the way the media interruption, once deployed, becomes the occasion for an altered regime of description, merely, installing another, seemingly less problematic process of reading that accounts for the media specificity.[6]

The quasi-messianic or apocalyptic coming or advent of the book as *thing* serves, in essence, as the staging ground for this or that narrative of "reading"-become-book use that can then serve as an input to yet more "readers" and the marks they leave in the margins of their books or the marks that once upon a time they recognized as meaningful but you've been writing off. Even in its ostensibly antiredemptive guises, such as when the butt of the reading is some "Holy Cow!" ideologeme of the field ("Shakespeare," the First Folio, anthropocentrism), which we discover is the product of an immanent set of practices (compositor error or the like), the redemptive cast migrates to the immanent sanctity of labor itself.[7] Such readings tend then to eventalize the performances of the critic, enabling us to point to our labors of reading as somehow proof of life, our lives, your life, their lives as lived—"life" having become some universal abstract exchange value—the good(s). Media interruption serves as little more than a blanking out of unreadability, then, installing the figure of not reading as a crossroads or crux, which it then cuts as it passes back to producing a reading. Through a very curious set of operations, the media interruption flickers in out of being to become the ground, say, for a recoverable materiality of a past world of book-use or some other social phenomenon, way of being, or practice that manifests as if a referent. Close reading (itself always an exercise in reading and not reading) is displaced by the management of the archive, the shuffling, sorting, and necessarily the reduction of an ever proliferating array of facsimiles or backups to whatever it was exactly that "Shakespeare" is said to have penned.

REBOOT: READING WILL RESUME IN THREE, TWO, ONE . . .

Rewind to Randall McCleod's ph/fantastic essay "Un '*Editing*' Shak-speare" (1982), and you will see what we mean.[8] McCleod examines a posthumously published (and improperly edited, according to him) poem written by John Keats, "On Sitting Down to Read King Lear Once Again." He points out that Keats wrote his poem in a portable facsimile edition of the First Folio (1804), perhaps the first unedited edition of Shakespeare since it had no notes or other textual apparatus. In a letter addressed to his brothers dated Friday, January 23, 1818, Keats transcribes his poem but drops the word *read*: "On Sitting Down to Read *King Lear* Once Again" becomes "On Sitting Down to *King Lear* Again." A narrative of Keats's composition exists in the letters, but the media event of the facsimile edition disrupts this narrative for McCleod, leading him to posit a different narrative for the poem. He points out that the title page of the book may also be part of the title of Keats's poem that he relates to Keats's signature written on the title page just above "Mr. William Shakespeare's" and dated 1817 (34). McCleod reads the signature not as a sign of Keats's ownership of the book but as his will, his "signing over" his copy to Fanny Brawne. McCleod criticizes editors of Keats's poem for ignoring the facsimile as icon, for following a "de-iconizing process of editorial transmission" (36). By contrast, McCleod resocializes the poem by unediting it, putting it back into the context of its "material" inscriptions and transcriptions. Yet McCleod's notion of unediting the social text depends on his turning facsimiles, reproduced in his essay sometimes as small parts of pages, sometimes of full pages of Keats's facsimile, into a blocking of one narrative in order to produce another narrative about the text in the age of "*photo*facsimiles" (37). The revelation of an earlier, Keatsian media interruption serves to naturalize another—McCleod's own use of *photo*facsimiles.

If Keats disappears the word *read* from his poem, McCleod disappears the question of how to read that elision and its dependence on both a facsimile of Keats's poem and a quotation from Keats's letter. The typography of McCleod's neologism is itself a symptomatic distraction: "un *Editing*" severs the *un* by a different font, spacing, and quotation marks from the capitalized and italicized *Editing*, but the title is then subject to maiming or reforming in the table of contents of the journal that published it and subsequent citations. Indeed, "un *Editing*," which refuses the irruption of white space, may be read as a condensed autoimmunizing antiaporia. But in the wake of McCleod's non/reading of what he dubs "Keatspeare," readers and editors do not know where to begin reading or editing—with print or after the handwritten date? Nor do we know where or when to stop reading. The poem appears on the same page that ends *Hamlet* (*FINIS*)—it erupts between plays. And precisely because Keats's 1804 facsimile has not been edited, the blank space on the page usually taken up by notes becomes writeable for a poem that is at the same time not publishable as a literary de/composition. Keats's poem becomes excessively literary, therefore, as its position within the facsimile edition renders its composition unnarratable, unreadable, and inedi/ta/ble—both "yum!" and "yuck!" How do we handle such irreducible "*thisness*"? Reduce the complexity of the fac/faux/simile and you lose everything. Try selling that?

In our view, the virtuoso McCleod pulls off a self-disappearing act even before he goes missing in the bibliographies of more recent scholars who clearly know and are influenced by his work: his essay goes missing because it quite corrosively exposes editing to a crisis by showing that the apparent difference between "editing" and "un *Editing*" cannot be kept in place by typography. Because Keats turns his Shakespeare facsimile into writing paper for his poems, composed in unpublished and unpublishable paratextual spaces, the resulting poem thus requires transcription and "facsimilation" in order to be assimilated into an edi/ta/ble narrative form—which is what McCleod does. And this "imagetexting" or what we will name in subsequent chapters "Bardoclash" derails any attempt to narrate and recover an uncorrupted, unedited "material" text written by Keats. All encryption models of the social text are wildly exceeded by the posthumographic status of "Keatspeare" for which McCleod and his readers serve as animating wetware, rendering the textual remains lively once more.

FAC/FAUX/SIMILES OF (NOT) READING

Fast-forward to Zachary Lesser and Peter Stallybrass's magisterial essay "The First Literary *Hamlet* and the Commonplacing of Professional Plays."[9] Lesser and Stallybrass show that the first quarto of *Hamlet* (Q1; 1603) is, much like the second quarto (Q2; 1604–5), a literary text and not the record of a theatrical performance it is generally assumed to be. By "literary" they mean geared to a world of scholar-readers on the lookout for *sententiae*—a model of the "literary" that emerges out of what represents an emerging community of readerly interest.

At the end of the essay, there appears an "Authors' Correction" page. "One play," it seems, "was inadvertently omitted from Table 1," and Lesser and

Stallybrass note that "we should have included this edition in our list." These things, it must be said, happen. Given all that they have done, who really could point a finger? It seems fair to note, however, that their brief bibliographical and unpaginated paratext serves to fund a belief that the archive may be positivized, errors corrected, and what went missing restored, if not joined. The correction page stands in for all the plays that may have existed but that are lost to record. It creates the sense of fullness. Our aim is not necessarily to question their essay's modeling of a particular historical practice of (not) reading *Hamlet* (scrolling through the text looking for sententiae) so much as to call attention to a lingering symptom of the serious (and totally infectious) case of archive fever that their essay contracts. In a joyful moment, this delirium takes us shopping. We pause with Lesser and Stallybrass to hallucinate the positivity of the first and second *Hamlet* quartos into a scene of buying. We enter Nicholas Ling's shop (*Ding*-a-Ling) in order to explain why he might have produced two very similar quartos instead of what always seemed like two very different quartos (and which therefore needed less explaining).[10]

Lesser and Stallybrass explain the apparent marketing blunder by imagining the scene:

> Ling's title pages have it both ways. A book buyer with enough interest in *Hamlet* to pay close attention will be alerted to the newer edition's superiority over the old—which, after all, such an interested reader could already have bought in 1603. This reader will thus be urged to buy the new version (as well). A more casual browser, on the other hand, might miss the distinction altogether, giving Ling a chance to sell off copies of Q1 (perhaps even at a discount) while still asserting the "new and improved" status of Q2. Ling's title page for Q2 thus seems an ideal solution to a particular, local problem: how should a publisher market a new version of a text he had printed only a year earlier, enticing customers to buy the new edition without driving them away from the old?[11]

The archive hallucinated here as a scene of book browsing provides a mirror image of the New Historicist anecdote. Instead of being derived from fiction in the archive, the archive itself is fictionalized, converted into a series of calculations the reader with "enough interest" will get back by converting his attentive reading into comparison shopping.

The mise-en-scène works, and artfully so. It's a gorgeously filmic moment that unfolds just on the edges of their sentences, as we are invited to glimpse at the past from out of the corner of an eye. But these aesthetic judgments disclose the way the essay itself serves as facsimile or backup, a sorting of textual data so as to summon up a past via the very great and much-appreciated labor qua fetish work that Lesser and Stallybrass do but readers *then* did not. Lesser and Stallybrass produce their facsimile in order to narrativize the data of what is said to happen in textual production; that is, they posit/conjure/hallucinate a scholarly community of readers in Renaissance London who read and write the same way they do without ever having done so—the actual labor of reading then and now differs. The vast labor entailed to produce their essay stands in reciprocal relation to the much different processes of reading or book use that they take to be and so constitute as a historical phenomenon. Q1 and Q2 of *Hamlet* are therefore re/constructed as a single and wholly reliable media platform for the delivery of sententiae. Value / use value for scholars in their imagined community is located less in the commonplace books and the literary tradition they are said to create than in the cut-and-paste operations that constitute them. The play itself—or at least the texts of Q1 and Q2 of *Hamlet*—may safely be forgotten: Lesser and Stallybrass don't have to read *Hamlet* (and neither do we), because its first readers didn't either. No one, it seems, read *Hamlet*. And in not reading the play, we come strangely to resemble Polonius as he replays himself replaying the contents of his commonplace book in Act 1, scene 3, almost making Laertes miss the boat he's been urging him to board. What a while ago Stephen Greenblatt called "the touch of the real" was, so we now discover, not only a desire for the referent, but always already the "touched of the real," a happy hallucination of the referent and the past through the drug of writing seemingly purified through the buffer of facsimiles.[12]

ENTER THOMAS MIDDLETON: BIO/ BIBLIOGRAPHY AS FAC/FAUX/SIMILE

Thus far we have treated two exemplary instances of media interruption in the hands of some of its most deft rhetoricians. We turn now to the labor of editing itself—understood, following Heminge and Condell, as a moment of recruitment, a moment at which it may be possible, by producing the correct bio/ bibliographical object, to orchestrate an "event" that alters the gravitation of the field. What does it take, for example, to launch an ideological counterweight to what Michael Bristol calls "big-time Shakespeare?"[13] How do you create a fetish object that might compete, that might deliver on the threat of a literal nonreading of Shakespeare by recruiting readers to bear someone else? It takes perhaps, at very least, the double whammy of *Thomas Middleton: The Collected Works* (2007) and *Thomas Middleton and Early Modern Textual Culture* (2007) and the addition, now, of *The Oxford Handbook of Thomas Middleton* (2012).[14] Tellingly, the editors inform readers that these editions are both like and unlike so-called complete or collected works of Shakespeare. A game is being played, a reorientation effected. The *Collected Works* begins by leveling the score and assuming the mantle: "Thomas Middleton and William Shakespeare were the only writers of the English Renaissance who created masterpieces in four major dramatic genres: comedy, history, tragedy, and tragic-comedy."[15] "Middleton was the only playwright trusted by Shakespeare's company to adapt Shakespeare's plays after his death." He also wrote the biggest "hit" performed by any company in London during the period. The narrative oscillates between affiliation and replacement, between the assertion of identity and a rupturing superiority.[16]

Thomas Middleton and Early Modern Textual Culture takes a different strategy. It crafts an editorial apparatus and approach not scripted by previous editions of Shakespeare's works. In the handy section titled "How to Use This Book," the editors reverse the temporality of the opening moves of the *Collected Works* to stage their project from the point of view of the reader. "Most modern readers of Middleton," they write, "will already have encountered editions of Shakespeare," acknowledging "Shakespeare" as a filter or model that might interrupt or arouse certain kinds of expectations that are unwelcome.[17] They assert the "irrelevance" of many of the editorial choices that concern "Shakespeare." In describing the protocol for the inclusion of texts in the *Collected Works*, they note that it "contains texts of all Middleton's known surviving works, and brief descriptions of what we know about his lost ones. It includes works written by Middleton alone, works written by Middleton in collaboration with other writers, and works by writers which Middleton later adapted."[18] The strategy then, which both is and is not the same as the one that produces the Oxford Shakespeare, subtly rewires the linkage between the figure of the author and his works to include everything that Middleton may reasonably be expected to have had a hand in. The logic makes fine sense but runs the (we think admirable) risk of counterclaims or objections over property rights that will be difficult if not impossible to combat.

Implicitly, the historical Middleton serves here less as a retrievable bio/bibliographical origin than as *Ursprung* or outpouring, the breathing and writing *bios*, the biological fact of an existence that requires remediation in order to render his textual corpus whole if not holy. *The Collected Works*, whose self-ruining completeness emphatically overcompensates for what is lost, proffers itself as a witting facsimile of an edition that claims to be *The Complete Works* but that is riven with writing gone missing. It registers its losses, the ash of the archive, as a series of descriptions that draw attention to the holes. One could, we suppose, choose to read this strategy as a compulsion to find signs of Middleton wherever and whenever is possible, and so to breathe life into him via the inflation of so many textual skins so that one day "he" may *live on*—but how could one not to want to join in? How could we not understand this as part of a strategy to alter the ideological field of Renaissance drama and value it as the intensive labor of a particular fetish community that wishes us to apprehend the past differently? The "Unintroduction" to the *Oxford Handbook* explicitly notes that "for Middleton there is no 'great tradition.' Yet"—offering the 36 essays that follow as proof of life, proof of critical traffic around the texts, proof that the world will now be different.[19]

As an exercise in bio/bibliography (the comaking of persons and books) the Middleton project provides no answers to the questions we seek to worry, but it offers a strategically different way of using texts and of conceiving of the edition and handbook as "backups" or "backing ups" to writing that maximizes its heft in our collective presents.[20]

THE NUCLEAR OPTION

Thus far, we have rehearsed an all too brief survey of some of our favorite media interruptions—which we read as deployments of unreadability in the service of an altered sense of the archive, the production of different effects of the past in our various presents. In short, they deploy a set of reading protocols that fundamentally do not change the Heminge and Condell business model of Renaissance drama. And so we come back to the question. What would it mean to confront a literal, brute unreadability and dwell within its yet-to-be-discovered limits? What does such a feat entail?

A little while ago or almost no time at all, someone tried to do just that. He wondered whether or not there might come a time when "Shakespeare" might "cease to be literature."[21] "It is . . . quite possible," he writes, "that given a deep enough transformation of our history, we may in the future produce a society which is unable to get anything at all out of Shakespeare. His works might seem desperately alien, full of styles of thought and feeling which such a society found limited or irrelevant." And "in such a situation," he adds, "Shakespeare would be no more valuable than much present-day graffiti" (10). "And though many people," he concludes, turning the knife, "would consider such a social condition tragically impoverished, it seems to me dogmatic not to entertain the possibility that it might arise rather from a general human enrichment." This is, of course, Terry Eagleton writing in *Literary Theory: An Introduction* (1983). As you recall, he is out to put "literature" under erasure, out to deface "literature" as a sort of liberal humanist gold standard or fetish object and with it the idea that reading made you a better person. Here he enlists Shakespeare's unreadability to his cause. Un-Shakespeare "Shakespeare," he implies, and you may picture what the future holds—a radical, blank future, it seems, a future that is not yet written but upon which you may like to project a future you'd prefer to the present. Deploying a rhetorical unreadability become literal nonreading, Eagleton leaves Shakespeare to be remaindered, moved to the library annex, put in the bin, or at least cancelled from the ideological menu. Shake-who?

At the end of the book, in the chapter "Political Criticism," the stakes get even higher. Having taken us on a tour of theory, Eagleton asks, "What is the *point*?" "Are there not issues in the world more weighty than codes, signifiers and reading subjects?" (169). Eagleton inputs the rhetorical launch codes and writes the following: "Let us consider merely one such issue. As I write, it is estimated that the world contains over 60,000 nuclear warheads, many with a capacity a thousand times greater than the bomb which destroyed Hiroshima. The possibility that these weapons will be used in our lifetime is steadily growing. The approximate cost of these weapons is 500 billion dollars a year, or 1.3 billion dollars a day. Five percent of this sum—25 billion dollars—could drastically, fundamentally alleviate the problems of the poverty-stricken Third World" (169). Eventalizing his own text with the pseudodeictic "as I write," Eagleton goes nuclear, and the future, or one version of it, dis/appears as a blinding flash of white light. But the trigger he pulls is a dummy. The nuclear moment passes and serves as a shock tactic by which an altered sense of the archive is installed. For his book, as we discover, serves "less an introduction [to literary theory] than an obituary," and he ends by "burying the object we sought to unearth" (178). The blast radius of Eagleton's going nuclear de-realizes literature and its parasitic theories along with it. His book, then, will have been a crypt, a closing off and down of a set of issues, that might inaugurate a political orientation to the vast archive named simply "writing," from which various positive agendas might provisionally arise: emerging national literatures, working-class/ethnic literatures, et cetera.

But where there should be a blank, the future drawing a blank, leaving us much like Walter Benjamin's angel of history facing backward, gazing out upon the wreckage that remains, it turns out that redemption beckons.[22] Shakespeare, Eagleton tells us, lives, rising like some phoenix from the ashes of literature. He did not, so it appears, have to die (again) for literature to die. The "Shakespeare" whose unreadability has been mooted was merely a body double for the pernicious "literature" that is now raining upon us as just so much fallout. "The liberation of Shakespeare and Proust," writes Eagleton, "may well entail the death of literature, but it may also be their redemption" (189). "Shakespeare" needed killing so that Shakespeare could live again. What actually needed killing was "literature"—and projecting Shakespeare's historical irrelevance was one of many rhetorical interventions in the ideological switchboard required to pull the trigger.

X MAR/S/KS THE SPOTS

Eagleton's book may be read as already choreographing a particular dance between what is called "theory" and "history" (language and reference/outside as mediated via various substrates/archives) and encoding thereby a set of strategies for prospecting or opening up new markets for "Shakespeare" (read "literary") reserves in a series of emancipated futures that are yet to be redeemed and that therefore offer the prospect of endless surplus values and (joint) stock options. In this sense, *Literary Theory: An Introduction* becomes readable as a moment of what Jacques Derrida might term "nuclear criticism," a set of moves that tax the present with the fabulation of a referent: either the mutually assured destruction of nuclear oblivion or the postivizing of textual traces in the name of "life"—an immanent ideology. For Eagleton, unreadability remains allied to the crypt or to the grave. It remains keyed to a marker or even a monument to which we could point, to which we could return to pull up the weeds, wipe away the dust or the grime, and read the inscription or write a new one. Or, in the event that the inscription has gone missing, we could exhume the contents and discover what lies beneath, what remains.

In "No Apocalypse, Not Now" (1984), Derrida speaks to such a question of radical, catastrophic unreadability as a question of archivability. In doing so, he posits a mode of unreadability not coupled to the grave but to an absolute loss. He links literature to the loss of a referent specific to total, nuclear destruction:

> Here we are dealing hypothetically with a total and remainderless destruction of the archive. This destruction would take place for the first time and it would lack any common proportion with, for example, the burning of a library, even that of Alexandria, which occasioned so many written accounts and nourished so many literatures. The hypothesis of this total destruction watches over deconstruction, it guides its footsteps . . . deconstruction, at least what is being advanced today in its name, belongs to the nuclear age. And to the age of literature . . . The only referent that is absolutely real is thus of the scope or dimension of an absolute nuclear catastrophe that would irreversibly destroy the entire archive and all symbolic capacity,

would destroy the "movement of survival," what I call "*survivance*," at the very heart of life.[23]

Under such circumstances, the symbolic work of mourning becomes impossible, for the "'*survivance*' at the very heart of life," an orientation to the future, to the possibility that our playing will replay, vanishes:

> This absolute referent of all possible literature is on a par with the absolute efface-ment of any possible trace; it is thus the only ineffaceable trace, it is so as the trace of what is entirely other, "*trace du tout autre.*" This is the only absolute trace—effaceable, ineffaceable. The only "subject" of all possible literature, of all possible criticism, its only ultimate and a-symbolic referent, unsymbolizable, even unsig-nifiable; this is, if not the nuclear age, if not the nuclear catastrophe, at least that toward which nuclear discourse and the nuclear symbolic are still beckoning: the remainderless and a-symbolic destruction of literature. Literature and literary criti-cism cannot speak of anything else, they can have no other ultimate referent . . . If we are bound and determined to speak in terms of reference, nuclear war is the only possible referent of any discourse and any experience that would share their condition with that of literature. If, according to a structuring hypothesis, a fantasy or phantasm, nuclear war is equivalent to the total destruction of the archive, if not of the human habitat, it becomes the absolute referent, the horizon and the condi-tion of all the others.[24]

With the destruction of both the archive and the referent, nothing remains. Such a loss of the referent (of the very possibility of reference) is different from "an individual death, a destruction affecting only a part of society, of tradition, of culture," which "may always give rise to a symbolic work of mourning, with memory, compensation, internalization, idealization, displacement, and so on. In that case there is monumentalization, archivization and work on the remain-der, work of the remainder."[25] By proffering a destruction of both referent and backup, of world and archives, nuclear criticism installs its own restricted prac-tices of not reading, reducing and thereby managing the textual dispersal that an archive effects. Indeed, the effect of such nuclear catastrophe would be to recall and obliterate all the fragments, all the bits and pieces that remain as they have been parceled out, as they have been lost and found. In the "event" of such an event, the chronological instant of such a cessation of happening, archive and ref-erent would, in a sense, merge, or the distinction between the two would become as fundamentally unclear as it would prove catastrophically irrelevant.

Here, Derrida's turn from the unreadability of literature to what we would call its "un-" or "an-" "archivability" depends on a media-specific notion of the archive: Derrida's archive is a written archive made of printed texts that "are" traces of *arche-writing*. Even in *Archive Fever: A Freudian Impression*, when he took stock of the impact of new media on the archive, Derrida did not theorize a shift in archive management from a referencing system with its retrieval and return protocols derived from a print archive and the assumed ontology of the book. The shift to a model focused by a facsimile archive, at a further remove from the textual referent, yet constituted also so as to be capable of being processed as or mistaken for the referent, remains to be thought. The surplus value of the facsimile as both "facsimile" and "faux-simile" constitutes the literary object, the book, always as an oscillating media event, an event that restitches unreadability in any act of reading. "*Survivance*," "the movement of survival," already, if you like, constitutes a winking in and out of being, a recrossing and cutting of the relations between the living and the nonliving, the organic, the machinic, and the inert. The backup of the facsimile is thus always in excess of the total destruction of any archive or paper machine.[26] It calls into question the distinctions between an archive and the world as we live it, the world as already keyed to an auto-archiving of itself as things unfold.

Here it seems important to recall that Eagleton's book resists itself and signs another road that it does not take. Against the move to liberation become redemption, Eagleton records but does not cite Marx in the *Grundrisse* worrying the "eternal charm" (10) of Greek art and, though Eagleton does not remind us, of Shakespeare. Marx writes that he will deal with Greek art first and then speak to the "relation . . . of Shakespeare to the present time" but never makes it back to him; forgets to do so; leaves him quite literally unread, citing him approvingly on the essence of money later in the text.[27] Greek art then does double duty. But the question of its charm is complicated. The relation between mythology as the "arsenal" to Greek art is interrupted by capitalism's growing technical mastery of the natural world. "What chance," writes Marx, aligning the Greek gods with their corporate equivalents, "has Vulcan against Roberts & C, Jupiter against the lightning rod, and Hermes against the Credit Mobilier"?[28] The problem posed by Greek arts and epic, then, and by an offstage Shakespeare, "is that they still afford us artistic pleasure."[29] Marx resolves this seeming contradiction by boxing it up in a narrative that reverses the genealogical cast to parenting. If parents derive pleasure from their children by reexperiencing their own childish naiveté, such is the pleasure afforded by Greek art, which serves up "beautiful unfoldings" summoned from "the historic childhood of humanity."[30]

By this inversion of genealogical time, our ancestors become our children. Interrupted by technological and media developments, their readability or retrievability is premised on the charm we derive from what is, in truth, their unreadability given our present situation and concerns. We recognize them, but they are not readable. We enjoy them, but that enjoyment manifests an apotheosis or exotic derivative of times past. The source of their attraction lies very precisely in how readily their readability is a given, gives itself to us so that it remains or goes unread. Marx retains the charm while boxing it up so that it may not speak to or of the future—which it cannot thereby infect. The judicious blankness to his model of the future speaks to us of the difficulty in knowing whether or not, when we speak, write, and read, we change scripts and how to reckon with the good and bad ghosts of those who were on the scene but who have departed and yet remain. We will, we know, find ourselves haunted—so how then do we own up to our futures as always already revivals, as reanimations of and by acts and thoughts past? With difference, or with the same old violence and exclusions, even as they are redistributed according to the latest demographics of race and species?

Marx warns of this difficulty in *The Eighteenth Brumaire of Louis Bonaparte*: "The social revolution of the 19th century cannot create its poetry out of the past, but only from the future"—a process he describes as like learning a new language. "It is like the beginner," he says, "[who] always translates back into the mother tongue, but appropriates the spirit of the new language and becomes capable of producing freely within it only by moving about in it without recalling the old."[31] Such a crossing over gets coded as a forgetting of the matrix / maternal language, as the speaker gains fluency in a language she cannot remember learning or by forgetting that she has forgotten the old one—a language that remains merely *next*, without origin or genealogical link to the father of her habits. As the emphasis on the materiality, difficulty, and potential failure of translation, reanimation, recalling, repetition, and so "renaissance," in Marx's brief narrative makes clear, the problem lies in discerning which phenomena are progressive and which retrogressive—a salvific lure for utopian energies that lead us to want to make good on an unfulfilled past that has been irretrievably lost. He posits the future therefore as constitutively unreadable and necessarily unwritable.

In our view, Marx's refusal to permit an archive of the future to cohabit with the archive of the dead and dying stands as a caution against dummy deployments of unreadability gone nuclear sponsored by media interruption or archival politics that close out the political. Such deployments rely on the flare of white light generated by the advent or messianic arrival of media specificity to inaugurate their own reworking or sorting of the archive so as to recuperate this or that fabulation of a referent—call it "future" liberation, for presentists; call it "history" in the guise of a referent, for historicists. Torn between both impulses, blinded by the successive flares of white light and drugged up by their juicy referents, we find ourselves stranded in the nonspace where conversion occurs, the *x* that mar/s/ks the spot.

THIS IS (NOT) A DRILL

"Warning!" "Media Interruption!" Or this medium is new—and different! "Quick," everyone says. "No time to lose." "This is it." "Look! You better get moving. Put your book down and pick ours up. If you don't you'll just be a botched facsimile of a reader." "Hang on," we say. "Slow down. No need to worry or head into the bunker. But you may want to check your purse."

Forget the rhetoric of urgency—there'll be another media interruption along in a minute. This time, you don't have to listen to the sirens. This time, watch (out) for the blank space, the blankness that's drawn in order to loop the interruption and return to a reading that does not read. Elude the gerund. Stick with the finite. Blank out. If you can accept that iteration is all there ever was or will be—the effect of the "original" a retrospective causation of the facsimiles/backups, and you its wetware—then what might we learn? Such a critical program would articulate the future as a fundamentally empty set that it is our job precisely not to fill because to fill it would merely be to fill it "againe" and "againe" in order to keep canceling it out and cashing it in. And so, instead, we seek to dwell in the blank spots unreadability discloses and covers over and to inhabit the question.

These blank spots are neither Marxian nor Derridean. They are best rendered as crossroads and cruxes—crossed out through data input operations that we perform all too quickly, hurried across by the "manifest danger" of apocalypse, the proffered hopes of redemption, or by a mode of academic production in which readings must prove vendible. Yet the "danger" of reading is not something that we can secure ourselves against or safely avoid. In their address to "the great variety of readers," Heminge and Condell may seek to amass readerly "friends" and "friends of friends"—the First Folio already a prima facie Facebook page—but no friendly firewall can contain the danger of unreaderly "foes." The "friending" of readers (and friends of friendly readers) already enfolds and inscribes a politics of friend and foe, the reader as p/artisan who is directed to reread, but whose rereadings are always after the missing manuscript that the First Foe/lio has apparently "left behind" in its salvific idealization of itself as Folio, as a printed archive of authorial impressions.[32] Instead of Heminge and Condell's instructions for use, we wish to reiterate their iterative schema, "againe and againe," and receive it as an invitation to play nonreading out as a blank check/ed.

To that end, we find ourselves embarked on a project of un/reading, a project that focuses on sometimes barely visible, often minute manifestations of media-specific interruptions of reading in print editions, film adaptations, and so on, of Shakespearean drama. In this first chapter, we have attempted merely to delineate this project. What it means to read (and not read) from our position necessarily remains to be seen.

In Chapter 2, "'O, Horrible, Most Horrible!' *Hamlet*'s Telephone," we begin by putting John Dover Wilson's *What Happens in Hamlet?* on the line with Avital Ronell's account of *Hamlet* in *The Telephone Book* to explore the ways in which editing smooths out a series of interpretive puzzles in the play keyed to the problem of voices that go missing or that are interrupted, that are relayed or recorded, or that appear in the play only as facsimiles of themselves. At the end of the play, Hamlet turns himself into a dysfunctional relay system, turning Horatio, his faithful answering machine, into a relay to the future. Such an ending stands as a stark or perhaps stalking companion to the haunting of the play by Hamlet's father and enables us to identify within the play a conversation about the nature of answerability that inflects current critical discussions of Shakespeare's response to matters of sovereignty and government. Ready to listen, we turn to the text of *Hamlet*, hearing in Barnardo's opening question "Who is there?" a calling of the ghostly sovereign to account, dialing him up, in order to settle outstanding accounts.

In Chapter 3, "*Romeo and Juliet* is for Zombies," we offer a reading of what we call *Romeo and Juliet*'s "equipment for dying" from the vantage point offered by a three-minute film short directed by Iranian director Abbas Kiarostami, *Where Is My Romeo*, screened at Cannes in 2007, translated to DVD, and now streaming on YouTube. We examine the orientation to mourning that takes shape in *Romeo and Juliet* and its founding as a structure of disturbed viewing that requires us to make or *do* something, as Capulet and Montague seniors signal by their construction of statues to accessorize and archive the story. Kiarostami's short film offers itself not as an adaptation of the play but as "spin-off," asking us to watch a series of women watch the end of the play, but refusing to screen *Romeo and Juliet*. The oscillating presence/absence of Shakespeare, the literal unviewability/unreadability of the offstage play, as *Where Is My Romeo?* unfolds, leads us to read contemporary cinephilia in conversation with the modes of reception that Shakespeare's play imagines to the tragic events it stages. The automaticity of mourning in the play figures an accessorizing of decay, an accessorizing or fetish labor that represents something both more and less than a reading.

In Chapter 4, "Drown Before Reading: Prospero's Missing Book . . . s," we take up the crux of Prospero's stated intention to "drown his books" near the end of the play, which, in defiance of the elements, sometimes morphs in commentaries on the play into a Faustian book burning. Placing filmic treatments of this crux alongside the play text, its editions, and its reworkings in postcolonial contexts, we examine the appearance of books being written/produced in the closing sequences of two adaptations of the play: Julie Taymor's *Tempest* (2010) and Peter Greenaway's *Prospero's Books* (1991). Analyzing the place of these films, which are concerned with the process of writing early modern books, in relation to two developments in the history of the cinematic paratext—first, opening and end sequences that show the credits printed on turning pages of a book and, second, the increasing expansion and development of end credit sequences since 1980—we examine the allure that Prospero's books, forever unreadable, have for us.

In Chapter 5, "*Anonymous / Anony/mess*," we raise questions of the so-called authorship controversy as it does (and does not haunt) Shakespeare studies by way of a reading of the "controversy" turned conspiracy or, better yet, disaster film *Anonymous* (2011). The film, we think, constitutes a complete mess, modeling the Shakespeare (or is it de Vere?) archive as a messy, massy morass out of which voices are summoned by the variously human or lively presences that breathe their words—the wetware to whom we have introduced you, or that we have asked you to consider yourselves to be in this our first chapter.

We conclude with a short weather report in place of the reshelving operations that we understand a bibliography or even, in our terms, a bio/bibliography, to constitute.

CHAPTER 2

"Oh, Horrible, Most Horrible!" *Hamlet's* Telephone

Barnardo: Who's there?
Francisco: Nay, answer me. Stand and unfold yourself.
Barn: Long live the King.
Fran: Barnardo?
Barn: He.
Fran: You come most carefully upon your hour.
Barn: 'Tis now struck twelve. Get thee to bed, Francisco.

—*Hamlet* (1.1.1–5)[1]

And yet, you're saying yes, almost automatically, suddenly, sometimes irreversibly. Your picking it up means the call has come through. It means more: you're its beneficiary, rising to meet its demand, to pay a debt. You don't know who's calling or what you are going to be called upon to do, and still, you are lending your ear, giving something up, receiving an order. It's a question of answerability.

—Avital Ronell, *The Telephone Book*[2]

IN OUR FIRST CHAPTER, WE OFFERED YOU the First Folio (1623) as the scene of a media event. Thus was "Shakespeare" launched as an ongoing splicing together of texts and readers, a viral recruitment of variously lively hosts, whom the Folio posits as friends to the textual corpus/corpse of "Shakespeare." The First Folio stands for us as a strategically imperfect archive. It offers a partial Shakespearean impression that requires you to splice together looking (at his image) and reading (his and others' words) and to summon up, by that exchange, a Shakespeare phantom that you take as a referent. Read hard and you will, if you read rightly, glimpse the man, and so receive his impression. His words assume the aura of a code. The living, breathing *bios* that he was becomes twinned with the *biblion* ("book" but also "niche" or "slot in a library") that you keep circulating, enabling him/it to live on.[3] By this recruitment, we become "wetware," the biosemiotic motor or substrate to Shakespeare's animation in our various presents.

In this chapter we offer an un/reading of *Hamlet* (c. 1600–1602) that posits the play as already a response to such recruitment and lesson giving by the un/dead. By its structure and handling of questions of reference the play seeks to capture the peculiar feeling that comes with finding yourself answering the call that John Heminge and Henrie Condell place, picking up the telephone from which issues the reproduction of a voice that is not itself but that claims to be so, and that, worse still, you treated as such merely by agreeing to answer. The insistent ring, hum, ping, or drone of your phone, whatever stimulus it is that demands attention, stitches you into the telephonic structure of the call. You find yourself on the line, waiting, on hold to the *phone* (voice). To write as directly as possible and to risk nonsensicality, we posit *Hamlet* as already producing what we can name today the effect of telephony, and exploiting (right royally) the telephonic dialing up of distant voices for its dramatic effects. *Hamlet* is a telephone book.

Beyond capturing, in advance of the fact, the peculiar effect of telephony, we argue that *Hamlet* ventures an order of telephonic resistance or unreadability. It resists the call. Even as Hamlet finds himself (and we find ourselves) compelled to answer, the play refuses to capitulate to the weak sovereignty of a dead father-king whose voice comes back complaining about something or other he got in his ear. Voices go missing and get interrupted, dropped, relayed, recorded, rerouted, and augmented through various writing devices such as tables, letters, and a dumb show and by the human component to writing technologies, actors, messengers, secretaries. Media proliferates and pools. These devices may, or may not, appear onstage as props. Such voices appear then always as facsimiles of themselves, as reports, or reports of reports read aloud, making some voices distorted echoes of themselves and others hallucinations.

Hamlet proceeds as a parade of these fac/faux/similes, multimedia renderings or reproductions, the action held hostage by what's not onstage, by what might, or might not, have happened, be happening, and remain to happen, as that is suggested by differently backed forms of evidence. By its ongoing deployment of different media, all of which fail, the play attenuates the call, strands us in the nontime of answerability, of finding ourselves recruited before the call, of being entered into a becoming wetware. It worries protocols of evidence, acts of reading (and not reading) that seek to refer to or to touch the world; it draws attention to the way these readings are only as reliable as their backing—the physical substrates of wax, skin, paper (rags or vegetable), and ink and the human witness that offers the report.[4] The play ruins Hamlet's own drive for a textual forensics, *CSI*, "gotcha" moment in the staging of *The Murder of Gonzago*, both under- and overproducing even as Hamlet seeks to shut things down; to set things straight. Such probing yields only phantom referents, fac/faux/similes of things that may or may not have occurred.

In offering the play to you as a telephone book, a fragmentary auto-archiving of what it is like to find yourself "on the line," we aim to account for the rich and varied responses to the play's resistance by reorienting critical attention to the play's tactical unreadability. Critics and audiences have long noted the play's obsession with writing technologies, with repetition, revision, reanimation, and revival.[5] But largely, such critical and creative efforts, imagining that "every exit

is an entrance somewhere else" or time-traveling un-*Hamlet*ings (filmic and critical), have sought to bandage up or smooth over disabling cruxes all in order
to reduce the static the play generates.[6] They supplement the play in order to
supplant its difficulties, generating a weak sovereignty over the text. The core difference between this wealth of artistic and critical fetish work and our approach
lies in the way we resist the urge to minister, positing the play, instead, as a
self-rending multimedia archive that will not resolve into a single, sovereign performance or reading.

You can try to keep your text of *Hamlet* straight, lining up the terms, by reading the play's writing games thematically, as Jonathan Goldberg has so deftly
done.[7] You can divide the labor; bust the cruxes by editing them away; and then,
with the text sedated, hallucinate a performance and simply declare, as does John
Dover Wilson, what happens in Hamlet.[8] Like Steven Ratcliffe, you can dwell
with the offstage world that haunts the play to very productive effect.[9] You can
claim the play as the first instance of the "whodunit" or the first film noir as Linda
Charnes has done in a brilliantly anachronistic rezoning of the play.[10] You can
stitch the play to the confessional confusion of the period and yoke the mobility
of voices to the "*hic et ubique*" of Hamlet Senior's ghost.[11] You can even own
up to the play's uncanny repetitions and self-revisions, spell the action and the
title backward as Terrence Hawkes does in his still inspiring "Telmah," finding
therein a "jazz aesthetic" that doubles as a politicizing *jouissance*.[12] You can posit
the play as a kind of psychoanalytic substrate or psychotropic flypaper on which
editors and readers rend their wings, as Marjorie Garber does in her readings of
the psychology of editing.[13] Or you can wax ecstatic and luxuriate in the mute-
ness that comes with finding yourself recruited as wetware and imagine a salvific,
new media history to come that would resolve all.[14] But as you do so, realize that
you are generating a weak sovereignty over the text by refolding cruxes, managing
an economy of reading and not reading, so that *Hamlet* coheres, and you can end
the call and put this telephone/book down.

But try as we might, even as we hang up, put *Hamlet* down, and tiptoe away
from its niche in the library/depository/crypt, lest that call come again, we're
never quite off the hook—hence all the labor that goes into managing the call
and the hallucinations of certainty or reference it produces. The problem is that
no matter what feats of editing or parceling out of media we attempt, the structure of *survivance* to which *Hamlet* responds and that it archives (badly) sports
objections to our attempts to sort the play into a series of mono-media operating on separate, static-free channels. We remain like Hamlet, Horatio, Ophelia,
and Marcellus, like Yorick, like all the various objects pressed to use as imperfect
answering machines in the play, going over and over the same telephonic cruxes
the play generates. And these cruxes do not derive from some imperfect translation from stage to print and back that might one day be resolved to create a
seamless set of reversible passages. Instead, the play exists as an irreducible set of
problems generated by its archiving of what was already a multimedia platform,
the public theater. Moreover, by its own auto-archiving, the text fractures itself.
Always too much and too little, *Hamlet* repeatedly threatens not to happen even
as it repeatedly does so.

In this chapter we offer an account of the play's rending or disabling across different media, pursuing lines of questioning that the play paradoxically opens up by closing them down as it becomes a multimedia archive: the text (first quarto [Q1], second quarto [Q2], First Folio); the editions; the critical apparatus; the creative elaboration in plays, on film, and so on. For us, *Hamlet* designates not a play but a burgeoning archive of the predicament of the citizen-subject forced to sift the differently mediated textual remains of acts past under the demands placed by a spectral sovereign-father whose call you have to take. Radicalizing John Dover Wilson's *What Happens in Hamlet*, we refuse to hear the declarative cast to his title or even to process it as a question. Instead, we ask perversely what is the meaning of *what* and what is the meaning of *happens*? What is the textual referent of *Hamlet*? These questions may strike some readers as strange. Yet to assume the transparency of the statement "what happens in *Hamlet*" or even to turn that statement into a question is to operate still within the impossible forensics framework that drives Hamlet and *Hamlet*'s action. What happened? Murder. Who did it? Claudius. Only by questioning the basis of the question can we perceive the choreography by which *Hamlet* constitutes itself as an archive and its ash.[15]

FIRST WORDS

The play begins, as you recall, with the posing of a question that is already an answer, a response to some *thing*. The action begins in reference to an absent word or sound, the intimation of a prompt or presence that comes before. A voice asks the dark to speak: "Who's there?" Are you noise or presence? Will you, can you answer? Friend or foe? But already there's a problem, a switch, a reversal. The yet-to-be-named Francisco answers with a challenge: "Stand and unfold yourself." Undo your cloak. Show your face. If I am to answer, you must answer first. We must both agree to be answerable. Barnardo answers the challenge not by name but by function. "Long live the King," he proclaims, speaking as he who bears the sovereign's mark. But which king is it exactly—Hamlet Senior, Claudius? Do such names even matter? There's always a king, isn't there? Perhaps it's safest for the likes of you and me to disappear and present ourselves as soldiers merely—as they who put teeth in the sovereign's mouth, who serve as mediators of sovereign violence. It's safest to hand off the call, own up to your recruitment, and pass the receiver along to another. "Hamlet, we think it's for you." Things settle down as Francisco posits the voice as the man he's expecting and names him in the form of a question: "Barnardo?" Barnardo agrees to be himself. Then they're down to familiarities, minor recriminations or thanks—Barnardo's either late or very punctual—"'Tis cold . . . not a mouse stirring" (1.1.6–7). Go on, go in, and get to bed. Yet even as the matter seems settled, we know that the two men have merely postponed an installed uncertainty with regard to such challenges and answers, for Horatio and Marcellus are on their way up, coming to settle a question, to speak to a thing that keeps coming back, to a ghost that, so it seems, "would be spoke to" (1.1.44).

Already, by its beginning, the play offers itself as an insufficient archival response to a word or noise that precedes the first words of the play. In terms of the structures of *survivance* that give us our daily Shakespeares, we might say that *Hamlet* unfolds quite precisely as a self-rending attempt to remember the word that comes before the first word (what was it again?), ensuring thereby that that word be forgotten, held at bay. The play documents the afterlife of some *thing* that precedes it, which is finished but the facticity of which always exceeds the play's attempts to reconnect its present to a moment that has passed.

In Derridean terms, we might say that what "happens" in the play derives from an "event" that produces not only "an act, a performance, a praxis, but an *oeuvre*, that is, at the same time the result and the trace left by a supposed operation and its supposed operator."[16] By this completion or terminus, some *thing* lives on. Indeed, its completion or "cutting off" was what "destined [it] to this sur-vival, to this excess over present life." The absent word or noise to which Barnardo responds figures this cut or cutting off, the trace of something that has passed and this "*cut* assures a sort of archival independence or autonomy that is quasi-machine-like," placing us in a realm of "repetition, repeatability, iterability, serial and prosthetic substitution of self for self."[17] Within the play, this "quasi-machine-like" matrix generates a structure of repetition and replay that comes to write what follows: the action, its translation to other media platforms, and its afterlife in critical discourse. The effect is "quasi-machine-like," in Derrida's terms, because even as we "live" the madness as our "own"—which is to say that it manifests as if "organic," "eventful," "human"—it responds to the afterlife or "sur-vival" of an operation that appears to us only as a trace that would render it "automatic," "machinic," in- or "non-human." The challenge remains, we think, to model the play outside or without such terms and so to tolerate the dis/ease it generates.[18]

For us, the play resists the naturalization of this ontological network of an always already technologized, hardwired and so haunted model of being into the elaborated forms of sovereign-subject and friend-foe and the generative familial relations of husband-wife, father-mother and son-daughter, and so on. All such models are deracinated by the play's telephonic structure, which foregrounds the inhuman cutting that marks any beginning, staging the "cut" throughout its structure as an interrupted or dropped call, the call's interruption, and the maniacal supplementation of voices by other media in order to keep them lively if not alive. Within the play, it becomes hard to know therefore by what ratio we can distinguish between an "event" and a repetition, between the organic and the machinic, for terms collide. Indexed to matters of voice, to its relay, at a distance (*tele/phone*), the play's staging of prosthetic substitution produces, on the one hand, a desire for a more complete archive, more and more evidentiary backups for the missing word, and by the same hand, a competing desire for an archival apocalypse that would cancel out the missing first word, time traveling back to fill in what has already gone missing even before we begin. The action remains hostage to these dual impulses even as the play sabotages both.

When, for example, at the end of the play Hamlet posits the "rest" or what remains as an absence of voices, a deaf and dumb "silence" that both he and the theater audience will endure, he turns himself into a dysfunctional relay system to some putative future to which he speaks: "Fortinbras," he insists "has my dying voice" (5.2.340), which Hamlet gifts to him, throwing his voice forward into the moment when Fortinbras may speak as Hamlet or augmented by the "sur-vival" of Hamlet's words. But such a voice requires a relay, an intermediary. Thus is Horatio, Hamlet's faithful answering machine, recruited as bearer, as he who keeps Hamlet's voice lively if not alive, enabling his gift to presence in the future. That is, as long as Horatio gets the words right—"I am dead," Hamlet says. "Thou livest: report my cause aright" (5.2.322–23). But such reporting remains an open question, for even Hamlet is loath to set down more than the impetus of his voice to remain or to come back, mandating nothing more firm than that Horatio sort out which events truly count—"tell him [Fortinbras] which th'occurrents more and less / Which have solicited.—The rest is silence" (5.2.341–42). What Horatio leaves out, what he neglects to relay, the gaps he introduces by his reduction or narration of the play, the transformation of Hamlet's "cause" into story, will be rent by silences, minor oblivions, holes.

Already, at the end of the play, it begins. Horatio will speak, so he says of "how these things came about," but the story manifests by its repetition as no more than a horror movie trailer, promising that we will "hear / Of carnal, bloody, and unnatural acts, / Of accidental judgements, casual slaughters, / Of deaths put on by cunning, and for no cause . . . All this can I / Truly deliver" (5.2.364–69). Such lessons as there are to be learned will only figure a traumatizing replay of a fractured archive. Still, the newly arrived Fortinbras says he will "haste to hear" Horatio's narration and calls "the noblest to the audience" (5.2.370–71). Stay tuned. He has "some rights to memory in this kingdom," so he says, and "of that" Horatio promises that he "shall have also cause to speak" (5.2.375). Rights to memory aside, it's always best to arrive with glowing references as well as an army. Cue the Hamlet tape. Speak that voice again. And Horatio promises that the dead Hamlet will speak for he shall provide the missing breath for "his mouth whose voice will draw no more" (5.2.376). Thus the play ends with the launch of the latest sovereign legitimized by the endorsement of the latest corpse animated by the latest witness.[19]

Such an ending stands as a stark or perhaps stalking companion to the haunting of the play by Hamlet's father. It discloses the way the play's scrambling of evidentiary protocols and their writing machines are keys to matters of sovereignty and government. What does it mean for Hamlet to take the revenant father's call? What is owed to a dead sovereign? What will it mean for Fortinbras to take (up) Hamlet's dead voice? We argue that the play offers an orientation to these questions from the position of those who are forced to interrogate the textual remains of a sovereign who is present but unavailable, compelling but unable to deliver a final or a first word. Indeed, we think that it is only by pursuing a double argument that thinks questions of media and mediation *in tandem* with questions of sovereignty that we can begin to grasp the play's choreography of what amounts to a zoo/bio/biblio/politics that examines the experience of the relay, of finding oneself recruited, of becoming "wetware."[20]

We take Francisco and Barnardo's opening exchange, therefore, to constitute the governing question that *Hamlet* poses concerning answerability and
the responsibilities that attach to it—questions that play out as a scrambling or
defacement of matters of sovereignty and succession, of generativity and generation. For already, before he is even launched, Fortinbras's words ring hollow.
Hamlet will be taken, he says, "like a soldier to the stage, / For he was likely,
had he been put on, / To have proved most royal" (5.2.381–82). Now he shall
be "put on" even in death, proved royal by Horatio's breath, with Fortinbras as
body double, the foil who tropes the protagonist. "The soldiers' music and the
rite of war / Speak loudly for him," Fortinbras promises, effecting Hamlet's translation as reanimated speaking property to the staging of another media launch,
a rebranding.[21] But we end not with speech but with the engulfing of all voices
(Horatio's promises notwithstanding) by gunfire: "Go, bid the soldiers shoot"
(5.2.387). The salute serves as the ritualized displacement and conservation of
the threat of sovereign violence, unless, of course, there are those still to be lined
up against the wall and shot.[22]

The future, so it seems, never looks brighter than when illuminated by gunfire.
But be careful, for your first words, never the first word, may still prove your last.

TELEPHON/E/Y

If *Hamlet* is a "telephone book," which is to say a multimedia archive, then the
word *book* must be registered in its full set of meanings, as *biblion* or niche in
a library or depository. In *The Telephone Book: Technology, Schizophrenia, Electric Speech*, Avital Ronell posits the play after this fashion, finding therein the
traumatized script of telephony, a switchboard of tropic actors that register the
"uncanny gathering of voices" (51) that issue from the receiver. Both more and
less than a reading, its lines from *Hamlet* simply appear from nowhere, as Ronell
renders the text of the play as a dis/continuous script that splices together different times and places. Putting through a call that Alexander Bell, inventor of the
telephone, placed to *Hamlet*, she writes, "*Hamlet* was swallowed by telephonics"
(285). "The father's umbilical cord couldn't cease naming itself and its ghostly
partner," she elaborates. "This perhaps explains why the telephone's most sacredly
repeated declamation before an audience was to be 'To be or not to be,' marking the interstice between ghostly conjuration and the voice of the other" (285).
Ronell describes how Sir William Thomson, speaking to the British Association
at Glasgow, Scotland, on September 14, 1876, recalls the demonstration he witnessed earlier that year at an exhibition in Philadelphia. "I heard," so he writes,
"'To be or not to be . . . there's the rub?' through an electric telegraphic wire; but,
scorning monosyllables, the electric articulation rose to higher flights, and gave
me messages taken at random from New York newspapers: 'S. S. Cox has arrived';
'The City of New York'; 'Senator Morton'." "All this my own ears heard," he says,
"spoken to me with unmistakeable distinctness by the thin circular disk armature
of just such another little electromagnet as this which I hold in my hand" (284).
Truth is, he confesses, he "failed to make out the S. S. Cox" (283), but happily
someone must have been taking notes so that in his dumb show reenactment up

in Scotland of the historic occasion in Philadelphia, the unplugged telephone he holds in his hand speaks still, its message coming through loud and clear. As Ronell remarks, putting through Thomson's call to *Hamlet*, "This is why when his father calls up, Hamlet has to write everything down. He pulls out a slate rather than a sword to commit to memory [external memory device] the telephonic inscription" (285).

Ronell's conception of telephony defines the ontological network of an always already technologized, hardwired model of being. There never was or could have been a moment prior to the mutual embrace of technology and biology, liveliness and life, the apparently inert and the apparently organic.[23] As Thomson's reenactment before the British Association in Glasgow makes clear, the organic and inorganic remain caught in an ongoing production of fac/faux/similes of each other, mimicking each other's effects, taking turns, if you like, in the crafting of a telephonic infrastructure. There's no problem here—such is merely the way things are and categories of being come to be (made). Such problems that derive do so from the dropping of certain calls and not others, from the static necessary to the transmission of those calls that go through, and from the ways we manage or police the static, attempting to eliminate what is endemic and necessary to the telephonic effect. Politics, therefore, finds itself routed through the telephone, through the various switchboards that connect and disconnect calls from certain groups, and persons. Accordingly, it's in the nature of calls to go awry, to connect different discourses and sites of enunciation as the effect gets rezoned or migrates. It's this mobility, the way missing voices and delayed messages pop up in the strangest times and places that proves key to understanding what it is *Hamlet* has to tell us about answerability and prerecorded Shakespeare effects as we generate them in our various todays.

In Thomson's reenactment in Glasgow, for example, and at the exhibition in Philadelphia, we can make out already this uncanny gathering of voices. The telephone's speaking back of *Hamlet* recalls actors variously past performing the edited words of a *Hamlet* text that flickers in and out of being—"to be or not to be . . . there's the rub." In 1876, in Glasgow, Thomson had to play all the parts, reenacting the occasion of the telephone's first performance minus the electric speech, *phone* minus the *tele*, and revealing thereby the human already as telephone, a telephone to the telephone, whose parts lie dead in his hands, and whose electric speech Thomson renders live/ly by his own differently neuro-electric speech. If, in his rendering, Hamlet's monosyllabic weighing of his "quietus" seems to make the crossing from human voice to electric speech and back more easily than other less familiar proper names (S. S. Cox), this derives, no doubt from the fact that Thomson and his audience already know the lines, have already taken their impression, have been recruited as readers or friends by the friendly readers of the First Folio and its editions. Here, then, in 1876, among friends and readers become listeners, Thomson recruits for the telephone, asking his audience to lend their ears to the voices that will issue from similar "thin circular disk armature[s]" that come to populate their parlors and offices, even as the one that lies in Thomson's hand seems a bit dead. The circuit was already complete, already equipped to pass from one relay to the next, which is what Thomson does, launching the telephone by speaking back the words he already knew and then heard again to an audience that knows them also. "To be or not to be?" What else could the telephone's first words have been?

Taken as read, and so unrecorded in Thomson's transcript, nearly all *Hamlet*'s soliloquy goes missing. We supply the missing lines in our heads—but these lines take no time to read as we skip to the "rub." The lines were chosen, so it seems, for their monosyllabic insistence. Enunciate. "The rub" signals the end to the speech. *Hamlet* appears only in order to disappear. Graham Bell and Sir William Thomson (soon to be Lord Kelvin) move on, as does their audience. Once upon a time, *Hamlet* was news, but what's crucial now is the way the telephone accelerates the voice, beating out the newspaper and all the clipping offices that transmit thousands of bits and pieces of newspaper *sententiae* across the Atlantic every week or month to those eager to follow this or that trend abroad. The telephone, Thomson dangles, puts pay to the earnest cut-and-paste operations of distant readers plugged into an infrastructure fuelled by print and steamboat and so dependent on their Polonius factors abroad. It rewires the infrastructure that translates words from place to place. You may miss the name of the ocean liner first time round. You may need to endure the static, but still the telephone beats the newspaper and its clippings, transmitting the voice across that distance while all those static clippings remain yet to be clipped, or sit inside envelopes on this or that liner, which may or may never arrive—what was its name again?

Such then are *Hamlet*'s appearances in *The Telephone Book*. The play keeps coming back as a telephonic citation of the enervating and exciting being and not-being of a voice that speaks at a distance, playing its part in getting Thomson's listeners to pick up the receiver and help normalize the device, render it just so much furniture in their homes and offices. Given that Ronell announces in the opening "User's Manual" (in place of a preface), "*The Telephone Book* is going to resist you," we should not be surprised that she does not settle into a conventional reading of the play. On the contrary, along with its innovative and sometimes literally unintelligible typographical play, its index as Yellow Pages directory, the radical shifts of place and text, and its oscillations between historical moments, the *Telephone Book*'s rendering of *Hamlet* follows the tropic logic Ronell posits for "the telephone [which] splices a party line stretching through history" (295).

Accordingly, she posits the play as telephonic urtext—Hamlet's response to his father's otherworldly summons provides the script for what it means to answer the call the telephone issues. Hamlet Senior provides the voice-over for the call that by answering the telephone we activate. This voice trades in "whispers, spectral transmissions of a legacy, the currency of charges, electric or legal, whose ghosts refer to the allegory of a lusty self faded into the distance, cut off in the blossom of their sins." We grow "tense," Ronell continues, "with anticipation to learn the charges; like Hamlet, one beckons it [the ghost / the telephone] to speak more distinctly" (303). And so she assembles from the play a set of keys or telephonic cruxes, modeling the play as a set of tele-traumas that undergirds the infrastructures we inhabit. Uncannily, then, *Hamlet* keeps coming back, lines from the play emanating from the telephone when other historical persons and actors place or receive a call. Jacques Derrida ends up on the line to Sigmund

Freud; Martin Heidegger takes a call from the National Socialist Party; Carl Jung tunes into flying saucers; Alexander Bell's inventions become a haunt for his deaf mother; and these calls are routed or connect to cruxes in *Hamlet*, instances when the text fails or appears to fail as a reliable relay.

When, for example, Ronell inhabits a May 31, 1976, *Das Spiegel* interview with Heidegger on why he accepted a call from the Nazi Party we find ourselves telescoped into the text of *Hamlet*. "So you finally accepted [the call]. How did you then relate to the Nazis?" asks the interviewer. "Someone from the top command of the Storm Trooper University Bureau, SA section leader Baumann called me up," replies Heidegger (29).[24] The interview moves to matters of philosophy rather than historical circumstance, or worse, to the ways in which matters of philosophy may be coconstitutive with historical circumstances, and Ronell renders Heidegger's replies thus: "to prepare to be ready . . . To be prepared for preparation . . . But it does seem to me that inquiry could awaken, illuminate and define the readiness we've talked about . . . to prepare to be ready . . . Even the experience of absence is not 'nothing,' but a liberation from what I call in *Being and Time* the 'Fallenness of Being.' To be prepared for preparation requires contemplating the present . . . and to define the readiness" (40). "Isn't this close to what Hamlets have to say before their causes are reported, aright or wrongly?" she continues. "Overcome by the state, they take a tool in hand which is no longer a tool but a moment in the structure of general relatedness. Replay Hamlet" (41)—which she does, dialing up his exchange with Claudius (5.2.197–203):

> *H:* There's a special providence in the fall of a sparrow. If it be now, 'tis not to come; if it be not to come it will be now; if it be not now, yet it will come; the readiness is all. Since no man knows aught of what he leaves, what is't to leave be-times? Let be.
> *King:* Come Hamlet, come, take this hand from me . . .
> *H:* A few days later someone from the top command called (41).

And from *Hamlet* we reenter Heidegger's response to his interviewer—the script has been established, a collation of differently historical moments via differently historical texts. Claudius becomes a Storm Trooper commander on the line to a Hamlet/Heidegger concerned with his inability to control what is said of him about a call he answered even as he might have not. Accordingly, Hamlet (or is it Heidegger? Who can tell?) attempts to install his own "rumor-control devices aiming to neutralize the proliferation of tabulations around the dead" (420).

This concern with having one's cause reported rightly, of living on as an object after one's demise, designates one relay or trope within the circuit of tele-traumas that Ronell constitutes. But the circuit itself was inaugurated by the return of Hamlet's father, "head of state, overdosed" by "oto-injection" (21), who dies "cut off even in the blossoms of my sin, / Unhouseled" (1.5 77–78)—forced, that is, to accept a poisonous injection through the ear, when all the time, had he known, he should have been calling on the divine to forgive his sins. For Ronell, this scene of irreversible "oto-injection" means that the play stages itself as a response or reaction to the trauma of telephonic or oto-addiction. Bell's mother was deaf, and he modeled the telephone on the ear of a corpse—which anecdotally sutures the telephone to the ear, become defunct or un/dead double, a prosthesis that introduces a doubled, defunct ear into the circuit that forms between speaker, telephone, and receiver. No wonder we all end up "fucked," as Ronell colorfully puts it, mainlining the telephone, unable to put it down, waiting for the call: "You'd wait for her call, like the Heidegger boy. Your father's voice often behind you: Get off the phone. As if one could get off the drug by the same paternal injunction that put Hamlet onto it. Getting off didn't mean then what it now does. You were all hooked up at an early age, even those of you with mothers at home" (353). Let's return the scene of alleged oto-injection. It's a story of being supplied with a *phone/y* while you were sleeping a sleep from which you will not wake, or from which you wake only to find yourself "dead," altered, on the line, answering but unprepared to answer, for you were cut off "in the blossoms of [your] sin," unprepared for your ending. Fittingly, this scene of addiction exists only as a reproduction or facsimile of itself—the ghost, who, by his own account, while he was present at his death, was fast asleep, like Thomson, a telephone to a telephone, recounting, after the fact.

THE PHANTOM REFERENT

It's nighttime again. And we are up on the "platform" on which the play begins (and ends). It's still cold. Hamlet, Horatio, and Marcellus are all ears—waiting and watching, but tuned for sound, counting an offstage clock, a sound effect that we either hear or do not hear, that comes before or comes not at all.

> *Hamlet:* What hour now?
> *Horatio:* I think it lacks of twelve.
> *Marcellus:* No, it is struck.
> *Horatio:* Indeed, I heard it not." (1.4.3)

Is it time yet? It's that time already. Are you sure? Let's listen very carefully. Trumpets sound. Two pieces of artillery go off. We will not hear anything now. An offstage drinking party ensues somewhere below us, Claudius's custom so Hamlet says. He offers a bit of late-night pop psychology about folks who get caught up in a repetition compulsion—"the stamp of one defect" (1.4.31) and such, earning Danes a drunken name—until Horatio shuts him up: "Look, my lord, it comes" (1.4.38). Enter the ghost "in such a questionable shape / That I will speak to thee" (1.4.43–44), says Hamlet—who describes the entrance.

Back in act 1, scene 2, Hamlet had had to keep quiet, keep an "attent ear" (1.2.92) as Horatio reported what Marcellus and Barnardo said they had seen twice and Horatio had seen once: "a figure like your father" (1.2.198) whose "solemn march" went "slow and stately by them" leaving them "distilled / almost to jelly with the act of fear" unable to speak to him (1.2.200–205). The same thing happened exactly to Horatio, he says, except he spoke to it, but "answer made it none" (1.2.214)—except that "it lifted up its head and did address / Itself to motion like as it would speak" (1.2.214–16). It moved in a way that—what?—leads Horatio to think that it registered his words, his presence, thought about speaking? Then the cock crowed and it was gone. Understandably Hamlet is full of questions, of "what's" and "wherefores." So together he and Horatio compile an identikit cum blazon of the ghost's "countenance"—eyes, beard, expression, and so on, which passes an unarticulated threshold of evidence such that Hamlet now is here on the platform, splicing looking with talking, speaking back to what amounts to three or more (how can anyone be sure?) messages left in the substrate of looking and talking become more talking that constitutes Horatio's report of Marcellus's and Barnardo's report, which we may paraphrase as follows: "There may or may not be a message from something that looks a bit like your Dad. It's for you (we think)."

Now in act 1, scene 4, Hamlet names the ghost: "I'll call thee Hamlet, King, father, royal Dane." He then reprises Francisco's demand to "stand and unfold yourself," imploring that the shape "answer me" (1.4.44–45). "Say why is this? Wherefore? What should we do?" (1.4.56). But is this a secular or a supernatural resurrection? Is it really you or what is now left of you that speaks or were you right all along and weren't one of those "maniacs who demand that they be buried with a telephone, a more or less mobile telephone, in order to tolerate the idea that they might . . . be buried alive?"[25] Is this you calling? "Hold off your hands" (1.4 80), Horatio, Barnardo, Marcellus—I have to answer the phone for "still I am called—unhand me, gentlemen" (1.4.84).

Hamlet and the ghost exit—Horatio and Marcellus, having agreed not to follow, do so. The call is always addressed, always "for you," but everyone registers its presence and likes to listen in. "Whither wilt thou lead me?" Hamlet asks; "I'll go no further," he insists. "Mark me," says the ghost. "I will," replies Hamlet (1.5.1–2). "Speak, I am bound to hear. / So art thou to revenge when thou shalt hear" (1.4.6–8). And it does turn out to be quite a story. And it makes so much sense—"O my prophetic soul! / My uncle!" (1.5.36). Hamlet always had his suspicions; he has never liked him. "'Tis given out that, sleeping within my orchard," Hamlet Senior's "custom" of an afternoon, "thy uncle stole / With juice of cursed hebona in a vial / And in the porches of my ears did pour" (1.5.59–62). "Lazarlike" blistering ensues—an Ovidian metamorphoses become time-lapse decay of the body to corpse. And having narrated the circumstances of his own death, the ghost is off: "Adieu, adieu, adieu, remember me" (1.5.91). What now? How to maintain the injunction to "remember me?" "Shall I couple hell?" asks Hamlet. "Oh fie [Fuck]!" (1.5.93).

The ghost was surprised to find Hamlet so "apt" to revenge; it had expected to find him "duller" than the "fat weed / That roots itself on Lethe Wharf" (1.5.31–33). He had expected a gorgeous, luxuriating forgetfulness or drowsiness—a slow growing vegetal rooting that would produce nothing other than itself. Such was the "custom" the ghost expected of Hamlet—a far cry from Hamlet Senior's afternoon nap and Claudius's nocturnal binges, which seem purposed, entered in some economic relation to the calculus of their respective political daytimes. But in the ensuing scene, the structure of the call, the injunction to "remember me," to replay voices at a distance within his being become medium or instrument for revenge, induces this vegetal growth. Hamlet passes very quickly from remembering to having his fellows swear that they will remember to forget, that all the time he is earnestly performing not remembering by way of an "antic disposition" (1.5.170), generating thereby all manner of noise or static: they will say, if asked, that they "know aught of me" (1.5.177). Remember me transforms to "Remember thee?" And then it's out with the tables—for how can he remember? How can he combat the story that is "given out" except by some order of device that preserves the ghostly call:

> Remember thee?
> Ay, thou poor ghost, whiles memory holds a seat
> In this distracted globe. Remember thee?
> Yea, from the table of my memory
> I'll wipe away all trivial fond records,
> All saws of books, all forms, all pressures past
> That youth and observation copied there
> And thy commandment all alone shall live
> Within the book and volume of my brain
> Unmixed with baser matter. (1.5.95–104)

Is Alfred Hitchcock's Mr. Memory in the house? By what backup or support can this injunction to "remember me" be observed? Already it is transposed into a "remembering of thee" figuring a problem of translation. Metaphorizing the theater as his own body; personifying memory as a temporary, insufficiently sovereign audience member in an otherwise "distracted globe"—here for the space of a few hours in the afternoon but then gone home—Hamlet starts writing or talking about writing. He wipes the "table of [his] memory" clean—empties his commonplace book or wax tablet. He figures a complete erasure—no ink blots, no knife marks from the razor that would cut away a layer of parchment and so mark the document as altered.[26] "All pressures past," all observations become impressions will be gone.[27]

Hamlet gets excited—"O villain, villain, smiling damned villain, / My tables! Meet it is I set it down / That one may smile and smile and be a villain" (1.5.106–9). "So, uncle, there you are," he goes on, capturing Claudius's essence in the form of the sententia he has written in the wax. Hamlet effectively "tables" the problem of memory through a writing device. We do not know exactly what he writes—instead, here, the tables script his voice as he and they form a relay or writing machine that produces the note-to-self sententia about smiling villains, an encrypted moniker that serves as mnemonic device translating the injunction "remember me" into a "remembering of thee." Thus recruited, Hamlet squirrels away a memory device, in case he becomes less "apt," in case a vegetal lethe-like rooting beckons. And so he will swear—"Now to my word. / It is 'Adieu, adieu, remember me'" (1.5.110–11)—except that he gets it wrong, misquotes the ghost, skips an "adieu." Does that still count? Then it's down to rumor control. Horatio and Marcellus enter on Hamlet concluding something—"So be it" (1.5.114). And so he makes them swear "never to make known what you have seen tonight"

(1.5.143), the ghost returning as a sound effect, "Swear" (1.5.149, 155, 179) and, "Swear by his sword" (1.5.60).

But memory and its external devices prove insufficient. They require further backups, a more elaborate set of devices in order to replay the message such that it may be understood to refer to more than itself. Hamlet needs further grounds to prove that Claudius is guilty. He doubts whether the spirit he encounters is his father. But how does one archive a ghost? And what, for that matter, exactly is *this* ghost? In one sense, Hamlet Senior figures as simulacrum, repeatedly referred to as being "like" the king: "In the same figure, like the king that's dead" (11.40); "Look's a not like the King" (1.1.42); "Is it not like the King?" (1.1.59); "Comes armed through our watch so like the King" (1.1.109). The ghost is referred to with gendered and neutered pronouns: *it* recurs frequently and is used interchangeably with *him*. Similarly, *ghost* and *spirit* are used interchangeably. The ghost spectralizes the specter, making the ghost's referent in excess of any identification of his body or spirit by collapsing both into an image. Consider Horatio's line "Our last king, / Whose image even but now appear'd to us." The adjective *last* rather than *late* works in two contradictory ways: on the one hand, it opposes king to image in order to differentiate them, making *image* synonymous with *ghost* and *spirit*; on the other hand, *last* does not limit the referent of *image* to the meaning of *ghost*, since the last king had an image before he was murdered.

In this sense, the historical difficulty posed by interpreting the quality or nature of ghostly speech in the period, which has animated so much criticism, stands as one way of posing a general problem of witnessing as tied to questions of reproduction.[28] As Derrida writes,

> the experience of ghosts is not tied to a bygone historical period, like the landscape of Scottish manors, etc., but on the contrary, is accentuated, accelerated by modern technologies like film, television, the telephone. These technologies inhabit, as it were, a phantom structure. Cinema is the art of phantoms; it is neither image nor perception. It is unlike photography or perception. And a voice on the telephone also possesses a phantom aspect: something neither real nor unreal that recurs, is reproduced for you and in the final analysis, is reproduction. When the very *first* perception of an image is linked to a structure of reproduction, then we are dealing with the realm of phantoms."[29]

The telephonic effect, here indexed to the phantom, designates a dizzying circularity or circuit between different orders of media. Hamlet progresses from "distracted globe," to "tables," to composing a sententia, to writing something down, back to swearing, to the present tense apparent surety of his oath, and then to the swearing of Horatio and Barnardo, backed up by his sword and urged on by the spectral sound effects of the ghost who repeats Hamlet's lines. But no backing or substrate proves sufficient, can hold the impression of the phantom's call. Instead, the play turns vegetal, as the ghost had expected, auto-generating phantom referents related to media in the form of writing games that program certain actions: Hamlet's unidentified, interpolated lines for *The Murder of Gonzago*; *The Murder of Gonzago* itself (there is no actual play, just possibly an allusion to one);

Hamlet's forged letter sending Rosencrantz and Guildenstern to their deaths; the recognition of Yorick's skull by the third Gravedigger; Yorick's skull itself calling up a kind of hallucination/flashback by Hamlet; Ophelia's ballad-singing media madness.[30] Even the ghost as a referent is unmoored. Is he already there before the play begins? Is he there when he tells Hamlet how he was murdered? Is he there in the closet scene?[31] The play ends up rooting itself "on Lethe wharf," as conflicting facsimiles of events past and present compete.

This spectralization of reference into a relay system by the ghost's call unfolds a problem of readability and audibility that is at the same time a problem of sovereignty in the play.[32] *Hamlet* asks what happens when the sovereign can't answer, when the speech of the sovereign is spoken from the beyond the grave, when the sovereign may be inaudible. And what happens when the sovereign doesn't take the call, doesn't answer at all? *Hamlet* routes sovereignty both through the logic of the fac/faux/simile and through the delayed or replayed and reported speech we call *Hamlet*'s answering machine. The play discloses thereby the way media platforms produce temporal and reference effects whose management constitutes the fabric of sovereignty itself.[33]

As Derrida points out in *Archive Fever*, living speech is always inscribed within a technical structure of repetition; the answering machine, when activated, speaks with a ghostly voice:

> A phantom speaks. What does this mean? In the first place or in a preliminary way, this means that without responding it disposes of a response, a bit like the answering machine whose voice outlives its moment of recording: you call, the other person is dead, now, whether you know it or not, and the voice responds to you, in a very precise fashion, sometimes cheerfully, it instructs you, it can even give you instructions, make declarations to you, address your requests, prayers, promises, injunctions. Supposing that a living being ever responds in an absolutely living and infinitely well-adjusted manner, without the least automatism, without ever having an archival technique overflow the singularity of an event, we may know that a spectral response (thus informed by a *techne* and inscribed in an archive) is always possible. There could be neither history nor tradition nor culture without that possibility.[34]

In *Hamlet*, the answering machine effect turns politics into a politics of the scene of writing or inscription (Should we be writing this down?). Phantom voices install themselves via various writing technologies, writ large, with the hope of reactivation. But we can never be sure that they were voices or that they actually happened. *Hamlet*'s telephones limit sovereignty then to various forms of dictation and instruction that are prone to dilation, forgetting, as they do and do not quite phenomenalize. All such lessons that Hamlet gives and receives and that *Hamlet* offers remain incomplete, botched, encrypted as they are by a party line to which you are connecting only just now.

Yorick's skull almost provides a model for the respondent's predicament. In act 5, scene 1, following the Gravedigger's knowledge, we suppose, of graves, Hamlet recognizes this Yorick (or claims to do so) and summons him up from memory. Hamlet takes *this* skull as Yorick's, and his speech memorializes Yorick's missing speech via words that are not remembered but whose effects are registered, rendering Yorick's skull a broken or inadequate playback machine for which Hamlet compensates: "Here hung those lips that I have kissed I know not how oft. Where be your jibes now—your gambols, your songs, your flashes of merriment, that were wont to set the table at a roar? Not one now to mock your own grinning, quite chapfallen. Now get you to my lady's table and tell her, let her paint an inch thick, to this favour she must come. Make her laugh at that" (5.1.179–84). Like Sir William Thomson at that meeting in Glasgow, here Hamlet must do all the voices—render the remains of this live wire of a clown lively again, putting Yorick's call through now. We do not know that it is Yorick on the line—the Gravedigger says that it is so and Hamlet decides to agree, trusting to his presence, to voice, but in doing so, rendering himself a playback machine that installs voices in things.[35]

This moment follows hard on the emptying out of surety from all forms of textual backing—"Is not parchment made from sheepskins?" Hamlet asks Horatio, "Ay, my lord, and of calves skins too," Horatio replies. "They are sheep and calves which seek out assurance in that. I will speak to this fellow" (5.1.107–10). Hamlet and Horatio then form a circuit as Hamlet narrates the graveyard, deploying an extended *ubi sunt* formula that renders each skull that the Gravedigger exhumes talkative by registering the absence of voice, the absence, in the case of the lawyer, of his various legal documents, and remarking on Alexander the Great's new use values in their present. The parade of skulls already borders on a game in which each new arrival sets Hamlet talking, striking new poses, impersonating this and that fellow as in some passionate archaeology. And this game might be said to capture the essence of conversation in the play, which threatens all the time to reveal itself as dictation or script giving, a lesson, that hopes to program some future action.

Like Yorick, Horatio finds himself reduced to minimal replies that enable Hamlet's continued speech. But such reduction to answering, to agreeing to become an ear, circulates through the play. It is not reducible to character—though characters may be reduced to this order of the digital, to speaking or not speaking—which does not mean that they are listening, hearing, or will agree to what we have heard them hear. Hamlet too had to be quiet and listen carefully back in act 1, scene 3; finds himself reduced to single words and phrases by the ghost in act 1, scenes 4 and 5; reduces his fellows to the same in the swearing that follows, the ghost serving then as literal playback machine, repeating his words. After advising the players on how to perform *The Mousetrap*, Hamlet leaves the first player with just three words: "Ay my lord" (2.2.475) during his instruction giving. After the aborted mousetrap, Horatio is similarly reduced to responding to Hamlet, "I did very well note him" (3.2.282). "Remember me"—the injunction transforms the figure of the sovereign, the ghost, into a literal dictator, an enforcer whose spectral fingers can only press *replay*. But such replaying of what was to begin with a phantom referent spawns only further backups and desire for backups that might lay hold of a certainty of reference that, caught in the logic of the freeze-frame, fragments further what was a fragment to begin with—the ghost's narrative, already a facsimile and partial rendering of his demise, rhetorically pitched against the story that's been anonymously "given out."[36]

As Ronell intuits by her splicing of Hamlet with Heidegger, their words become versions of each other's, spliced into a dis/continuous script, to understand sovereignty in such terms, as the play invites, is to come up against the limits of our ability to make sense of this play as producing any singular script that might be said to inaugurate the "human," our predicament, "modernity," and so on. For the play inscribes its account of sovereignty through the spectralization of character, rendering characters not as dialogical units or a network but as vocal functions on a party line without an operator.[37] Such is the static that the play would have us endure—provoking or demanding further supplementation or repair or radical inquiry in every *here* and *now* ("*hic et ubique*") that looms. Character criticism, such as would suture *Hamlet* to Hamlet, and by extension derive thereby a variously historicizing script for us from the play, manifests as a symptom of the play's telephonic de-centering of sovereignty. The play conserves a desire for a master's voice that can dictate the truth but voids its content by partially revealing such scripts to be only further hallucinations, the further production of fac/faux/similes of reading and not reading. To remain within this structure amounts to operating in a world without events, a world of continuous, dissimulated being that disguises the primary antagonism, the event, that was the sovereign state's violent articulation of itself and its citizens.

But how, other than through a self-rending auto-production of voices that do not quite coincide with their points of enunciation, voices that always seem to be coming from elsewhere, might we respond? What orders of compensation or counterproduction does the play imagine or stage in response to finding ourselves enmeshed within the structure of telephony? Hamlet's "antic disposition" codes his letters to Ophelia and his manner, revealed in act 2, scene 2, as further examples of noise or disinformation, rogue affect relays that generate static or simulate "Hamlets" "*while this machine is to him*" (2.2.121). Such letters and performances amount to facsimiles of facsimiles. But what of *The Murder of Gonzago* and Hamlet's warranting of the deaths of Rosencrantz and Guildenstern? What order of writing are these? They seek to alter the relays of his world and to rewrite the text of a sovereign violence that demands an extrajudicial killing.

Enter the dumb show.

HAMLET'S SPEECHLESSNESS

Hamlet: Can you play *The Murder of Gonzago*?
1 Player: Ay, my lord.
Hamlet: We'll ha't tomorrow night. You could for need study a speech of some dozen
    lines, or sixteen lines, which I would set down and insert in't, could you not?
1 Player: Ay, my lord.

(2.2.474–79)

The players appear out of nowhere. Hamlet has been running interference with Rosencrantz and Guildenstern. Here, he sends them packing—"follow him

[Polonius] friends. We'll hear a play tomorrow" (2.2.472–73). He then turns to his "old friend" and we learn that *The Murder of Gonzago* will be collated with a text that Hamlet will write. But those lines go missing; we have no empirical proof of their arrival; only Hamlet and the players can know if they've been said. The speech arrives quite precisely by not arriving, by splicing one text into another such that it passes as unseen and unheard even as it is seen and heard.

This order of anonymous writing aims very precisely to counter the anonymity that signs the passive giving out of stories such as the circumstances of Hamlet Senior's death. The only writing that counts will be writing that is not perceived as such. In act 2, scene 2, we watch the creation of this anonymous text—a text that we will never know for certain has been spoken. This speech, so we are told, will be written and inserted. We may judge therefore that it will have happened—but we will not hear it even as we do. Much like the player, reduced here to Hamlet's *phone*, we serve as ears merely, ears that will listen but not hear, judging that the speech has occurred (perhaps) with our eyes by watching Claudius's reaction. When *The Murder of Gonzago* is performed, then, the play unfolds as a facsimile of the collation, a collation that remains forever unavailable even as it is performed. Hamlet's speech of 16 lines going missing in order to prove effective, writing coming back as speech and thus constituting what will prove, he hopes, to be, for the first time, the repetition of an event for which the only referent is a phantom.[38]

Rather than default, as critics traditionally have, to psychology and character criticism or its avatars by asking what motivates Claudius to interrupt the performance or deriving a metaphysics or ontology of speech from the scene, we want to insist on the way the play structures the relation between performance and text as a relation between performance and phantom referent.[39] *The Murder of Gonzago* inverts the relation between the murder and the ghost's facsimile narration—it aims to recreate it in and by this difference. Something occurs, as we all remember, to make Claudius rise and end the performance:

> *Ophelia:* The King rises.
> *Queen:* How fares my lord?
> *Polonius:* Give o'er the play.
> *Claudius:* Give me some light, away.
> *Polonius:* Lights! Lights! Lights! (3.2.257–62)

But that thing, whatever it may be, remains absorbed into a texture we cannot know, that the play renders unavailable. What then is to be made of the dumb show, the crux that animates so much critical traffic? What is the dumb show exactly? What is its status? Crucially it is not a repetition, an equivalent of *The Murder of Gonzago*, itself the equivalent of the ghost's speech about his murder. Its media relation cannot clearly be sorted out. Its singularity consists in its designating an event. The dumb show happens, and happens only once. Strictly speaking, it reads as a long stage direction: "*The trumpets sounds. Dumb-show follows*":

Enter [Players *as*] *a king and a queen, the queen embracing him and he her. He takes her up and declines his head upon her neck. He lies him down upon a bank of flowers. She seeing him asleep leaves him. Anon come in* [*a* Player *as*] *another man, takes off his crown, kisses it, pours poison in the sleeper's ears and leaves him. The queen returns, finds the king dead, makes passionate action. The poisoner with some three or four* [Players] *come in again, seem to condole with her. The dead body is carried away. The poisoner woos the Queen with gifts. She seems harsh awhile but in the end accepts love.* [*Exeunt*] (3.2.128ff)

Within the play, the dumb show is not a transcription of a past performance. Neither is it a script. Instead, the stage directions both archive a performance to come and describe a performance that has already occurred. The effect proves dizzying. For the dumb show calls into question the economies of reading and interpretation that have thus far prevailed in the play.

"What means this?" Ophelia asks immediately after the dumb show ends. But when are her lines supposed to occur? Is she addressing what Hamlet has said to her or the dumb show itself? The nontemporal status of the directions is registered by the editorial habit of not including the dumb show within the line count for the play. It simply occurs during the performance—designating its timing but not prescribing its duration or exact content. Assuming they know what the dumb show means, W. W. Greg, John Dover Wilson, and other critics who have followed in their wake formulate the problem as one of redundancy. The dumb show plays as a disposable surplus or worse as static. They justify its inclusion by variously differentiating it from *The Murder of Gonzago*, despite the dumb show's singularity in early modern drama and the obvious differences between the two versions of the same story: the dumb show has no revenger, and the actors are mute.[40]

Yet in what structural sense does the dumb show "follow," as the textual note dictates, when the players "enter"? Hamlet provides no advice to the players about the performance, as he does for *The Murder of Gonzago*; and, as many critics have pointed out, it's not clear whether Hamlet even knows about or wants it to be performed.[41] It voids its origins by and in its appearance. The dumb show simply happens. Even more strictly speaking, the dumb show is not exactly stage directions or even a plot summary. The king does not "die"; instead it registers results—a "dead body" is "carried away." It serves then as a loose facsimile of whatever a given cast performs or a given reader imagines is performed. The dumb show's resistant status renders it the perfect example of *Hamlet's* recurring spectralization of a multimedia "text" that does not speak, that does not answer a call or even place one. It stands as an archive to the play's own procedures, its unfolding as an ongoing archiving of its own encryption of events.

The Murder of Gonzago can never be the *CSI* trap Hamlet claims he wants it to be because the trap is already caught, as it were, in this spectral economy where every repetition is like one to come and in which every performance must constitute its own origin that it is then understood to be repeating.[42] Consequently, no one can actually "answer"; all that the players and the audience can do is remain on the line, on hold to a speech that may or may not be happening even as the call ends and Claudius, in this case, disconnects. All we can do is report in fac/faux/simile form. And here we begin to broach the political implications of our account: no one, so the play seems to say, is ever really in the position of sovereign as Carl Schmitt defines sovereignty—"sovereign is he who decides the exception."[43] Instead, like the audience watching the play, clued in by Hamlet to a moment that appears as if it should trade heavily on dramatic irony as some sovereign technology on sale daily at the Globe, sovereignty finds itself disconnected by the telephone. As such the dumb show stands in relation to the missing word that begins the play before it begins. It designates the play's traumatic archival kernel that very precisely is not there, but present only in and by its performance of what is missing. The dumb show remains strictly unreadable. It is not "there." It refuses to reside in a single substrate or medium. Lacking even the Ghost to personify its structure, it remains arguably the most deeply haunted scene in the play, the most in need of exorcism if not excision. We may venture, then, that the asymmetrical structure of the dumb show as unrepeatable "event" that the text archives and *The Mousetrap* as repeatable happening constitutes the machine, in the play's sense of the word, which generates the coproduction of the fac/faux/simile and the phantom referent that is *Hamlet*. The play begins before it begins with a call from beyond the grave: an unmarked grave whose occupant therefore must be "remembered," and this "quasi-machine-like" logic corresponds to the critical crux the dumb show generates by and as its an/archiving of a performance. The two "cuts" or cruxes stand as the generative core of the play's spectral / telephonic / tele/technomedia economy of hallucinated reading in which speech detaches from is referent and words simply "live on" and come back.

In this sense, the inverted double to the dumb show may be located in Hamlet's other key moment of writing, the forging of a letter with which he replaces Claudius's letter to the king of England, condemning him to "present death."[44] In act 4, scene 6, Horatio receives a letter from Hamlet, siphoned off from the packet that is then passed on to Claudius. This letter testifies to Hamlet's existence and alludes to a set of circumstances that are too sensitive to put in writing. "Horatio, when you have overlooked," it begins; as Horatio must read aloud, we discover the turn that the plot has taken: pirates, jumping ship, a return voyage. "I have words to speak in thine ear will make thee dumb"—which, of course, Horatio both is and is not, as here he reads Hamlet's words aloud. These words for which Horatio's have substituted, as if themselves a dumb show, are delivered in act 5, scene 2, as Hamlet concludes the narrative alluded to here in the letter:

> Up from my cabin,
> My sea-gown scarfed about me, in the dark
> Groped I to find them out, had my desire,
> Fingered their packet, and in fine withdrew
> To mine own room again, making so bold,
> My fears forgetting manners, to unfold
> Their grand commission; where I found, Horatio,
> A royal knavery, an exact command . . .
> My head should be struck off. (5.2.13–24)

Hamlet gives the original letter warranting his death to Horatio for him to "read at more leisure" (5.2.26), but then goes on with his narrative reporting what happened on the ship. He describes, in effect, an offstage scene of writing and revision, a dumb show of writing or a crime scene of writing that redesignates bodies by the vacancy to the word *bearers* (5.2.46). Having discovered Claudius's letter, Hamlet sits himself down and "devise[s] a new commission, [writes] it fair" (5.2.31–32) even though once upon a time he disdained such secretarial work, the effect of which is that "those bearers [of the letter should be] put to sudden death / Not shriving time allowed" (5.2.46–47). "So Guildenstern and Rosencrantz go to't" Horatio remarks. "They are not near my conscience," Hamlet replies, at which Horatio exclaims, "Why what a king is this!" (5.2.62), referring uncertainly to the excesses of Claudius or to the cool, self-governed discipline of Hamlet.

Here, Hamlet parasitically inhabits Claudius's writing structure, becoming "like a sovereign," producing forged facsimiles of letters warranting a death sealed with his dead father's signet ring "which was the model [likeness or copy] of that Danish seal" (5.2.50). The letter has gone. It remains now as a further instance of writing gone missing, present to the play only in the form of the allusion, the absent narration designated yet to come in the letter of act 4, scene 6, which comes to us through the voice-activated audition of Horatio, in the reporting Hamlet provides, and in the dead but uncanceled letter that Horatio may read at some putative leisure to come. There remains, as Hamlet observed to Horatio in act 5, scene 1, no "assurance" in writing and its substrates. The elaborated infrastructures of *survivance* remain intact. They may, as in the case of Claudius's dead letter that would reduce Hamlet to an object to be handed over into "present death," or that has him hand himself over, be interrupted, but the relays, even if parasitically reinhabited, may not be canceled. Your time, finite being that you are, will run, the "rest" may be "silence," but still, your words may be speaking long after you are not. "I do prophesy th'election lights / On Fortinbras: he hath my dying voice," says Hamlet (5.2.339–40). And "from his mouth whose voice will draw no more" (5.2.376), Horatio will, so he says, summon up the words. Hamlet's words shall be spoken (but not quite) again even as he rests in silence.

In order to escape this structure, a time-traveling, wish-fulfilling cancellation serves as the ultimate hallucinatory lure for readers of the play—from Dover Wilson's *What Happens in Hamlet*, which severs editorial matters from performance, to Margreta de Grazia's astonishing Hamlet *without Hamlet*, which aims to suspend the last two hundred years of *Hamlet* criticism that would stitch him into a post-Romantic predicament of the "modern."[45] Rather than replay or repeat, such apocalyptic editorial or postal cancellations deliver prequels or sequels, whole parallel worlds. They fill in the missing word/world that comes before the first word, exploding the text as they reconstitute it. The un/reading they install must overcompensate, however—must secrete an excess of presence to make up for the phantom referent they see off. The symptoms they generate take the form of an overproduction of sense, a sense that they must constitute over and over again, constantly recrossing the crux in order to bandage the cut. They remain hostage then to same logic of the fac/faux/simile that we have identified.

CANCELLATIONS: *HAMLET 2*

This urge to cancel the past, to assert one's agency in the present via a time-traveling return that revises the referent finds filmic treatment in the mall comedy *Hamlet 2* (2008), in which Jesus and Hamlet join forces in order to fix their relationships with their fathers. Parodying the inspirational teacher genre, the protagonist of the film, Dana Marschz (Get it?), is a failed actor turned drama teacher in a high school in Tucson, Arizona, which, as the narrator at the beginning of the film announces, is where dreams "go to die." Haunted by "his bad relationship with [his] father," Dana translates Hollywood films to stage, as in his two-person adaptation of *Erin Brockovich*, to blistering reviews by teenage drama critic Noah Sapperstein. When funding cuts mean that drama will be cancelled, Dana seeks out Noah for advice. Noah minces no words, telling Dana that he has "produced nothing worth saving" at which point Dana offers, "There is this one other thing. It's a piece I've been working on . . . It's called 'Hamlet 2.'" The gist of the plot responds to Dana's insight that *Hamlet* is so very sad and that had everyone had a lot of therapy, then the story it tells might have been avoided. So much more than a sequel, *Hamlet 2* seeks to trump the play's telephonic interruptions with a two-way, static-free or static-friendly conversation with Hamlet's father. And if it were to succeed, inserting its prerecorded therapeutic messages into the past, then *Hamlet* would simply never have been. *Hamlet 2* offers an un/making or un/reading that would leave us all with, quite literally, nothing to read, and nothing for Horatio to report: Hamlet without *Hamlet*.[46]

At the beginning of the stage production of *Hamlet 2*, Jesus, played by Dana Marschz, returns from the dead and gives Hamlet a time machine so that he may go back in time to save the lives of Gertrude, Laertes, and Ophelia, whom Hamlet also marries. Claudius is left out of the plot, but Old Hamlet turns up on a huge movie screen near the end to tell Hamlet he forgives him. After Hamlet forgives his father, Jesus, in turn, forgives his "higher Father." The only difference is that God does not respond, but his silence is in effect replaced by the audience's enthusiastic applause. In *Hamlet 2*, calls go through unimpeded, everyone has the right number, and Jesus becomes a holy switchboard operator whose number is available for the asking—or better yet, at the moment you think you might need it, you discover that you already have it:

> *Hamlet:* Where are we going?
> *Jesus:* 33 AD.
> *Hamlet:* Got it!
> *Jesus:* Hold on!
> *Hamlet:* Okay.
> *Jesus:* You know, sometimes even I feel like my father's forsaken me.
> *Hamlet:* Really?
> *Jesus:* Good luck.
> *Hamlet:* Thanks, Jesus.
> *Jesus:* You got my cell number?
> *Hamlet:* Yeah.
> *Jesus:* Okay. My dad finds out what I've been up to, he's gonna crucify me.

Yet an excess of specters haunts Marschz's salvific sequel. A visual echo of 33 AD, the time Jesus tells Hamlet to set his time machine for, appears on a large screen at the back of the stage just as Hamlet starts the machine—namely, Leni Riefenstahl's 1935 film *Triumph of the Will* chronicling the Nazi Party Congress in Nuremberg in 1934 (Figure 2.1).

Adolf Hitler appears in the second of three shots, as if heiling Jesus and Hamlet. This footage, however, is effectively hidden both because of its brevity and because our attention is directed to the action in the left side of the frame.

Hamlet 2 splits the screen in half, letting in, though effectively making invisible, a spectralization that haunts the apparently successful revisitation of Old Hamlet that would exorcize traumas past. A res/in/surrection of two world historical crime scenes, the Riefenstahl footage links the crucifixion of Jesus and the Holocaust and structures the narrative sequencing of *Hamlet* and *Hamlet 2* as unhappy play and then happy sequel (as a do-over of the play). Choose the film over the play, stick with its *diegesis* that completes the old, and these momentary images, along with the troubling parade of anti-Semitic and misogynistic references throughout the film, flicker in and out of view like some troubling static that will simply pass. The silent and invisible God Jesus addresses at the end of the stage production is the flip side of the footage from *Triumph of the Will*. The negative of negation is in turn negated as theological evidence; however, the ghost of Old Hamlet does not spectralize enough: he appears as a father speaking entirely new lines, but he cannot double as an invisible and inaudible and never incarnated higher Father.

Beyond reconfirming the out-of-joint temporality of the play that we have already offered as a symptom of its telephonic structure, by its ending, *Hamlet 2* produces a visual structure that depicts the blanking out of a traumatic cut in the service of decoupling the present future from past traumas. But by that blanking out, by the decision to look to the future, a past crime scene lives on. Offered under the rubric of forgiveness, of a son forgiving a father, such a moment of elation comes freighted with its traumatic double, an elision that lets something of the past through. Such moments of forgiveness, the film seems to offer (or maybe it does not), remain connected, then, to a textual apparatus that remains inhumanly neutral—rerouting those calls you wish to put through or parasitically allowing still others to go through unwanted. The return to 33 BCE, if you like, calls forth also all the other possible '33s including Riefenstahl's, whether you like it or not, by the currency of numbers. The film's deployment of time travel, its splicing together of Hamlet and Jesus following an oedipal script, remarks the danger we found brooding in our first chapter in Marx's sense of the future in the *The Eighteenth Brumaire of Louis Napoleon*, a future that cannot be imagined.

Hamlet 2, of course, turns out to be a success. Fathers and sons are both forgiven. The play is translated to Broadway with the original cast mostly intact. Dana Marschz strolls down a New York street impersonating a Jeremy Irons who's been on the phone to beg for a part in the play. Surprise, surprise, by its *Hamlet*-fixing finale, *Hamlet 2* offers to cancel the "old" and authenticate the "new." *Hamlet 2* has launched; it has amassed friends and foes—witness the billboards to the Broadway launch. Within the structures of repetition and revision we have

Figure 2.1   Leni Rienfenstahl's *Triumph of the Will* (1935) appears on-screen in *Hamlet 2* (2008).

been accounting, the un-*Hamlet*ing of 'Hamlet 2' accomplishes something that no one else has managed to do. In supplementing the play, it disambiguates the title, quite literally producing Hamlet without Hamlet Senior, Hamlet without *Hamlet*, as it were, repatriating the Dane, and giving him a play that finally bears his name as successor to his father, the sovereign Hamlet II. Thus, finally, the economy that pertains between character criticism and management of the text via editorial procedures would transform the faulty phantom referent of the title into a true haunt—playing two shows a day, matinees and nights, on Broadway.

END OF CALL

Thirty or so years before the media launch that was the First Folio, four hundred years before the fictional translation of *Hamlet 2* (the play) to Broadway and the release of *Zombie Hamlet* (2012) in movie theaters, prose polemicist for hire Thomas Nashe tried out a defense of plays and play going in his *Pierce Pennilesse* (1592), which imagined, somewhat strangely, how the dead might respond to seeing themselves bodied forth onstage. Actor-zombies, he offered, walked the London stages. The pitch runs as follows: "The pollicie of Playes," writes Nashe, proves "very necessary" for it generates "light toyes" that will "busie [the] heads" of those people who find themselves with too little to do when a "State or King-dome that is in league with all the world . . . hath no forraine sword to vexe it."[47] There's just nothing quite like "feare of invasion" "every houre" to keep people on their toes, he thinks, to enervate and so animate the multitude and ensure that the state is "confirmed to endure." War, or better yet, "feare of war" keeps people busy. Plays are not the cause of civil disorder, then; they do not, as certain detractors may remark, "corrupt the youth of the Cittie" (214). Instead, they serve a "necessary" function—to provide one of the four pleasures that "men that are their owne masters" (212) "bestow themselves to" during "the after-noone," which is "the idlest time of the day": "game playing, following harlots, drinking or seeing a Playe." "It is very expedient," he continues, "they have some light toyes to busie their heads withall, cast before them as bones to gnaw upon, which may keepe them from having leisure to intermeddle with higher matters" (211).

Enjoying himself immensely, the virtuoso Nashe further takes on the counter-factual burden to "prove Playes to be no extreame; but a rare exercise of vertue." Follow his argument and play going becomes the privileged writing machine of the state. It offers up moral lessons that will ensure by their happening that nothing actually happens that has not happened before. Writing of Shakespeare's chronicle plays, Nashe offers that "first, for the subject of them [plays], it is bor-rowed out of our English Chronicles," resuscitating the "acts" of our "valiant forefathers" "that have line long buried in rustie brasse and worme-eaten bookes" (212). Reclaiming the acts of the dead from the "Grave of Oblivion," as John Michael Archer notes, Nashe proclaims plays (histories at least) "reliquaries of aristocratic honor."[48] He summons up "brave Talbot (the terror of the French)" from *Henry VI Part One* and asks "how would it have joyed the brave *Talbot* . . . to thinke that after he had lyne two hundred yeares in his Tombe, hee should triumphe againe on the Stage, and have his bones newe embalmed with the teares of ten thousand spectators at least (at severall times), who, in the Tragedian that represents his person, imagine they behold him fresh bleeding" (212). And therein lies the power of plays that Nashe offers as their defense. He proclaims, "There is no immortalitie can be given a man on earth like unto Playes" (212), offering the public theater to London's City Fathers as something on the order of a secularized chantry cum Star Chamber, the audiences it draws the biosemiotic affect relays that ensure that "Talbot" remains a household name, living on, in their mouths and by their tears. Our sighs or our censure will decide who and what lives on and who and what gets forgotten. No reading here, no parsing of a text; just an economy of remembering and forgetting wedded to the continuance of the city, its governors, and its theaters.

What tends to go unnoticed in Nashe's repositioning of plays and play going as a kind of virtuous or moral calisthenics, perhaps because it appears so cli-chéd—of a piece with the cult of memorialization in the period—is the emphasis on the manner in which plays transport their audience. Momentarily inhabiting the skin of the now defunct Talbot, Nashe freezes the tragedian's performance and the "spectators'" reaction as something Talbot does not see but would have "joyed" to think on. Nashe's subjunctive rendering completes the impossible circuit and communicates the "joye" Talbot never felt but we now anticipate for him. The reanimating power of Nashe's katabasis stands surety for the stage as a machine for producing various kinds of "pasts" in the "present," rendered less as a spectacle than as an impossible thought or feeling imagined in the bones of a dead man, "newe embalmed with the teares" of the audience. Andrew Gurr has written persuasively of this passage as the "first description of mass emotion other than laughter in any London playhouse," citing Nashe's defense as a key fragment in understanding the shift in stage practice during the Armada years. Nashe's logic seems more complicated, however. For if plays are reliquaries, forms that somehow distil or preserve past virtue, enabling it to be reactualized in as many "presents" as there are metonymic shows or showings (at "several times" in this case), then plays and play going become the privileged means by which to provide the successive doses of reference once provided by the actual threat of Armada or any "forraine sword." For Nashe, then, public theater becomes a device by whose contiguity with the dead, whom it dusts off and causes to walk again, the state is able to access the referential powers of violent acts of marking or history making but in idling or leisurely guise. Such resuscitations, he contends, will tend to "distract the globe," to replay Hamlet's words, to keep their audience quiet, dumb, like that fat weed that luxuriates on "Lethe's Wharf." After all, there is so very much we needs must forget to remember.

Come Judgment Day, of course, the dead will (for Nashe) actually rise and final accounts will be settled, but in the interim, public theater remains your best hope for living on (unless, that is, you can get Shakespeare to write a sonnet about you).[49] By this theatrical technology and its infrastructure, the growing number of theaters in London, the state, Nashe suggests, may produce terror effects on the order of a Spanish Armada or a foreign invasion. Support the theater (or simply let it alone), he seems to say, and theater companies will serve up shows that sedate the idle by allowing them to revive past glories. Talbot shall terrify the

French daily, Henry V shall take Harfleur again and again, and every day may be St. Crispian's Day. Certain very special proper names collecting dust in the chronicles will find voices to name them and bodies to flesh them out onstage. And such names and the affect relays they form with their hearers will prove so much more effective than tear gas or some such technology of punishment. Theater, Nashe implies, convenes a crowd in order to disperse still other crowds that might one day assemble, producing tears of idiotic joy, now, before the fact, which keep certain names fresh, circulating, newly embalmed.

Then again, as Nashe's delight in his own performance makes clear, while it may seem that he offers theater to the state as a tool for revising the past, or writing the present and the future, what's getting sold here is the public theater itself, along with Nashe's own pamphleteering, as sovereign media platforms.[50] It is they that constitute the privileged technologies by whose recruitment of watching, listening, and reading or scrolling audiences, the names of "Talbot," "Henry V," and "Hamlet" will continue to circulate, living on in spite of and because of their various states of arrest as objects. Tuned to the currency to be found in proper names and their serial revival, Nashe's deal comes with the hardly veiled threat also that if support is not forthcoming, then those to blame (read: City Fathers) may find themselves tragically unremembered or worse lampooned onstage. Public theater may offer up doses of awe and terror, but it can also produce deforming laughter and worse. What's at stake, then (and it remains unclear how high or low those stakes actually were in the 1590s) is the business of keeping readers reading, theater audiences showing up, and the City Fathers regulating rather than closing theaters. Nashe's defense naturalizes the fact of theater in relation to a collective archive, asserting its sovereignty as a framing device, a neutral or tactically unstable technology for summoning up names, their stories, and their aphoristic or ideological quotient. Such performances may prove edifying. They may find imaginary labor for idle hands and minds. They may incite a riot.

Admittedly, Nashe's defense gets high on a discourse of anticipation, written from within Talbot's tomb. Here, Talbot is summoned as a kind of exotic derivative from times past—a repeatable future that the plays access in order to make sure that nothing can finally happen. To borrow a phrase or two from Richard Doyle's reading of the rhetoric of contemporary cryonic technologies and the complex financial arrangements they require in order to maintain the un/dead, we could say that the contract Nashe proposes here between the state and its players offers up theater as an "engine of anticipation"—an anticipation here felt by the dead Talbot, kept freshly dead, "sur-viving," by the production of affect in the theater of Nashe's "today." Time appears here as a reversible and contingent effect of a particular technology, making Nashe, "Shakespeare," and theater more intensely "present" *here, today* in a debate about its future.[51] In effect, then, Nashe's "policie of plays" depends on positing the stage and its plays as part of an extended multimedia platform, a generalized structure of *survivance* that forms between the grave, official histories, the public theater, and its plays, backed in quarto and folio, edited, translated now back to stage, to film, to your home entertainment centers, or to the clouds where you archive such things and serve them up in classrooms.

If today the rhetoric of cryonics, whose feasibility remains to be decided, has no choice but to "exchange an economy of reference for an engine of anticipation," Nashe has it much easier. As self-appointed rhetorician of a viable technology, already pulling in bodies left, right, and center, such that the City Fathers are protesting at the traffic generated by just two operating theaters in the early 1590s, Nashe subtly offers public theater up as an agent of distraction, an enervating recipe or confection that will provide the commonwealth with the doses of phantom referents it needs in order to remember to forget. Of course it is all very improving. Virtuous action will be worthy of replication and reembalming, producing fake (i.e., animal) blood and real (i.e., human) tears. In addition, "spectators" (City Fathers included) will be chastened in the present by the negative examples as well as the virtuous.

But don't get too distracted. What you have been reading will have been Nashe, "Shakespeare," and the whole company engaged in a project that they hope, and that did, exchange an "engine of anticipation" for a valid economy of reference: the existence of so many public theaters in London, plays entered at the Stationer's Register, and their collection in the First Folio. By that same token, however, the translation of now defunct human skins from parchment to stage, reanimated by the shadows of the company, whose performances cast off variously backed texts, generates still a host of figural possibilities as each iteration fails to agree. There never was or will be a *Hamlet*, only variously unreadable and irreconcilable *Hamlets*. It has been this order of resistance that we have sought to discern in *Hamlet*'s self-rending archiving of itself in different media, the texts themselves resisting and inhabiting the lures of what Nashe describes as a technology of secular resurrection, theater as *telephon/e/y*.

Fittingly, the crux offered by Hamlet's dying words as delivered by the First Folio serve as an emblem for the life-and-death effects produced by a multimedia archiving of the end of the call. "O, I die, Horatio," he announces (5.2.336). "The rest is silence" (5.2.342), but he continues to emit sound effects that the Folio captures via a series of "O"s. Typically, this crux (what is Hamlet doing at this moment in the play?) is simply suppressed by editors—Hamlet's trailing "O, o, o, o" excised from the play. What, then, is the status of such a crux? Is it the archiving of a particular performance (by Richard Burbage, perhaps)? Is it a missing stage direction that has been folded into the play, requiring a further disambiguation by the addition of the editorial "Dyes?" We end by sponsoring no particular reading but instead by offering this "O, o, o, o," as a very particular symptom of the textual monstrosity that is *Hamlet* (with Hamlet) and that is produced by the glitches and hang-ups of media translations and our attempts to generate weak sovereignty over them. "I am dead." Yet still I shall speak, make noise. I may even prove "royal." The fetish labor of textual editing and critical reading remains bound to this crux, to the virtualization of speech, a virtualization that resists our attempts to assert sovereignty over a text other than by its reduction and refolding. There really is no assurance to be found in media (or their histories), and for this reason we assert a disabled, aporetic politics of the crux against the parceled-out sovereignty of the editorial crutch.

But we have to go now—there's another call coming through: it's Juliet. She's on her own up in her bedroom and she's feeling rather low. She tried calling the Nurse back but stifled her own call, for "what should she do here?"[52] "My dismal scene I needs must act alone" (4.3.19), she says, but "faint cold fear thrills through my veins" (4.3.15). Vial and knife before her, she previews waking up in the Capulet family tomb-cum-movie theater and finds herself terrorized by a spectral montage of disgruntled Talbots become Tybalts. How she feels about Nashe's offer of theatrical reembalming we do not know, but "joy" does not quite describe what she expects when she wakes or finds herself woken. Shrieking like a mandrake torn from the earth, instead she imagines that she shall "madly play with [her] forefathers' joints, / And pluck the mangled Tybalt from his shroud / And, in this rage, with some great kinsman's bone, / As with a club, dash out [her] desperate brains" (4.3.51–54): "Where is my Rome/O, o, o, o" (5.3.150)?

CHAPTER 3

ROMEO AND JULIET
IS FOR ZOMBIES

38. Another series, which cuts across all the others: the name, the law, the genealogy, the double survival, the contretemps, in short the aphorism of *Romeo and Juliet*, Shakespeare's play of that title. It belongs to a series, a still-living palimpsest, to the open theater of narratives which bear this name. It survives them, but they also survive thanks to it. Would such a double survival have been possible "without the title," as Juliet puts it?

39. The absolute aphorism: a proper name. Without genealogy, without the least copula. End of drama. Curtain, Tableau (*The Two Lovers United in Death* by Angelo dall'Oca Bianca). Tourism, December sun in Verona ("Verona by that name is known" [V. iii, 299]). A true sun, the other ("The sun for sorrow will not show his head" [V. iii. 305]).

—Jacques Derrida, "Aphorism Countertime"[1]

AT THE END OF OUR LAST CHAPTER, we left Juliet up in her bedroom, imagining what it might be like to wake in the grave world from which Thomas Nashe claims public theater summons up the dead. As you recall, Nashe imagines that such a wake-up call will prove highly satisfactory to all concerned. London's authorities shall witness the distraction of its idle multitudes; said multitudes shall get high on successive hits of affect; public theater and its avatars shall grow and prosper. Nashe summons up "brave Talbot (the terror of the French)" from *Henry VI Part One* to illustrate theater's appeal and invites his readers to contemplate the "joy" Talbot would have felt, had he known, that two hundred years on "his bones [are] newe embalmed with the teares of ten thousand spectators at least (at severall times)" provided by London's theaters.[2]

For Nashe, theater becomes akin to a mode of archival tourism or touring. It takes you everywhere and nowhere. Its chief currency lies in the "proper names" it keeps in motion and the stories they condense. By its employment and recruitment of biosemiotic wetware (actors, writers, and spectators), public theater keeps the likes of Talbot "freshly dead," periodically opening the grave for successive revivals. The company's "shadows" or actors body forth such names and deeds whose bones were long since picked clean. And, come the end of the play, those names, twinned with the faces and names of certain actors, perhaps, find themselves inscribed in the memories of the audience—the audience become wetware to theater as a mnemotechnical relay to the grave.[3] By their theatrical translation, Talbot's dust-bound deeds are rescued from the kinetic dead zone or media purgatory of the unturned, worm-eaten pages of a chronicle. Welcome, we might say—fanfare, please—to the public theater: that latest, new-and-improved apparatus of secular resurrection. That's Nashe's pitch, anyway.

But Juliet's not so sure. Up in her bedroom, vial of sleeping potion by her side, she's still wedded to the thought of actually waking up. She's turned off by the thought of Talbot Tybalts. Revivals, she thinks, prove scary: "a faint cold fear thrills through [her] veins."[4] She wants to live, plans on dying so as to live. Unfortunately, the play she's in seems headed into Nashe's tomb world, and she worries that she and it might get stuck there, that the theater might become, in effect, a crypt. We join her at the moment she wakes or "rises," as the stage directions have it, in the tomb (5.3.147). But we do so obliquely, via the cinematic delegates recruited to her survival in Iranian director Abbas Kiarostami's *Where Is My Romeo* (2007). This short, three-minute film depicts a series of women in an unidentified movie theater watching the last minutes of Franco Zeffirelli's *Romeo and Juliet* (1968). At no point in its three minutes does *Where Is My Romeo* give us direct access to the Zeffirelli film. Neither does it deliver its soundtrack. Instead, we watch the film as mediated by the women in the movie theater. We hear the soundtrack by way of a muted, muffled, distanced rendering of the dialogue and music but with no guarantee that this accords with what the women hear. Juliet's suicide unfolds, therefore, through the film's succession of reaction shots, through these women's faces, as we listen in on the auditory stimulus that augments the screen images they see and we do not. Even as it completes a set of familiar circuits—*Romeo and Juliet* may be recognized; Zeffirelli's film comes to its end; the audience emotes on cue—*Where Is My Romeo* does not allow us to move beyond the scene of cinephilia (the on-screen image of an audience watching a film) that it takes as its habit and its haunt. We do not make it out of its movie theater. We struggle and fail to motivate the images it offers, to transform them into the semblance of a narrative.

Our aim in this chapter is to inhabit *Romeo and Juliet* (c. 1595–97) from within the uncertainties, the mis/recognitions, and mis/directions that *Where Is My Romeo* produces by its off/staging of the play, by its summoning of Shakespeare to a scene of metacinematic commentary and reflection. We are interested in the film's own investments and contexts, but more so in what might be said to be its unintended or chance consequences for the play. Crucially, for our purposes, we think the film represents back to us the function of the spectators in Nashe's sales pitch, offering to our eyes one iteration of the so very many audiences that have served and serve still as the biosemiotic relays to what Derrida names the "still-living palimpsest . . . the open theater of narratives which bear the name[s] "Romeo" and "Juliet" and so also the title, *Romeo and Juliet*.[5] The film attenuates our access to the play, this yoking together of two proper names to form a third, a third that takes on the form of a title, a title keyed to a story, to a niche in our archives and libraries become tombs. It asks us to approach the play by way of the emoting wetware that we both are and now, by the film's cinephilia, are not. We "watch" *Romeo and Juliet*, but the tears we cry are cried for us by the women it screens, tears that, once upon a time, Nashe offered to London's City Fathers in order to sell public theater. We are interested in this partial estrangement, this awareness of media as a relay, which strands us in the "cut" or crux of not reading, in a moment that remains strictly unreadable.

Where Is My Romeo invites us to focus on the role of successive audiences become substrate to the program *Romeo and Juliet* installs and so to redescribe the play from the vantage point they afford. The scene of cinephilia it screens serves as a moment when film as medium loops back on itself, coming to serve thereby as a substrate to the theatrical medium. And this cinematic capture or hosting of the play as it has been translated to film enables us to foreground *Romeo and Juliet*'s own formal properties and peculiarities. In what follows we dwell with what we take therefore to constitute the film's deforming or partial wrecking of the play even as it renders it recognizable. Its title, for example, misquotes Juliet's waking line—"Where is my Romeo?" (5.3.150)—dropping the form of a question so that the line takes on the role of a figure or topos, a declaration of the film's haunt. Such a deformation—perhaps an accident, perhaps a signature; how should we tell?—seems of a piece with what we take to be the distancing of the play signaled by the withholding of the film image and the attenuation of the soundtrack to Zeffirelli's film. But the effect of these disorientations remains unclear.

We take such instances of partial wrecking or wrec/k/ognition as examples of what sociologist Bruno Latour names "iconoclash." "With iconoclasm," he writes, "one knows what the act of breaking represents, and what the motivations of apparent destruction are."[6] The icon is broken because it is taken as a false idol. The act of breaking demystifies; it breaks one relay in order to promote what it takes to be a healthier attachment, a better icon or idol. Accusations of fetishism or a pathological relation to things or objects fly. But "for *iconoclash*," Latour continues, "one does not know: one hesitates, one is troubled by an action for which there is no way to know, without further inquiry, whether it is destructive or constructive."[7] *Where Is My Romeo*, we think, inhabits this zone of hesitation. It troubles the play, but it does not break it. It enables us to sidle up to Shakespeare, to watch as we reach a threshold at which a minimal unit or particle of Shakes/ appears, in this case, proffering one of three proper names—Romeo, but not yet Juliet, or *Romeo and Juliet*. For, even as we may fill in the missing names in our heads and so complete the title, the film refuses to deliver them, leaves them tactically un/read, pushes the play away as it invites it in, by retarding our ability to eliminate the medium that backs the story in the iteration we encounter *this* time.

If for Latour "we can define an *iconoclash* as that which happens when there is uncertainty about the exact role of the hand at work in the production of a mediator," we go further and suggest that an iconoclash, or here more precisely a Bardoclash, serves to foreground the presence of media itself, in this case in the proliferation of this "still living" but dead-alive "palimpsest," *Romeo and Juliet*. Unlike Latour, we are not particularly interested in attempting to judge whether or not the "hand ready with a hammer [plans to] . . . expose, denounce, debunk, show up, disappoint, disenchant, dispel one's illusions" or if, "on the contrary, [it is] . . . a cautious and a careful hand, with palm turned as if to catch, elicit, educe, welcome, generate, entertain, maintain, or collect truth and sanctity."[8] We understand that, from his point of view, he wishes to defend models of reference and translation that proceed on the basis that deformation or transformation are necessary to any act of mediation—"no transport [translation] without trans-formation" might constitute a slogan to this effect.[9] We understand also that he considers interrupting a cascade of images, breaking the chain of mediators, and forcing one "freeze-framed" instance to stand impossibly for the whole to constitute an act of critical violence or stupidity.[10] We remain sympathetic to these positions, but what intrigues us is the way the successive remediation of a text across several platforms may generate deforming effects, serial iconoclashes, that are not reducible to a strong, agentive, intentional act of critical breaking or postcritical loving.

Media transfers or migrations tend to add and drop actors all the time. The recognition they produce comes with a certain wrecking of what they transport. Indeed, we venture that *Romeo and Juliet* might be understood itself to constitute a programmatic breaking of an image or refusal to produce a particular order of iconographic effects. And by that breaking, it inducts its audiences into a quasi-automatic, compensatory set of iconophilic or iconophobic gestures. *Where Is My Romeo*, we speculate, marks one spinning off and away of the *Romeo and Juliet* thing that renders this program visible, the structure of the play a delivery mechanism, the film, in effect, siphoning off the play to serve as the occasion for its own image making.

For us, then, an icon or Bardoclash manifests as the momentary retarding of the actualization of a text in cascade, as it is performed, and as a making available of the variously lively (human and not) mediators that translate or transmit some *thing* (text, story, image) to inquiry. Bardoclash signals the intervening function of the media that mediates, which permits the Shaky translation, and raises a question therefore as to its functions. It is political in the strict sense that it requires us to decide on its status, but it communicates also the madness of deci-sion, the way in which deciding relies, as its Latin root recalls, on an irreversible cutting.[11] An iconoclash raises the stakes of reading and deciding but offers no mimetic political program. Instead it acknowledges that whatever we decide will have consequences and so impedes the act of deciding, the act of knowing.

For example, we tend to share Juliet's concern about the uncertain status of revivals and the epistemic violence that may attach to them, and so we are tempted to find in *Where Is My Romeo* something on the order of a prophylactic inoculation against the bio/bibliographical program that the yoking of Romeo to Juliet to *Romeo and Juliet* installs.[12] The play is a virulent mode of *survivance* that keys the biopolitical management of sex lives to the bibliographical living on of books and media. As Derrida writes, in addition to "missing" one another, Romeo and Juliet "both survive . . . one another."[13] And by missing one another, they both live to see the other dead, coming to serve therefore as each other's substrate. Thereafter, both, in Derrida's terms, live on and over, and above—into a succession of forevers, backed up by the play's title such that we cannot fail to recognize them and it, and find ourselves, like it or like it, reviving this un/dead, never living, always lively, super- or supracouple.

The play's eponymous self-naming creates, in this sense, an auto-referential, self-grounding program that it will not be possible to disinter. Romeo and Juliet remain tangled with the title, yoked to each other, and to the play, by what seems like a mutely serial "and." And this program begins and ends, as Juliet guesses, in the tomb, the archive cum vault of stories, which the public theater circulates and today migrates to successive media platforms via serial revivals. Its power lies in the fact that the only bones at stake are ours, as well as those of the actors that body their proper names forth. For, if Nashe was able to predicate theater's viability on the supposed referential outside grounded on and in "brave Talbot's" bones and deeds, then, in *Romeo and Juliet*, theater subsumes the grave, eats it, such that its program, that *Romeo and Juliet thing*, becomes unmoored from state or sovereign and takes on the heft of an apparatus or writing machine. The tomb it stages is always empty even as the theater may (or may not) be full.

But we're not sure. We hesitate. It remains to be seen and not seen. In order to find out, we need first to embark on a redescription of the play on our way to Kiarostami's movie theater—a redescription tuned to the cascade the play sets in motion, by its own act of breaking, by its self-interrupting, self-ruining structure of *survivance*, its equipment for dying.[14]

Accessorize That!

At the end of *Romeo and Juliet*, the watch raises the city, and Verona converges on the Capulet tomb. "The people in the street cry 'Romeo', / Some 'Juliet', and some 'Paris', and all run . . . toward [the] monument" (5.3.191–93). The ballistic clamor of these as yet singular proper names—"Paris," "Romeo," "Juliet"—punctures Verona's early morning air as the names explode serially from anonymous mouths. The names remain unmoored. The three have yet to enter into a significant relation. They hang in the air without conjunctions, but by their naming they signify that something has happened. Verona congregates. Those who bear the names "Capulet" and "Montague" or who, like the Prince, stand with Paris, find themselves summoned by the watch or drawn by the clamor. They are presented with the bodies: "County Paris slain, / And Romeo dead, and Juliet, dead before, / Warm and new killed" (5.3.195–97). Capulet's wife says she will die. Montague's wife, so we learn, is already dead—Romeo's outlawry and exile killed her. Accordingly, the Prince seals the tomb, "till we can clear these ambiguities" (5.3.216–17). Clear the crime scene. Silence the cries. Inquire into the syntax that we lack and that will enable us to enter these names into some set of relations that we may understand.

Nothing, so it seems, was as they thought. The Capulets woke two days ago to find Juliet dead. They buried her. They choked down the "baked meats" that would have been the "wedding cheer," and felt the word *cheer* (food that is happy, akin to happiness) fracture into the "sad feast" of mourning (4.5.84–87). They did not understand, but still they grieved and buried their daughter. Now they find her warm and dead. Again. Now they must revive their grief.

Montague suffers also. Romeo? Is he back? Come home to die? How comes he here dead, already? He offers the scene uncertainly as a pedagogical, parental, or filial failure—how could his Romeo, "untaught," "press before [his] . . . father to a grave" (5.3.214–15)?

Likewise, the Prince—does he know that Paris frequents the tomb, plans, "nightly," "to strew [Juliet's] . . . grave" with flowers and tears (5.3.12–17)? Probably not, for Paris "would not be seen" (5.3.2); gets spooked by Romeo's torch (5.3.21); and has his page keep watch though he's "almost afraid to stand alone / Here in the churchyard" (5.3.10–11), what with all that loose ground "with digging up of graves" (5.3.6).

Now all that remains are the three bodies. What can the Prince do but "seal up the mouth of outrage for a while" (5.3.216)?

A voice supplements the scene. Friar Lawrence turns epilogue, confesses, apologizes. His words come quickly to enumerate the plot that the parents have missed and so to parse out the agents involved in the errant course events have taken. Juliet was suicidal and came to him alone in his cell; he gave her a sleeping potion and wrote a letter to Romeo explaining everything about the "form of death" he "wrought on her" (5.3.244–46), but "Friar John / Was stayed by accident" (5.3.250–51); he came to the tomb himself, but there was a noise, within or without, and he was frightened; Juliet would not leave; "her nurse is privy" to the marriage (5.3.266). If it is his fault, punish him.

Besides or before this minimal revelation of the turn events took, Friar Lawrence's words serve to couple and uncouple bodies, to provide the syntax that the Prince and surviving family members lack. Friar Lawrence rewrites the scene and reanimates the corpses and in doing so we witness a scene of writing, the writing of the play's title, *Romeo and Juliet*, the title we already know, whose composing we may never encounter for the first time even as we do so:

Romeo, there dead, was husband to that Juliet,
And she, there dead, that Romeo's faithful wife.
I married them, and their stol'n marriage day
Was Tybalt's doomsday, whose untimely death
Banished the new-made bridegroom from this city:
For whom, and not for Tybalt, Juliet pined.
You, to remove that siege of grief from her,
Betrothed and would have married her perforce
To County Paris. (5.3.231–39)

If the watch was able to produce the bodies, to summon up a static tableau, but not to provide an animating narrative that explains the scene, the Friar's emphatic "there"s and "that"s suture his voice to the scene. His voice-over re/couples Romeo and Juliet; decouples Juliet from Paris; recodes Tybalt's role in the drama. He provides the syntax, reinstates the dropped or missing relations.

The first two lines fold upon one another, rendering Romeo and Juliet in and by their relation to the other. Romeo and Juliet come to figure a singularity as Friar Lawrence's words and perhaps hands gesture to where they lie together, the phrase, "there dead," "there dead," by its repetition, punctuating the lines. Tybalt enters as the first agent in the chain of their destruction. Their "marriage day" was Tybalt's "doomsday." He figures as the occasion for Romeo's exile, not for Juliet's pining. The parents also figure—for by marrying her to Paris they sent Juliet "to me . . . with mad looks" (5.3.239–40). Interruptions and errors mount. But the Prince says he trusts the Friar—or, reprising Juliet's earlier trust back in act 4, scene 3, says, "We still have known thee for a holy man" (5.3.270).[15] Balthasar corroborates with the letter Romeo sent to the Friar. The Prince reads and reports. "Some shall be pardoned and some punished," he ends. And so, the play returns to its beginning as he offers up its title in reversed form, recognizing thereby the constitutive yoking or coupling and uncoupling of bodies that Friar Lawrence sets in motion: "For never was a story of more woe / Than this of Juliet and her Romeo" (5.3.309–10).

Moments prior to the Prince's estranging couplet, Capulet offers Montague his hand for "this [his hand] is my daughter's jointure, for no more / Can I demand" (5.3.296–97). But Montague goes further:

> For I will raise her statue in pure gold,
> That whiles Verona by that name is known,
> There shall no figure at such rate be set
> As that of true and faithful Juliet. (5. 3. 299–302).

To which Capulet adds, "As rich shall Romeo's by his lady's lie / Poor sacrifices to our enmity" (5.3.303–4). And so it begins. Icons shall be raised. Rival icons, perhaps. It's hard to say, as the play ends, what order of "peace this morning with it brings" (5.3.305), or how we are to reckon with the incipient iconophilia that Capulet and Montague set in motion. As Jonathan Goldberg comments, tempting as it is to wax lyrical and insist on the "'purity' and transcendentality of their love, and, by extension, of Shakespeare's art," Capulet and Montague's lines may be read as disclosing that "the corpses . . . continue to have a social function: indeed that they make possible the union of the two opposing houses."[16] It remains almost impossible, however, to judge their gestures, the quasi-automatic supplementing of the dead couple by a parade of coupled copies into successive media—statues; puppets; action figures, courtesy of Mattel; movies; and so on and so forth. Capulet and Montague may play at dress-up; they may enter into a tit-for-tat accessorizing of the dead; but so what? In one register the demystifying revelation that the corpses acquire a social function seems upsetting, but where, exactly, comes the surprise? Corpses have social functions—otherwise there would be no need for tombs, or libraries, or archives. Perhaps all that remains to do at the end of the play, when presented with this dismal crime scene, is to enter into some order of blocked mourning that needs must unfold as fetish labor.

After all, where were you and what were you doing the night before and morning of the Juliet's un/wedding to Paris? The Capulets were wrapped up in the arrangements: the burgeoning guest list, the fray of hiring "twenty cunning cooks" so skilled that they cannot help "lick[ing] their fingers" (4.2.1–4) while they make pies for the "wedding cheer" (4.5.87). They had to send the Nurse off with the keys to fetch more ingredients. Come morning, they rose to find Juliet dead: "She's dead, she's dead, she's dead," wails the Nurse (4.5.25). But now all that's canceled. Moments ago, Juliet woke from "the form of death" only to die, again, for the first time, and so now they must grieve again, begin again to grieve all over, as if for the first time. Juliet revived in order to die. No wonder they all end up hooked, embarked on rival feats of icon making. Accessories to the crime scene, they accessorize the dead couple by and in their translation to a different order of media than flesh.

Set aside the ideological heft the story is said to have as the "'preeminent document of love in the West'"—straight, queer, otherwise, with time, inter- or transspecies, we have no doubt.[17] Forget the way the play may be said to stage "a conflict between the lovers' individual desires and the reigning demands of family, civic, and social norms in relation to which those desires are formed."[18] None of that was primary or constitutive. Indeed, it might be said that whatever ideological quotient or predicament you wish to derive from the play has been the legacy we have constituted by our rendering and augmentation of the plot to which it recruits us. The play begins and ends in the crypt, it detours into the crypt, before its time, playing a shell game, with which we all now have to reckon, breaking or emptying itself, so that we are left to pick up the pieces. The play ends and begins wedded to an infrastructure of *survivance* that Derrida names "a groundless ground from which are detached, identified, and opposed" life-and-death effects "that we think we can identify under the name of death or dying . . . as opposed to life."[19] *Romeo and Juliet* constitutes a "living-dead machine, sur-viving, the body of a thing buried in a library, a bookstore, in cellars, urns, drowned in the worldwide waves of a Web."[20] But the survivals it programs constitute the spinning or sloughing off of a series of freeze-framed images, holiday snaps, and video nasties, as it breaks itself to pieces.

Before Shakespeare, there come the folk tales; Italian and French versions follow channeling Ovid's Pyramus and Thisby; Arthur Brooke freely translates Matteo Bandella's *Giulietta e Romeo* (1554) as *The Tragicall Historye of Romeus and Juliet* (1562); Shakespeare's *The Most Excellent and Lamentable Tragedy of Romeo and Juliet* (1595–97) appears, adding the balcony scene.[21] That play ends—"Curtain" (well, no curtain at the time, but still the play ends, insert your desired frame effect, and the audience leaves)—then come paintings, operas, guest appearances in novels such as *Nicholas Nickleby*; films, so many films; Broadway shows—*Westside Story*; animated features such as *Gnomeo and Juliet* (2011); songs—by the Angels, Dire Straits, Lou Reed, Melissa Etheridge, the Indigo Girls—and now the zombie version of the play complete with balcony scene, *Warm Bodies* (dir. Jonathan Levine, 2013).[22]

The touring, the fetish labor, the accessorizing begins and continues—writ large or small. For, maybe, on occasion, you find yourself rereading certain scenes—sneaking off to the library or to your bedroom alone or with a friend. Eventually, your fingers might wear out certain must reread pages like some worn icon of a saint whose hand the lips of the faithful have kissed away. As anecdote has it, when the First Folio that had been chained to the shelves of the Bodleian Library in Oxford in the seventeenth century for students to use was returned to the shelves and opened in the early twentieth century, having been switched for a third edition Folio in 1664, it was found that "the most handled page of all was the lovers' poignant parting at dawn in 3.5."[23] Such is the form that bio/ bibliographical intimacies take—pleasures of the flesh conjoined with those of the text. And so, like Juliet, we find ourselves continuously kissing and kissed "by th' book" (1.5.109). Or, maybe, if you've a bigger budget, one year, you find yourself taking a trip to Verona, planned or on spec, and decide, for a lark, to find the couple's haunt, their balcony. When you get there, of course, you find them already gone or supplemented by mannequins, their absence amended or marked in the form of plaques quoting lines from the play, street signs, a stunt balcony, which, from time to time, all require maintenance and repair from the traffic.[24] Or maybe you allow yourself to play mannequin and wake up one morning to find yourself Juliet to someone's Romeo ("ooh!" "Ah!"—"Here comes the sun"). "Ever fallen in love (with someone you shouldn't've)?" If so, no worries; the Friar mixes a heady brew.[25]

Understandably, the news that when we love, we play zombie to a possible revival of this un/dead couple, that, in fact, when we love, we continue to mourn them still, produces a confusing mix of pleasures, including desires for cancellations—such as the happy ending in *Nicholas Nickleby*, in which even Tybalt makes it out of the play alive.[26] Critical readings likewise share in this confusion, attempting to reprogram the play so as to derive from the pair of lovers a different orientation: a more historical, which is to say less hetero-normative account of desire, for example, that fractures the couple into a series of substitutions, or a script that manages to recognize, for once, two free individuals where we had mistaken a "single pair."[27] But it's hard to pull the two apart, for, as Juliet knows already, by the irony of her demand in the balcony scene to what she thinks is an absent Romeo to "doff" or "refuse" his name, uncoupling persons and names proves impossible, even as the two do not properly coincide (2.2.38–50). Romeo and Juliet, *Romeo and Juliet*, constitute an "absolute aphorism," "a proper name," which itself couples two names with the name of a play. And by this coupling, which the play wrecks, by this folding together of the proper names that designate characters into a title that tropes or trumps them, the series appears "without genealogy, without the least copula." The title figures an irreducible, inexhaustible structure, unfolds as a story and a semiotic chronology, that always turns out the same.[28]

Such, then, is the impression Romeo and Juliet and *Romeo and Juliet* make on each other that subsequent iterations may only replay the terms or seek to transpose them. The two lovers serve already, in and by the story, as each other's substrate. The biopolitical yoking of sex lives to state formation comes bound to a bibliographical coarticulation of persons and texts that crafts a niche or slot in the library / archive become crypt. Each actualization, ruined from the start, broken as a condition of its coming into being, ends by returning the story to its niche. As Friar Lawrence's voice-over in act 5, scene 3 makes clear, the two coexist "there dead," in the non/space to which he points. So "raise her statue in pure gold," if you want; make one "as rich" for Romeo, too. Choose whatever frame or medium you will to summon them back. You may even decide to go looking for them—"December sun in Verona," your vacation their holy day. What may we do other than continue the serial augmentation and memorialization of this doubled proper name across differing biomedia, living on, by, over, and above, our lives and loves contributing to the play's ongoing amassing of equipment for dying? The play has already broken its icon and in offering us this broken, fragmented, defaced story, it recruits us to successive acts of iconophilia/phobia. So no worries; everyone who watches or reads the play shares in the fetish.

The play itself telegraphs a caution against charges of fetishism at the very beginning of act 5, scene 3, as Romeo breaks open the Capulet tomb to gain entry to the vault. Paris looks on from his own interrupted equipmental mourning, as Romeo begs Balthasar for a "mattock" and a "wrenching iron" (5.3.22) to break open the vault. Paris recognizes that the man before him is the "banished haughty Montague / That murdered my love's cousin, with which grief / It is supposed the fair creature [Juliet] died" (5.3.49–51). Paris then wonders why Romeo has come and what his breaking open of the tomb intends—or worse, he assumes that the gesture betokens some further violence, some urgent and compulsive mutilation or desecration that he must prevent: "here he is come to do some villainous shame / To the dead bodies" (5.3.52–53). Paris, bent on what he assumes to be the opposite course of action, extending and prolonging his own order of mourning, intervenes to stop him. "Can vengeance," he asks, "be pursued further than death" (5.3.55)? The act of breaking and entering, the violence of the act that Romeo must accomplish in order to keep his appointment, to make it to the grave on time, here gets mis/read as a compulsive, frightening, violent order of fetish labor. Paris, who augments, whose hands adorn the tomb, looks on and judges that the hand with the mattock intends to break and to do violence to the bodies within the tomb. He misjudges the affect, the velocity of Romeo's blows. Paris intervenes. Romeo kills him. Paris begs for admittance to the tomb—"lay me with Juliet" (5.3.73). Romeo obliges and only then looks at his face, identifying him as "Mercutio's cousin, noble County Paris" (5.3.74–75). Such misdirections and partial recognitions wreck the play. Here Romeo breaks into the tomb too early, and, missing Friar John and the letter, finds Juliet dead (so he thinks).

By these several mis/readings, that of Paris and that of Romeo, the act of making—or is it breaking?—assumes an impossible, specular status. The two men become misapprehended mirror effects. Indeed, their serial mis/readings stage the process by which the madness of decision renders their recognition of the name—"Montague," "Capulet," "Paris," "Juliet"—a convulsive wrecking in the name of right reading. The play permits nothing more than the production of these wrec/k/ognizable figures/fragments, smashed icons, summoned from the archive-crypt that theater has become. Under such circumstances, charges of fetishism cease to signify. For everything depends on the crafting of an altered set of objects—successive, differently mediated "statues" that seek to program Romeo and Juliet, *Romeo and Juliet*, differently—the play never a referent that preexists them but a cascade of images that we keep in motion. What Derrida calls the "still-living palimpsest," "the open theater of narratives which bear this name" constitutes a cascade across different media that *Romeo and Juliet* formalizes—the play itself a strategic rendering or icon building that splices the failure and wrecking of its own image to its attempts to render that couple anew.

The tomb was and remains empty. There are no bones to the story.

MISS AND MEND

Rewind; start again; maybe this time things will turn out differently. But even before the play begins, by its prologue, the process has already begun, the program complete. "[*Enter* CHORUS]." Just voice this time, bodied forth. Or, rather, an actor's voice figuring that of the company or the corporation that brings us this play and that editions render now as a variously paratextual "prologue" folding it into act 1 or not, as the case may be. The lines we know already—we complete them in our heads even as the prologue may stutter them, as in the tailor plucked to fame in *Shakespeare in Love* (1998). We may all variously nod in agreement, then, as to the facts of the case. Cue the opening lines:

> Two households, both alike in dignity,
> In fair Verona, where we lay our scene,
> From ancient grudge break to new mutiny,
> Where civil blood makes civil hands unclean.
> From forth the fatal loins of these two foes
> A pair of star-crossed lovers take their life,
> Whose misadventured piteous overthrows
> Doth with their death bury their parents' strife.
> The fearful passage of their death-marked love,
> And the continuance of their parents' rage,
> Which but their children's end nought could remove,
> Is now the two hours' traffic of our stage;
> The which, if you with patient ears attend,
> What here shall miss, our toil shall strive to mend. (1–14)

It's slow going at first, the rhymes too close, the syntax overly exact. And yet already the prologue tunes an audience's ears to the sonnet speak that will characterize Romeo and Juliet's encounters and the accelerated, syncopated temporality of their bid to exit normative and normalizing chronologies underwritten by familial, social, generational, and generative programs. It posits the form but estranges the pace. Focus on the plot for now, on lining up the terms.

The prologue posits the "pair of star-cross'd lovers tak[ing of] their life" as the biopolitical loss or trauma necessary to "bury their parents' strife." Household enmity endures, especially when both households are "alike in dignity," and, except for "their children's end, nought could remove" it. The as yet unnamed pair's death, their coming to nothing, figures a traumatic interruption of the generational and reproductive cycles that lead to the automatic enmity of the "ancient grudge" between Capulets and Montagues, suggesting something on the order of a biopolitical balance sheet underwriting the return to health of a city in which "civil blood" issuing from "fatal loins" breeds "uncivil"—that is, bloody—"hands." Such then is the regimen the play recommends. Generative and generational loss, so the prologue declares, may void the uncivil scripts that wreck Verona and make possible something "new" that would be also a return to something lost—though it remains uncertain come the end of the play with Prince Escalus's words "all are punished" echoing in our ears the extent to which the play offers anything more than a dead loss or dead end.

Telescoping from the city, which is one, a single thing, that fractures into the two households from which the pair issue—these families, the loins of the city turned "fatal," such that reproduction becomes an outpouring or loss of blood—we encounter the lovers, who never appear singly and who, from the beginning, from before the beginning, are already a "pair." The prologue treats them collectively, positing "their life" (two lives impressed into one course), their "death" (two deaths, two survivals of each death), as the necessary condition of fair Verona's renewed singularity. Already the prologue programs Friar Lawrence's voice-over in act 5, scene 3, where he narrates the crime scene—where he points to the pair "there dead" onstage. But in the last three lines, there's a pause. The prologue advertises the play that is coming; recruits the audience (which stands already recruited); and, in doing so, asserts the efficacy of the theatrical medium as host to what the prologue "misses."

The prologue, so it turns out, was a stunt or stunted sonnet—it lacks something essential to this story or loses it in its telling. The enervated temporality of the "star-crossed" pairing hovers uncertainly, then, in the conjunction of sonnet media and theatrical performance, which do not quite connect and that serve as different frames for launching a story that plays always, from its first telling, as a revival, a bringing back to "life," on the condition of a death—a naught, a nothing, an encryption, the aphorism, the proper name—the program already little more than an archive and a crypt, an empty tomb. All this "is now the two hours' traffic of our stage"—it will take place "here." And if you listen carefully, patiently ("ears"), or sit still ("arse"), "what here [in and by this prologue, this sonnet] shall miss, our toil [labor onstage] shall strive to mend." The prologue ends with a moment of sensory recruitment, listen and sit still, that stands in relation to the "toil" by which the actors shall minister to and perhaps "mend" what goes missing. And in doing so, it turns an audience's attention to the theatrical medium, which, merely by coming second, aims to mend what has been missed.

Pitching itself as a remediation, nodding, perhaps, to the currency of the story, already, the prologue programs the action and its aphoristic certainty, keying the outcome to a generational and generative politics that yokes scripts for loving, living, dying to the "life" or facticity of various media: the lyric countertime of the sonnet and the linear unfolding of a play in performance. It does so within the balance sheet of biopolitical loss and gain that the prologue's sonnet calculates. Incompatible or variously compatible frames intervene, superimposing themselves on this story whose temporality is measured already as "ancient," cosmologically underwritten, and yet also as the spans of two lives, the few years the lovers live, and the few days they spend together. Already, then, the prologue produces an order of freeze-framing that reduces the proper names, cuts them off from the series as still lively, un/alive nodes to be performed, taken as inputs to our acts of making or simply acting out—"he's such a Romeo!" The story never phenomenalizes exactly in any of the successive "here"s offered by media platforms but migrates to the next available frame effect. Miss and mend; miss and mend.

Baz Luhrmann's rendering of the prologue in *William Shakespeare's Romeo + Juliet* (1996) offers a compelling instance of how the migration of the play to film further complicates its layering of media. In his film, the last two lines of the prologue are cut or, better yet, translated into the enframing devices of the televisual broadcast as figured by the television set on which an African American newscaster offers a monotone exaggeration of the iambic pentameter of the sonnet, spliced with the cadences of her profession, transforming the "story" into the empty casting or shell of an "event" (Figure 3.1).

The television hovers within the frame of the film as *William Shakespeare's Romeo + Juliet* asserts its sovereign ability to deliver the story, to amp up the affective and sensory routines necessary to let you feel "their life" and "their death." The camera slowly closes on the television set such that when the announcer

Figure 3.1   Televisual prologue in Baz Luhrmann's *William Shakespeare's Romeo + Juliet* (1996).

speaks her final line—"Is now the two hours' traffic of our stage"—the image on the television set merges, synchs up, or is eaten by the frame of the film and we are catapulted into its diegetic world with its kinetic, syncopating, fast cuts.

The prologue then repeats as an end-stopped, male voice-over ghosts the modes of repetition that characterize television news programs ("in case you're just tuning in") as they cater to and attempt to capture an audience. Key phrases such as "Fair Verona," "Grudge," "Mutiny," "Civil Blood," appear as subtitles on screen, in various fonts, miming the captions of print media alongside words that have for us, by their appearance in our built word, the force of proper names—such as the way "Police" appears on a black and white police car. The civil disturbance of the "ancient grudge" appears as a close-up of so much stock footage of burning buildings and the like captured by an eye-in-the-sky camera from one of the Prince's or the network's helicopters. The "fatal loins" are per-soned as we see newspaper and magazine photographs of the Capulets and the Montagues; the prologue is now unpacked to produce a *dramatis personae*, the film then introduces its own signature font in which the letter *t* appears as a cross in the blazoning of certain phrases, such as "star cross'd lovers" against a black background, the sequence ending in the appearance of its own title, *William Shakespeare's Romeo +Juliet*.

In Luhrmann's rendering, the noncorrelation between prologue and per-formance on the "stage"—the way the prologue offers the performance as a supplementing, mending, or reparative act of what "here shall miss" in the prologue—is translated into a cinematic omission of the lines that plot the noncorrelation. The eventalizing language of performance goes missing but is conserved in the multiple frame effects generated by the citation of television and print media (eye-in-the-sky cameras; news programs; features; newspaper headlines; a host of static print media). What's "missing" from these kinetic dead zones—akin to the dusty pages of the chronicles from which Nashe's public the-ater rescues "brave Talbot"—shall be provided, indeed, is provided immediately by our explosive entry into the in medias res beginning of act 1, scene 1, by way of the film's fast cuts. Uncivil blood spills quickly within the film's mutinous choreography.

But if the film introduces itself, inaugurates itself, as an immersive experi-ence that delivers the death-seeking couple whose story the television "misses," its fullness remains predicated on the presentation of television, the impossibly deracinated, extraterrestrial television set, held there by the medium of film. Entering the movie, giving oneself over to the film, entails a discarding or media ingestion of the television set. And yet, the film remains haunted by the televisual in that the first sounds we hear and the first images we see are something that even the film may not capture or render: three short bursts of dyspeptic static and three images that dissolve before they are able to take shape—the television com-ing to life and going silent of its own accord.

Iconoclasm or iconoclash, we may ask. But let's not decide. Let's hesitate, for—like Nashe's defense of public theater, like the play's advertisement of the serial replacement of the prologue or extratextual sonnet by the play itself, with its dialogic production of sonnets, as in act 1, scene 5—*William Shakespeare's Romeo*

+ *Juliet* transposes the life and death of Romeo and Juliet into the serial generation of successive orders of media that enable an audience to reexperience the hits
of affect on which the story trades. It seeks to prolong, to amp up the equipment
for dying (ooh! Ah!) by pitching the story's transmission as the correlative genesis
of different media that revive key "proper names" and the stories or aphoristic
programs for being and not being that they designate. Here, film delivers the
televisual broadcast up to view, "mending" what it "misses," recruiting its audience by positing its own technical enframing of the "star crossed lovers" against
a televisual absence or stasis. Romeo and Juliet are dead—never lived—but from
their proper names issue forth whole orders of media deaths and birth effects
(and defects), as successive orders of media archive one another according to a
nonlinear, looping chronology that renders them "old" and "new" by their serial
replacements.[29] The founding or generative trope of *Romeo and Juliet*, then, as it
successively mediates its protagonist "pair," manifests as a strategic enframing of
one medium by another—sonnet to play, television to film, lively to dead, corpse
to statue—in which whatever media precedes that which mends is pronounced
"dead" or old and newness a product of the sequence and parasitic upon it.[30] The
capacity of one medium to deliver or to revive, more vividly, to veridicate the
Romeo and Juliet thing, to reinflate their proper names, which migrate so easily
because they are empty, aphoristic, "never arriv[ing] by [themselves but] . . . part
[always] of a serial logic," depends on the willed forgetting or ingestion of one
medium as it enfolds another.[31]

As Derrida shows in *The Truth of Painting*, frame effects of this order are never
medium specific, even as they take on different forms as canalized by the technical possibilities of a medium.[32] Consider the case of the 3D animated feature
film *Gnomeo and Juliet*. Like many films, *Gnomeo and Juliet* was simultaneously
released in three digital editions, the most expensive of which says on the cover
that you can watch the film four ways: on Blu-ray 3D, on Blu-ray 2D, on DVD,
and on digital copy. (Another, cheaper edition includes the Blu-ray DVD and
digital copy, and another still cheaper edition includes a DVD and digital copy).
Such multiple releases require the production of a technological pedagogy for
would-be users in order to optimize their viewing experience—replay the prologue's recruitment of your patient "ears" or "arse," lest you "miss" what the latest
medium "mends."

Just as Blu-rays include stickers telling the potential buyer that they do not
play on a DVD player, so 3D Blu-rays include information about the new equipment they require: a 3D-enabled HD flat-screen television, an HDMI cable, a
3D-enabled Blu-ray player, and a special set of wraparound dark glasses, different
from the ones used in movie theaters (which don't work with 3D Blu-rays that
one can play without a 3D-enabled Blu-ray player) and that differ depending
on whether they have been made by Sony or Disney. All this equipment is now
on the market. In order to market a product that requires marketing new equipment, however, Disney and Sony 3D Blu-rays begin with what we call media
trailers that showcase the benefits of the new upgrade of the disc (some DVDs
did the same thing in relation to video when DVDs first arrived on the scene, and
the DVD edition of *Gnomeo and Juliet* begins with a media trailer about Blu-ray,

and the 2D Blu-ray begins with a trailer about 3D Blu-ray and 3D equipment since each disc is also sold separately).

The media trailers promote the format of DVDs and 2D Blu-rays by using clips from existing releases and then identifying them by name at the end. 3D Blu-ray trailers go a step further, however, taking narrative form, showing characters or people watching the Blu-ray on a home theater. The aim of the trailer is convince the buyer that "Sony 3D brings the theatrical experience back to your home."[33] Yet the trailer makes that case by differentiating the home theater from the movie theater. A television set is shown in both the Disney and Sony media trailers, for example. More interestingly, the home theater experience is reproduced through various kinds of special effects. For example, Sony shows a family at home watching a Blu-ray: shot from behind the family, the image shows us the television image from *Toy Story 3* (without its soundtrack audible) they are watching in front of them and placing us, in effect, in a row of a movie theater behind them. The media trailer compensates us for our greater remoteness, however, by making the family and the living room almost invisible and the television frame extremely visible.

The special effects make the media trailer into something like a simulation training film, helping us understand how immersive 3D Blu-rays are by making the world in the films far less visible and by bringing the film frame toward us. Yet, by detaching the television frame from its location on the wall in the living room, the trailer creates a double frame, with the "real" but less visible frame, exposed behind the "imaginary" but more realistic frame foregrounded for us. The dimensionality of the image in the frame gets distorted (there is no single vanishing point). The better image is being sold not only by returning the image to the frame but by dividing the frame in two. The frame thus becomes as much an obstacle to clarity of the image—an obstacle you may overcome by allowing the "new" medium to "toil" on your behalf.

The frame is not medium specific; in short, and the multimedia formats through which "film" is presently delivered are permutations, re/divisions within and between film and media. Accordingly, the story of successive media and their media citations cannot completely be historicized as a linear sequence or accommodated by existing accounts of the history of film and (new) media. The ontology of different platforms (play, print, film, digital image, etc.), their metaphysics, can only be imaged and imagined by and through their capture by other media. If you like, we are and we were never seeing a play, or watching a film, even at the Globe or in a movie theater that projected nitrate or celluloid prints that made up what self-described new cinephilics call "old" cinephilia. For that media-specific experience was and remains grounded in nothing more than a series of variable frame effects predicated upon other media. Rumors of media deaths (and births) have, as the saying goes, been "greatly exaggerated." For, instead, they constitute technical relays within a generalized economy of living on. To anticipate Juliet's self-medicating suicide, they constitute only the "form of death" (5.3.246) and life.

It's from within this story of media replacement or succession, as forms migrate across platforms, that *Where Is My Romeo* emerges—tuned to the metacinematic genre of film moments that screen the moviegoing audience back to itself (cinephilia/cin-off), sometimes granting access to the film image they watch, sometimes not, sometimes enabling us to hear the soundtrack, sometimes not, layering sounds, layering frames, and so causing film to close on itself. The film plays host to *Romeo and Juliet* as a citation within its own metacinematic commentary as film goes global and digital, as film might be said to "die" or already to be "dead."

BARDOCLASH

Where Is My Romeo belongs to the genre of world cinema. It addresses itself very deliberately to cinephiles, but the "worldness" of the world cinema it enters is not easily circumscribed by the words *global* or *universal*.[34] The film was screened at Cannes in 2007 as 1 of 33 films edited together as a "Cannes-pilation" film titled *Chacun son cinéma: Une déclaration d'amour au grand écran* (*To Each His Cinema: A Declaration of Love to the Big Screen*) and then released on DVD in a one-disc edition and a two-disc French edition. Both editions are out of print, though still for sale on various websites. Kiarostami's three-minute film has been extracted, compressed into streaming video, and uploaded by multiple versions onto You-Tube.com. The status of the film remains complicated therefore. Each of these iterations, the multiple editions, the successive migrations and extractions of the film from DVD to YouTube, itself a commonplace practice, complicates our sense of the ontology of film or media generally. What is the status of this film? Does it constitute already an adaptation or a spin-off from Shakespeare's play or from a filmic adaptation of the play? Do the multiple YouTube extractions constitute "editions" or further adaptations insofar as they isolate the film from its cinematic source?

The title *Chacun son cinéma* serves as a preemptive exercise in ontological damage control. The title cancels out a thinking of the global in favor of a universal assumption that we already know what cinema has been and still is, dividing cinema up into discrete units of narrative films directed by single persons from single nations: each person, whether a director, cast or crew member of a film, or spectator gets his or her own singular cinema. And that cinema is available, if not at Cannes, then on DVD. The "universality" of "world" cinema thus celebrated is composed of a nationally bounded geopolitics, each film exchangeable in the same universal currency. Indeed, we could reasonably say that the entire film is a compilation of cin-offs since each film is in some way about film.[35] Unlike spin-off, or full-scale film adaptation, the cin-off is limited to a single sequence in a narrative film in which characters watch a single sequence of a film in a movie theater. All have scenes in movie theaters, though one of the thirty films stops at the ticket window and another ends at a bar after the film is over. One film shows clips from the cin-off in Jean-Luc Godard's *Vivre sa vie* (*Her Life to Live*), in which the prostitute Nana (Anna Karina) and her john go to the cinema to see Carl Theodor Dreyer's *Jeanne d'Arc* (a.k.a. *The Passion of Joan of Arc*, 1928), shifting the narrative focus to Antonin Artaud playing a priest away from Maria Falconetti playing Joan. And the film plots a course toward a "happy ending"—for film we take it—offering its final title in the DVD menu as the emphatically promising "Happy Ending."

If you choose this option, however, you go to a comedy directed by Ken Loach about a father and son standing in line deciding which film to see only to change their minds at the last second and to go to a football match instead. The last fade-to-black shot of Loach's film carries over a roar of soccer fans from the last shot, with credits in white type. Yet the "Happy Ending" title and the happy ending arrive in the form of a short clip from the end of René Clair's *Le Silence est d'Or* (a.k.a. *Silence Is Golden, Many about Town*, 1948) that shows Emile (Charles Boyer) asking his young date, Lucette (Dany Robin), while they are watching a hand-cranked projection of a silent film, if she likes happy endings. She replies, "Yes," and he says, "So do I." Play music, fade to black, followed by a thank you to René Clair and then by a citation of the film's French title. Endings, terminations, fade to black, and death effects become thereby a matter for cinephilic discussion—what order of ending do you like—happy or sad?

Where Is My Romeo significantly contributes to the cine-"wreckage" of *Chacun son cinéma* by interrogating the ontology of the film medium.[36] The title of Kiarostami's film is conspicuously missing the question mark that follows Juliet's question in the play. By improperly reciting a question from *Romeo and Juliet* as an unpunctuated and nonsensical declarative sentence, Kiarostami pressures the viewer to hallucinate the question mark and hear the silent title as a question. Indeed, the French subtitle underneath the film's title on the two-disc DVD edition succumbs to this pressure and supplies the missing question mark, as if emending the film, repairing and correcting its unwitting error.

This correction is itself something of an error, however (Figure 3.2a). For Kiarostami's film puts cinema's ontology into question by reproducing yet disturbing the citation practices that underwrite its apparently specular economy.

Much the way Jean-Luc Godard cuts from Dreyer's close-ups of Falconetti in *Vivre sa vie* (1964) (Figure 3.3c) to Nana (Anna Karina) watching her in a movie theater (Figure 3.3d), both of whom shed tears, *Where Is My Romeo* lets us identify with the anonymous women in the audience who are identifying with Juliet, as in a hall of mirrors. Kiarostami follows Godard in making film spectatorship into an archival and auratic effect. In Godard's *Vivre sa vie* no extradiegetic music plays on the Dreyer soundtrack of Dreyer's film, nor does any extradiegetic music sound play on the Dreyer soundtrack of *Vivre sa vie* as the central character Nana, shot in close, watches mirroring close-up shots of Joan (Maria Falconetti). The theater showing Dreyer's film seems to be in disrepair. Only the neon letters "cine" of "cinema" to the left of the marquee are lit (Figure 3.3a). Only three people are watching Dreyer's film (one woman walks out just as Nana and her john sit down; Figure 3.3b). Godard represents the specularity of two beautiful, young women actors in two different films as a cinephilic effect, a fantasy of auratic immediacy that is no longer, perhaps never was, available and that is grounded in the total silence of the soundtrack of *Vivre sa vie*. Godard did not say that cinema was dead until the 1980s when he filmed his eight-part *Histoire(s) du cinema* (*Histories of Cinema*), but he had already seized on a kind of cinematic death in *Vivre sa Vie*, adding the title "Le mort" a second time to his rendition

Figure 3.2a and b   Title sequence to Abbas Kiorastami's *Where Is My Romeo* from *Chacun son cinéma* (*To Each His Own Cinema*) (2007) and closing, "Thank you so much Mrs. Kheradmand."

Figure 3.3a, b, c, and d   Carl Theodor Dreyer's *Passion of Joan of Arc* (1928) as archival effect in Jean-Luc Godard's *Vivre sa vie* (*Her Life to Live*) (1962).

of Dreyer's film (it appears only once in *Jeanne d'Arc*).[37] A different analogue medium, which Godard deployed in *Histoire(s)*, made it possible to keep cinema intact, something that had a history that began and ended even if what cinema was remained an open question.

In *Where Is My Romeo*, Kiarostami goes further, staging film spectatorship as a tropic, archive effect that constitutes a form of mourning. Like *Vivre sa vie*, *Where Is My Romeo* focuses on a series of women (18) in a movie audience who are shot successively in close-ups of approximately the same length. They watch a woman (Juliet) commit suicide near the ending of Franco Zeffirelli's film adaptation of the play. The crucial difference is that Kiorastami never shows the film the women are watching, intensifying the auratic immediacy of the emotional responses we see on the screen by withholding the image of the film to which they react. The reaction shots pose a problem, then, inviting us to sift the faces for an implied narrative or progression even if they are randomly ordered. The first and last women we see are quite old, in contrast to the other women, who are all young. Some women stare fixedly at the screen. The last actress turns her head to her right as if looking at the person seated next to her, but we can't tell what she sees, or if she is seeing anything. This final actor gets a line of text at the bottom of the frame thanking her by name: "Thank you so much Mrs. Kheradmand" (Figure 3.2b). Most of the women cry as the film gets more dramatic. Juliet's line "O happy dagger" (5.3.169) provokes tears. These shifts from many young women to one old woman, from women sad to women sad enough to cry, may be interpreted in a number of ways (e.g., even a very old woman may still be young enough to identify a 14-year-old teenager; women may be deeply moved by a film about a woman; the film is really a tribute to the Iranian actress it names who appears to accept this tribute by turning and nodding her head in reference to the succession of reaction shots to which she reacts). Yet these shifts do not constitute a narrative shift: their multiplicity and heterogeneity prevent one from totalizing *Where Is My Romeo* either as a random series or as a narrative film. The film's last shot is not an ending (no one gets up to leave), and the music from Zeffirelli's film plays over the two credits that end Kiarostami's film. The initially diegetic soundtrack of the film becomes extradiegetic during the end title sequence.

By redividing *Where Is My Romeo*'s cuts in their relation to the content of their images and its film soundtrack and by dropping the question mark to the film's citation of Juliet's line, Kiarostami invites us to read the film in philological terms. Whoever added the question mark after Romeo in the French subtitle was not merely resisting the film. Philology is essentially a reparative operation, emending texts, preserving and saving them, making sense of them, rendering them readable. And in this case such a discourse of repair would plug up all the cuts and divisions, mending what goes missing. Using YouTube, we could, if we were so moved, restore the unseen Zeffirelli film. All you have to do is to open two browsers and place them side by side, almost as if the film had been shot in split screen, to see the one clip and the other at the same time.

We "have the technology" to complete the circuit that *Where Is My Romeo* interrupts. Synchronizing two browsers and screening both films—imaging, thereby, precisely what the film refuses—enables a certain order of philological

Figure 3.4   Synching up Abbas Kiorastami's *Where Is My Romeo* (2007) and Franco Zeffirelli's *Romeo and Juliet* (1968) via Youtube.com.

inquiry into the process by which Zeffirelli's *Romeo and Juliet* adapts Shakespeare's play. He cuts Friar Lawrence and also two lines from the Prince's summation, reassigning the lines that remain to the male voice-over narrator who delivered the prologue, the lines serving as the film's epilogue. And such a focus on the restoration of what has been cut, on the violence to adaptation, may prove very powerful.

Kiarostami's use of the Prince's lines shorn of "Go hence, to have more talk of these sad things; / Some shall be pardon'd, and some punished" (5.3.307–8) so that "All are punished" (5.3.295) resonates most loudly and has been read as keying an audience to the film's deeper topical allegory, offering up the series of emoting women as a symbol of the universal oppression experienced in his Iran.[38] The reading is supported by the fact that the film replays in small the strategy of Kiarostami's feature "Shirin" (2008) in which "a hundred and fourteen famous Iranian theater and cinema actresses and a French star" appear as mute spectators at a theatrical representation of *Khosrow and Shirin*, a Persian poem from the twelfth century, put onstage by Kiarostami. The development of the text—long a favorite in Persia and the Middle East—remains invisible to the viewer of the film; the whole story is told by the faces of the women watching the show." Shirin Ebadi, happens also to be the name of the Iranian human-rights activist who won the Nobel Peace Prize in 2003.[39]

As compelling as a topical reading of *Where Is My Romeo* may prove, even as it tends to universalize the series of reaction shots the film offers—the philological become ally to a roman à clef decoding ring—the strategy that Kiarostami describes, of having its 18 actors stare at a blank sheet of A4 paper as opposed to watching *Romeo and Juliet* (1968), illustrates the purely technical function of actors as biosemiotic relays or wetware to a media platform. Kiarostami says he shot the women looking at the paper first and then added the soundtrack from Zeffirelli's film later.[40] *Romeo and Juliet* quite literally remains unscreened, therefore, unseen, and unread throughout the course of film, its presence supplied as supplementary and supplanting intertextual circuit completed by certain of but not all the film's audiences. The film, the play, reduced to the moment of Juliet's suicide, become citation, becomes a point of transfer between different media and a set of political concerns both to do and not to do with Iran today. Indeed, even as the film invites this order of philological repair and allegorical transcoding, it's hard to see that it authorizes such modes of philological archive fever or *mal du cinema*, accessorizing the wrecking upon which it embarks.

In this sense, the film's formal fracturing of itself (image from sound, intertext from audience, audience from on-screen audience) designates a problem at the center of cinephilia—namely, the relation between readability and mourning. As Anselm Haverkamp writes, "the death of Mnemosyne exhausts the possibilities of lyric in that it grounds the impossibility of reading in the inability of mourning . . . Without memory and the defensive abilities of understanding ('to re-collect'), there is no possibility left for a future hermeneutics."[41] *Where Is my Romeo* stacks a series of noncoincidental terms or terminuses: the death of cinema; the death of human rights in Iran; the literal, prosaic death of the actor it memorializes, "Mrs. Kheradmand," become proper name; and the death of Juliet hard upon the death of Romeo. The film might be read, therefore, as a kind of funeral procession, anticipating the mourning of the Mrs. Kheradmand who, perhaps, already mourns, in advance, for her own death as she watches Juliet end hers. Along the stations of this parade, we mourn for all that the film splices together, in discontinuous series. But any such thematic reading (privilege whichever death you like) runs aground on the fact that *Where Is My Romeo* has already serialized mourning. Kiarostami returns to a film that ends with mourning, but the shots of Zeffirelli's *Romeo and Juliet*'s funeral are registered only through music and hence cannot be registered in *Where Is My Romeo* other than in the audience's recognition of Olivia Hussey's voice on the soundtrack singing the "Where Is Love?" theme turned pop song as it plays at the end of the film. The referent of mourning, whether that referent is alive or already dead, fictional or real, finds itself forestalled.

In refusing to make mourning into an entirely knowable or narratable sequence with a single object, Kiarostami's film deconstructs the presumed ontological integrity of cinema, the central issue being whether or not film is indexical. *Where Is My Romeo* offers us both a specular deafness (the film we watch has no soundtrack; the actors in the film heard nothing) and blindness (the film we hear has no image track; the women in the movie theater are staring at a blank sheet of paper). Yet blindness and clarity, deafness and hearing, do not map exactly to what is on or off screen. Under such circumstances—whether we encounter the death of cinema, of civil society, of an actor, or of Juliet, for that matter, reading may continue, narrative may reappear only by way of an allegorical, philologically fuelled detour, an iconophilia/phobia such as takes shape at the end of Shakespeare's play.

By withholding *Romeo and Juliet* (1968) from view, Kiarostami collapses the movie theater into the screen the film's women are watching, directing our attention by using the film soundtrack of a film adaptation of a play to a difference between theater and movie theater audiences we ordinarily cannot see. Yet phantom effects of a frame return. If you assume (mistakenly yet correctly), for example, that the audience in *Where Is My Romeo* is watching *Romeo and Juliet*, you may find yourself scratching your head and wondering where the camera has been placed even though you know it has obviously been placed in front of them. The film so totally resists the diegesis-completing convention of shot reverse shot that instead of the camera becoming a static given, more and more pressure gets placed on our understanding of each shot that unfolds as a fragment itself rather than as one segment in a series that may be replaced or interchanged with any other. The women never look at the camera or acknowledge it in any way so it is clear we are not watching a documentary of a live performance. But it is clear that the immediacy of the women's responses depends on something like a phantom fourth wall: an invisible proscenium arch between the camera and the women, shown on-screen, that the women cannot see, just as we cannot see what they are (not) watching. In effect, for the film's three minutes, the movie theater becomes a tomb, empty, refusing to acknowledge or to deliver up a complete circuit by which we may mourn properly and instead forcing us to sift its fragments and to risk, in allegorical or philological mode, breaking them further.

Such a nonplus or breakdown, we suggest, serves as the conditions that *Romeo and Juliet* sets in motion, staging the process by which mourning is translated into successive orders of broken media and frame effects. Such also are the productive effects of *Where Is My Romeo*, when modeled as Bardoclash—as an uncertain object within the cascade that *Romeo and Juliet* sets in motion. For by its broken quotation become title and withholding of the film it watches, *Where Is My Romeo* speaks back to the play's own engagement in the practice of citing other media—especially of the (anti-) Petrarchan sonnet tradition, which the prologue begins and that Romeo and Juliet enact at their first meeting:

> *Romeo:* If I profane with my unworthiest hand
>> This holy shrine, the gentle sin is this:
>> My lips, two blushing pilgrims, ready stand
>> To smooth that rough touch with a tender kiss.
> *Juliet:* Good pilgrim, you do wrong your hand too much,
>> Which mannerly devotion shows in this,
>> For saints have hands that pilgrims' hands do touch,
>> And palm to palm is holy palmers' kiss.
> *Romeo:* Have not saints lips and holy palmers too?
> *Juliet:* Ay pilgrim, lips that they must use in prayer.
> *Romeo:* O then, dear saint, let lips do what hands do—
>> They pray; grant thou, lest faith turn to despair.
> *Juliet:* Saints do not move, though grant for prayer's sake.
>> Then move not while my prayer's effect I take. (1.5.92–105)

"You kiss by th' book," Juliet replies to Romeo's begging that she "give me my sin again" (1.5.109)—citing both the rules of the sonnet tradition as script and also perhaps troping the prompt-book from which actors recite their lines.[42] But what speaks here—book or person, *biblion* or *bios*? And by what ratio or rationale should we ever decide, ever manage to decouple the biopolitical from the biblio-graphical coarticulation of life and death and love effects?

"'Where is my Romeo?" The question, real or rhetorical, by Kiarostami's logic of faulty citation, becomes a haunt, a topos—*Where Is My Romeo*. It processes the question as a moment or a place to which we may return, where we straggle or dwell. Juliet wakes in the tomb. Dwell there. Strike the pose that is her question. Keep the title at bay. The film advertises but retards the auratic function that yoking of Juliet to Romeo by the play's title effects. And so, following *Where Is My Romeo*'s logic of faulty citation, its transformation of citation into a cul-de-sac or dead ending, we ask who or what should we understand as speaking Juliet's question and reenter the play by way of her suicide, her revival into a "thing-like death."

"A THING LIKE DEATH"

So Juliet rises. She wakes in the tomb, wakes to find her Romeo dead and gone— "Where is my Romeo?" (5.3.150). Friar Lawrence bolts. She stays—"I will not away" (5.3.160). She moves in, takes the tomb as her haunt, and proceeds to narrate the scene:

> What's here? A cup closed in my true love's hand?
> Poison, I see, hath been his timeless end.
> O churl! Drunk all, and left no friendly drop
> To help me after? I will kiss thy lips.
> Haply some poison yet doth hang on them,
> To make me die with a restorative. [*Kisses him.*]
> Thy lips are warm. (5.3.161–66)

Winking, Juliet reads Romeo's death as a failure of hospitality, an overindul-gence. He has feasted without her. So she kisses him, condensing the variously erotic senses of "die" such that it will become a "restorative"—restoring her not to life but to death. She renders her death thereby lively, enlivening, revives into death. But the watch interrupts. "Yea, noise? Then I'll be brief. O happy dagger," she continues, "this is thy sheath; there rust, and let me die" (5.3.167–68). "Cut!"

We never know if the poison works, if enough remains that the kiss would indeed have killed. Cue the noise—the noise that trumps the scene, that spoils, that would interrupt. And so, Juliet calls for the "cut," a cut that completes, that ends the circuit and penetrates her own body with Romeo's "happy dagger." The act of cutting here assumes an unstable valence. On the one hand it will kill, cut her off—freeze-framing her in this moment, and by that freeze-framing escape the return to the sovereign syntax of Verona, of the world beyond the tomb. But by the same hand, this cut repairs what has been broken, cut off by the absence of Romeo, by his too early coming and his too early dying. Capulet's first words in the scene take up Juliet's metaphor but are unable to undo the cut that she completes. "O heavens! O wife," he says, "look how our daughter bleeds! / This dagger hath mista'en, for lo his house / Is empty on the back of Montague, /

And is mis-sheathed in my daughter's bosom" (5.3.202–5). Capulet's words draw the dagger out. They seek to undo the cut. He surveys the scene and traces the blade back to the absence, the empty scabbard, that marks Romeo's body. But the dagger remains: his daughter bleeds. His recognition of the act that is not yet readable replays Juliet's words, catches them at a remove, but wrecks the sense, registering the dagger as a misplacement, a wrecking of sense.

But such is the view from without the closed circuit that Juliet's calling for the "cut" completes. The metaphorical exchange or aligning of terms in Juliet's lines leads to the mutual coding of life and death, of dying and restoration. This metaphorical circuit, which never rests, which can only keep on shuffling the terms, replays the logic of Romeo's suicide moments earlier. Arriving both late and early, and always, always, on time, he toasts Juliet and drinks: "O true apothecary, / Thy drugs are quick [lively, fast]. Thus with a kiss I die [by which he means die, but also "come," and live on]" (5.3.119–20). Romeo narrates Juliet's body, misrecognizing it as her still lively corpse, playing the scene out with mock jealousy: "Ah, dear Juliet,"

> Why art thou yet so fair? Shall I believe
> That unsubstantial death is amorous,
> And that the lean abhorred monster keeps
> Thee here in dark to be his paramour?
> For fear of that, I still will stay with thee
> And never from this palace of dim night
> Depart again. Here, here will I remain
> With worms that are thy chamber-maids. O, here
> Will I set up my everlasting rest,
> And shake the yoke of inauspicious stars
> From this world-wearied flesh. (5.3.101–11)

Romeo can't quite believe that Juliet looks as good as she does in death—that "beauty's ensign yet / Is crimson in thy lips and in they cheeks" (5.3.94–95), so he fantasizes death as his rival, a rival he can only out do by joining Juliet in death, detouring into death with her such that he and she may live on.[43]

Romeo and Juliet, we know, "miss each other," "but they also survived, *both of them*, survived, one another."[44] Here, in the tomb, they bear witness to each other's deaths, and in doing so come to serve as remainders, delegates to each other's survival, living on in and by their deaths, positing death itself as a restorative, a remedy. Neither mourns exactly, but neither do they exactly forgo "any funerary rite for one another," as Paul A. Kottman suggests. Instead, their transcoding of life and death renders mourning indistinct from the living on into death that marks their choices. Each of their suicides functions as the substrate by which and within which to register the life/death of the other. Each death serves as a way of entering into a closed relay with the other, such that each lover's suicide serves as a revival into death.[45] Death, it seems, requires a medium. It does not mark an end exactly nor a cancellation of the problems of material backing. Here, in the tomb, Juliet calls for the "cut," a cut that defines, ends, and begins. We watch (and live out) the decisions, the ongoing production of cuts, successive orders of framing, necessary to preserving the cut.

But how can this be so? "Our thoughts of our death are always, structurally, thoughts of survival," writes Derrida, "to see oneself or to think oneself dead is to see oneself surviving, present at one's death."[46] No wonder, then, to return to where we began this chapter, that up in her bedroom Juliet has doubts, worries as to what will happen in the event that she wakes in the tomb, and projects herself forward into the tomb become screen for a traumatized sense of futurity. The plan as pill-pushing Friar Lawrence told her was to enter a "thing like death . . . that cop'st with death himself to scape from it" (41.74–75). To "cope" means Juliet shall meet, face, battle, buy off, dwell with, or detour with death in order to make possible a literal survival.[47] Death or death effects prove necessary, he counsels, to cancel out the marriage to Paris upon which her family insists. Death will enable her to rise again and as if for the first time as "Juliet." She must enter, so the Friar thinks, into a becoming "dead" to her family in order to wake to a future that is not scripted by them or the conflicts of their present. She must embark upon a becoming corpse, a becoming *thing*, gathering her family to her, so that by their handling of her, by the care they take of her body in mourning, they shall unwittingly become delegates not to her memory but to a literal survival.[48]

If, as Derrida suggests, death figures a blanking out or erasure of habeas corpus, the legal writ "which accords a sort of proprietorial sovereignty over one's own living body," Juliet's "thing like death" works in reverse.[49] Only by becoming corpse may she attain some measure of sovereignty over her living corpus. At Father Lawrence's urging, she enters into a literal, impossible, emptying "*habeas corpse*" so that, "two and forty hours" on, she shall "awake from a pleasant sleep" (4.1.105–6). By dying, she shall rise and possess her own self as prop. The corpse shall render up her own corpus to her, to have and to hold so that she may give it to Romeo to have and to hold. In the interim, she will have lived on as if dead, having given up any control over what will have happened to her body when she finds herself woken. Back in the Friar's cell, this prospect renders Juliet eager, reckless. Bent on suicide, high on the strong sovereignty of deciding her death, she demands that Friar Lawrence "hide me nightly in the charnel-house, / O'ercovered quite with dead men's rattling bones," or "bid me go into a new-made grave, / And hide me with a dead man's shroud" (4.1.81–85). She wants the drug now. "Give me, give me," she demands (4.1.121)—give me the drug that will give back my family to me such that by mourning, by caring for me in my "thing-like death," they become unwitting delegates to my literal survival. Fearing that she may self-medicate too early, Friar Lawrence demands she "Hold" and "Get . . . gone" (4.1.122). He will have the vial sent round.

But up in her bedroom, like it or not, she can't help but fantasize about the living death she will have endured when she revives. She worries that the poison won't work, that she will wake in her bed to the living death or zombie wedding to Paris. She worries that Friar Lawrence is merely out to dispose of her. She doubts the narrative the Friar supplies for what will happen to her in her "thing-like death." Back in act 4, scene 1, he tells her as is the "manner of our country . . . Thou shalt be borne to that same ancient vault / Where all the kindred of the Capulets lie" (4.1.109–12). "In the meantime . . . against that thou shall wake . . . Romeo shall by [Friar Lawrence's] letters know [their] drift" (4.1.113–14) and the two "will watch thy waking" (4.1.116). But such assurances do not assuage the thoughts that race on to fill in the void of sleep that a "thing-like death" entails. She wonders also "how if, when I am laid into the tomb, / I wake before the time that Romeo / Come to redeem me? There's a fearful point" (4.3.30–33). She shall "stifle," "strangle," in the "foul mouth" of the tomb that breathes no air (4.3.34–35). Worse still, she may not suffocate; she may, in terror, "run mad"

> And madly play with my forefather's joints,
> And pluck the mangled Tybalt from his shroud
> And, in this rage, with some great kinsman's bone,
> As with a club, dash out my desperate brains. (4.3.50–54)

In the event, she drinks because she thinks she sees Tybalt's ghost "seeking out Romeo that did spit his body / Upon a rapier's point" (4.3.55–57). Death comes calling but not for her. "Stay, Tybalt, stay!" But Tybalt won't wait or cannot hear her. And so she drinks. Toasts Romeo. Passes over into a "thing like death" (4.1.74). Juliet goes after Tybalt, blacks out, blanks out—a delegate to a spectral revenge plot she hallucinates and aims to prevent.

But here, in the tomb, the tie of the human subject to an automatic projection into the "will have been" of the future anterior (this is what my death will have looked like) comes unmoored from its speaker as the living body that speaks the words projects its future in reference to the corpse of the loved one mis/apprehended as still living and lively.[50] The proper names, if you like, shed their actors, their hosts. And by this shedding they take each other as host, name for name, medium for medium, both insufficient and in excess of the other as their death becomes an enlivening iconoclash that freeze-frames the other dying into life, living into death. Instead of reading the suicides as an individuating process, then, we read them as the moment at which, by positing each other as substrate to the death of the other and so living and loving on into death, Romeo and Juliet enter into a bio/bibliographical circuit—the fatal conjunction by which the two couple to form the title of the play, *Romeo and Juliet*. What we witness therefore in act 5, scene 3 will have been the production of the serial conjunction, the *and* of the play's title, the mechanism that constitutes the play as a third *thing*, a quasi-machinic survival.

Such a script as we find rehearsed in the play, what we have called the play's equipment for dying, is neither exactly "human" nor a personification of the "life" or "death" of media itself. Instead, we take the play to serve as notice that it will prove impossible to decouple the biopolitical as articulated in terms of plot and affect from the bibliographical. As Derrida puts it in the title to an interview, "Paper or Me, You Know . . . ," the choice between "paper" and "me" will prove impossible to make or to decide (cut).[51] And this script, this equipment for dying, runs no differently than the very many prosaic routines we inhabit already within the infrastructure of *survivance*: come your death, for example, shall you be burned or buried?[52] What do you plan to do with all your stuff? What will happen to all your data, on websites, in the "cloud," in your home, your storage unit, in all the adumbrated extensions in space that describe the circuits we travel? And how do you like to picture yourself being handled, waking, reviving, or living on into death, dying on? But choose as you like, as the play shows, the terms will merely circle back on themselves: corpse and corpus, *bios* and *biblion*, become substrates to the other, a mutual, coextensive enframing, such as we have seen constitutes *Romeo and Juliet*'s generative matrix as it parleys out across different media.

What would Nashe's Talbot make of the scene? Was he, in fact, the lurking presence in Juliet's bedroom that she mistook for her departed cousin? Who knows? If the living remain wedded to imagining themselves living into death, entering a living death, living on and over and above as a series of variously mediated *things*—animate only to the extent that we are hosted—then, even as *Romeo and Juliet* offers us a script for living on in the wet death of theatrical revival, your name hosted by so many wormy actors playing chambermaid to your corpse and corpus, such questions, in an irony that our next chapter explores, find themselves shelved, put on hold. For when Romeo and Juliet end, when *Romeo and Juliet* ends, its program complete, the bio/bibliographical relay returns to its niche, or reveals itself to be a storing of a potentiality and a corralling of an enlivening series of trace effects that, from time to time, we summon from the library or archive.

Then again, there might be some way to stop the dust from settling, to have the story run continuously, and so to escape the confines of the "book" or whichever medium plays host. Perhaps, to reprise a line of Romeo's, it will be possible to "give" us our "sin"/ema again, and again, and again. But such a translation or migration to a yet-to-be-imagined medium might require or manifest obliquely in our successive presents as an archival loss or injury, a total loss or oblivion— *bios* and *biblion* become bits and pieces of bio/bibliographical flotsam and jetsam floating on the flood—all wreck and no recognition.

Cue the special effects: "A tempestuous noise of thunder and lightning heard; enter a Shipmaster and a Boatswain."[53] Cue the line: "Boatswain!" "We split, we split!" (1.1.60).

CHAPTER 4

DROWN BEFORE READING

PROSPERO'S MISSING BOOK . . . S

It is a tribal habit in certain reserves of the B.B.C. to pay for the Resurrection of the Dead. The ritual is expensive; but it describes a need. It relaxes our hearing. It keeps us in touch with the past, and provides us with subjects for future conversation. Through the perfected necrophily of the living, we are allowed to tune in on the forgotten secrets of the Dead. The Dead are now honoured by their absence; preserved in our memories, summoned by engineers to inhabit the little magic box of sound. Prospero may have thrown away his Book; but the art of radio will rescue his weariness from despair; immortalize his absence; remind us that poetry is a way of listening. The art of radio may be too mortal for belief, but sound has its echoes whose future is eternal.

In the meantime, the divers loiter, bribing the sea to release its Dead for an interview with the living . . . Prospero may have thrown away his Book; but the art of radio will rescue his voice from the purgatory of the Ocean which is and may always be a neighbor to eternity. . . .

Announcer: "Tomorrow, at nine-thirty, you can hear again . . ."
Studio Engineer: "Stand by, stand by, we will go ahead in ten seconds from . . ."
—George Lamming, *The Pleasures of Exile* (1960)[1]

Like every trace, a book, the survivance of a book, from its first moment on, is a living-dead machine, sur-viving the body of a thing buried in a library, a bookstore, in cellars, urns, drowned in the worldwide waves of a Web.
—Jacques Derrida, *The Beast and the Sovereign, vol. 2*[2]

FOR THOSE OF YOU JUST TUNING IN, there has been a storm. Things have gone a bit awry. There we were moments ago in Juliet's family tomb-cum-movie-theater, watching her and Romeo die (again and again), but then there was all this noise and now we're wrecked. We thought that the phrase "wetware" was only a metaphor—a way of insisting on the living, fleshly, liquid, animate component to media platforms. But now we're well and truly soaked, just bits of variously animate flotsam. There might once upon a time have been a ship, but if so, it's gone. We heard talk of an island, but instead, we seem to have been landed with this book. It certainly feels like a book, looks like a book, but we're not sure; every time we start to try to read it, it multiplies or goes missing. There's no title on the cover. No author. And we're really not sure what's "in" it. When we try to open it images take shape and then dissolve, but there's a lot of audio, a lot of noise. The thing is radically, literally, prosaically unreadable.

Might be wisest to keep your eyes closed and listen—just to get oriented.

TUNING IN (AND OUT)

All sorts of noise and noises coming through now, a lot of static; but the signal's getting stronger, coming through loud and clear: ambient effects of rain, instruments, voices, but at a distance, just on the edge of hearing:

> Be not afeard. The isle is full of noises,
> Sounds and sweet airs that give delight and hurt not.
> Sometimes a thousand twangling instruments
> Will hum about mine ears; and sometimes voices,
> That if I then had waked after long sleep,
> Will make me sleep again; and then in dreaming,
> The clouds methought, would open and show riches
> Ready to drop upon me, that when I waked,
> I cried to dream again.[3]

Caliban, we know, speaks these lines, speaks them back to Trinculo and Stephano's unnerving by the invisible Ariel's sonic effects: "This is a tune of our catch, played by the picture of Nobody" (3.2.127). "If thou be'st a man show thyself in thy likeness" (3.2.128), demands Stephano—or, if a devil, do as you please. Trinculo is scared—ready to repent: "forgive me my sins" (3.2.130). But Stephano will have none of it—"He that dies pays all debts. I defy thee," but he doesn't quite convince, entreating, "Mercy upon us!" (3.2.131). Caliban, however, is habituated; consoles; waxes lyrical; reports on his own out-of- and into-body experiences as he passes between waking and dreaming, dreaming and waking, waking to wish that he might dream again. The noise won't hurt, he says. Relax. May as well allow the noise, the acoustic effects the island's full of, to recalibrate your bodily rhythms, the way you take your sleep, live on in and through dreams. They will do so anyway. So, give in; give over. By the end of the scene, they do: "This will prove a brave kingdom to me, where I shall have my music for nothing" (3.2.144–45), ventures Stephano, which Caliban takes as a goad to their present labor—the "destruction" of Prospero. He says, "Let's follow the noises . . . and after do our work" (3.2.149–50). And so they exit, taking the remote-controlled playing for a soundtrack, an accompaniment to the labor of their revolt.

But why begin *here*? Why begin in act 3, scene 2 with sounds that ambiguously differentiate themselves into variously technologized, sonic, musical, and vocal effects, which synch and do not synch up to the action? Why tune in and out to the noises to which Trinculo and Stephano reconcile themselves with what amounts to a boozy, metaphysical shrug and that Caliban takes as a given, a fact of the island, agreeing, if you like, both to hear and not to hear them? Why stage the island and the play as some sort of ham radio or series of broadcast effects?

We take our cue here from West Indian novelist George Lamming, who opens the first chapter of *The Pleasures of Exile* (1960), his reckoning and reversal of *The Tempest* (1611), by quoting Caliban's lines from act 3, scene 2, which describe "the noises" "the isle is full of." As Lamming makes explicit, but we, disoriented as we were from the storm, were slow to recognize, he offers the island's noises as somehow indexed to the book that Prospero says he drowns or will drown near the end of the play: "I'll drown my book" (5.1.57). "Prospero may have thrown away his Book," writes Lamming, "but the art of radio will rescue his weariness from despair," bring back his voice or voices "from the purgatory of the Ocean."[4] Taking on the disinterested and distanced tone of the mock ethnographer observing the island's natives, he remarks the "tribal habit" by which the BBC functions as a technology of secular resurrection or "necrophily," allowing or making or insisting that the dead continue to speak in and by their absence. Still, the radio does not quite convince. It's nice, it's pleasurable, but the dead don't quite sanction its serial summonses or prerecorded repetitions. It remains beset by problems of absence. The announcer and the studio engineer who work the magic become technicians merely, or, better, "divers [who] loiter, bribing the sea to release its Dead for an interview with the living."[5] And we, the listeners, constitute the crowd gathered on the sea's edge, gazing out not at a shipwreck but in anticipation of an act of bibliographical salvage.

Lamming's prose oscillates positions, locates this sea in our various kitchens and living rooms tuned in to the "set" from which the announcer speaks, transports us into the control booth where the studio engineer counts down until the air turns "live." The program? Who knows? It's withheld. What do we assume: a reading or performance of *The Tempest*, an interview with an increasingly famous West Indian writer, the latest chapter in a *Book at Bedtime*?[6] It really doesn't matter. The radio figures the noises of this island. The box that speaks has some relation, posits Lamming, not to the drowning of a book per se but to some generic act of "throw[ing] away," discharging, ejecting, or projecting—an outward movement that nevertheless, like it or not, comes back, turns back on itself. In terms of the memoir, the scene before the radio sets the stage for Lamming's description of a world programmed in relation to voices that code or intrude upon the island he explores. When the announcer reassures, for example, that if you have missed something or tuned in late, the program may be heard again "tomorrow at nine-thirty," Lamming comments that it's good "to know that Tomorrow will not desert us; that Tomorrow cannot refuse our habitual waiting," but still this programming of our days, this temporality lived in relation to the technical relays that enable voices to speak to us, at a distance, remains haunted by a desire for something else. That drowned, or as Lamming has it, "thrown away" book still beckons, remains out there, forever gone, forever (not) coming back, even as it does so. Don't worry if you miss it; you can catch it, or miss it (all over again), tomorrow.

Lamming's aim in the memoir is to speak back to his earlier use of the Caliban-Prospero dynamic in crafting his aesthetic. He does so by inhabiting or troping the play's trajectory. The island in question is England. The natives are English. He arrives as an exile from another island. "I am a direct descendent of Prospero," he writes, even as "I am [also] a direct descendent of slaves."[7] But such exile as he experiences is hardly without pleasures—among them the world of books, broadcasts, interviews, poetry readings, performances, and so on and so forth that make up the literary scene of late 1950s London. The memoir unfolds as a series of bibliographical topoi, anchored by the initial radio broadcast. The withheld script of the broadcast comes back as so many other voices recorded in scenes from the everyday life of the working writer, Lamming's interlocutors become walking books or bio/bibliographical effects. To read Lamming's memoir is, in effect, to watch books accumulate around him, to watch the way he negotiates the adumbration of bibliographical circuits that a visiting writer lives within. In the same chapter, for example, he narrates his experience as the "guest in the house of an English family," finding himself entertained by their nine-year-old son whose "first question was: 'Where are you from?' I replied, 'The Caribbean.'" At this point, the boy abruptly gets up, leaves, and, returning momentarily, "set[s] about spreading a great carpet of paper over the floor. Without explanation or apology, he simply [says]: 'Now let's see where we are talking about.' He had brought a map."[8] Lamming addresses the rest of his memoir to this boy, rendering his experiences as a bio/bibliographical impression—a life lived through and in relation to the circulation of different forms of media, a life lived in relation to a conflicted, sometimes abusive, sometimes ecstatic archive.

Throughout *The Pleasures of Exile*, Prospero's "Book," always capitalized, remains "thrown away," never "drowned," though the ocean remains a key figure, "always . . . a neighbour to eternity."[9] The act of drowning becomes therefore more of a launching or projection or jettisoning of a text or program that keeps on coming back in encrypted forms, its reactivating returns constituting the bio/bibliographical circuits in which Lamming lives his exile and takes his pleasures. The memoir inhabits this aftermath to the play, the time that comes once *The Tempest* ends, completes, cuts itself off as *thing*, with Prospero's book continuously drowning and emitting voices that arrive in a variety of forms and locations. That book remains, for Lamming, an unreadable, submerged entity that governs all, its presence registered only by its imperfect arrivals or in the variety of bibliographically mediated experiences he recounts. For Lamming, then, Prospero's book drowning functions as the constitutive act of the play's generative matrix to which he must himself write back. The book drowning inaugurates the play. Caliban and he (and we also) approach it through the figure of a compensatory, only partially readable, sometimes melodic, sometimes cacophonous, sometimes painful, sometimes, just plain missed or unregarded "noise" or static.

Like Lamming, whose radio we tune into, our aim in this chapter is to replay *The Tempest* from this uncertainly phrased scene of book drowning, hearing therein an invitation to think through the play's relationship to the figure of the archive and the conjoining of *bios* and *biblion*, of life and book become library, filing cabinet, dossier, file, shelf, radio, or storage device. Like Lamming we're tuned to the way in which *The Tempest* acquires a burgeoning paratextual addenda of books and sources, but whereas Lamming crafts his own writing as an attempt to rezone the play, to write through its storm, we remain focused on what we take to be the generative crux of what it means to speak the line "I'll drown my book." It remains hard for us to understand exactly what is at stake in Prospero's stated intention (perhaps, at some yet-to-be-determined and unstaged point in the future to drown his book). For how and by what logic of metaphorical transfer may a book be said to drown, to find the lungs its does not have inundated by a foreign medium, by water, to suffocate, or, as the *Oxford English Dictionary* allows, to find itself overwhelmed?[10] To what, we wonder, could such a sentence refer? Does Prospero do it? If so, how, where, and when? And what, we ask, does such a putative, metaphorical drowning have to tell us about the coarticulation of different forms of life (human and not) and different forms of media, especially when media are themselves said to "die" and find themselves "born"? What order of metaphorical, which is to say material-semiotic, transcoding is at work here?

It's no coincidence, we think, that bibliographical metaphors surface in the decolonizing responses to *The Tempest* as colonialist enterprise. As Jonathan Goldberg has argued, Prospero and Miranda's description of Caliban as a "failed pedagogical project," as a being "which any print of goodness wilt not take" (1.2.354) locates the play firmly within the circuits of humanist educational projects. Caliban proves resistant to Prospero's inscriptive regime—their writing of him will not take. Not surprisingly, then, the matter of impressions and of "printing" qua media effects come back in the play's biopolitical afterlives as enacted on countless actual islands.[11] If, the entire project upon which Prospero embarked, showing "kindness" or "humane care" to Caliban, figures a misapplication or misrecognition of Caliban, who by his resistance reveals himself, from Prospero and Miranda's point of view, to be some order of self-predicating "filth"—"Filth that thou art" (1.2.346)—then *The Tempest*'s bibliographical metaphors are primed, from their inception, by the biopolitical capture of "life" that marks and makes distinctions between persons by the articulation not simply of races but species. Indeed, Prospero's sovereign command of the island, by this gesture, comes to look very straightforwardly like the accumulation of various technical and administrative advantages backed by the media that underwrite his attempts at "printing." The mode of sovereignty he enjoys derives from the comparative advantages of technology and resources that allow him to broadcast his effects.

While Prospero and Miranda may regret that their Caliban pet project does not work out quite according to plan, their pedagogy cannot be judged, even by their own standard, a failure. It remains cruelly productive. For it comes to serve as the litmus test by which they may come to know the boundaries of what deserves and does not deserve "humane care." In the terms Michel Foucault develops in the lectures at the Collège de France published under the title *Society Must Be Defended*, *The Tempest* opens a window onto the procedures by which "a population [may be treated] as a mixture of races, or more accurate," the state may "treat the species . . . subdivide the species it controls, into subspecies known, precisely, as races. That is the first function of racism: to fragment, to create caesuras within the biological continuum addressed by biopower."[12] And beyond or beside or within the question of species lies the constituting of serial differences between so-called human animals and their nonhuman animal compeers. What *The Tempest* offers, then, is an opportunity to think through and with the bibliographical quotient or backing to these biopolitical articulations of living and dying in ways that suggest how the caesuras that constitute a biological continuum as an internally divided line spit out, at different historical moments, variously papery or mediated non/persons.[13] Such an orientation to the play, we think, discloses an awareness of the ways in which the "life" and "death" of books, technology, and media cohabit with the lives of persons and animals—"life" lived, read, stored, and archived in the form of some proliferating, hybrid, dead-alive zoë/bio/bibliography or writing machine.

Accordingly, the book Prospero "throws away" surfaces in a variety of media-specific guises in texts that share in Lamming's counterpedagogy. In *Black Skins, White Masks* (1967), when Frantz Fanon describes the de-structuring of the psyche that colonization provokes, he offers this anecdotal idiom: "In any group of young men in the Antilles, the one who expresses himself well, who has mastered the language is inordinately feared; keep an eye on that one, he is almost white. In France one says, 'He talks like a book.' In Martinique, 'He talks like a white man.'"[14] The book that talks, the figure of embodied fluency, disappears or dematerializes only to come back as a figure of whiteness—the book drowning in one particular pool of racially marked wetware—reversing thereby the technological progression from wax, to skin (parchment), to paper (rags then paper) in what amounts to an epidermalization of the bibliographical become racial metaphor. Fluency becomes equivalent to a tattoo that you lack or cannot get, but to which your voice or vocal prowess belongs. And such a tattoo, or "skin ego" recalls quite precisely the figure of the "print" that Miranda says Caliban will not take.[15]

You find a similar orientation to the play in Aimé Césaire's *A Tempest* (1969), whose dramaturgy carefully resists the script it sees *The Tempest* as installing. "The dossier is," as Césaire writes in another context, "indeed overwhelming"—and so *A Tempest* opens tactically with the "*ambience of a psychodrama. The Actors enter singly, at random. Each chooses for himself a mask at his leisure.*"[16] The Master of Ceremonies narrates the costuming—"Come gentlemen, help yourselves. To each his character, to each his mask. . . . Ready? Begin. Blow winds! Rain and lightning *ad lib.*" Césaire begins as he does with the Master of Ceremonies inducting and announcing the arrival of the cast because he's out to deprogram or to reveal that there may be more (and less) to the Prospero-Caliban dynamic than the figure of linguistic and cultural dependency upon which Octave Mannoni insists in his *Prospero and Caliban*.[17] Césaire's Master of Ceremonies insists on the fungible and so transferable quality of all the roles. They decouple from their expected designees and move around, actors picking them up and putting them down in a mode that seeks to de-essentialize the paradigm. The casting scene with which the play begins comes complete with mock commentary from The Master of Ceremony on his surprise, admiration, or consternation at the actors' choices and his commiseration on the roles left over for latecomers.

This alienating, prophylactic coding of theatrical performance as psychodrama, hopes Césaire (the title of his play already posits an indefinite *Tempest*, a serializing of the play), will open the text to something other than a deadly reiteration of a master-slave dialectic. And, as Césaire's deforming or rewriting of the play's title reveals, such an altering of the paradigm or reshelving of the dossier as it is understood to write the relations between populations as well as individual-ized bodies, proceeds by a calculated strategy of bibliographical intervention that seeks to alter the biopolitical circuit that attaches to *The Tempest*. Goldberg notes, for example, the way Césaire "transfers the language lesson [Caliban is said to receive from Miranda] to Prospero" in the play allowing "Caliban to refuse the point: 'You didn't teach me a thing! Except to jabber in your own language."[18] And like Césaire, Goldberg's own modus operandi in his *Tempest in the Caribbean* unfolds as the reworking of editorial or bibliographical cruxes, opening a crux, in order to open the text to other signifying possibilities.[19]

The ending of *A Tempest* remains instructive in this regard. Prospero enters, as the stage directions outline, "*aged and weary. His gestures are jerky and automatic, his speech weak, toneless, trite.*"[20] He stands onstage defending "civilization" from the encroaching peccaries and opossums that take over this now less-trafficked island. He lets off volley after volley in every direction. The jungle is "laying siege" to his cave. He's cold, and he calls for Caliban to make him a fire. But he's only got himself to talk to now. Just some old, loony castaway, shouting "Caliban"—"it's just us two now, here on the island . . . only you and me." His voice falters. The Prospero-Caliban dyad dissolves, or better still, turns out all along to have been the mutterings of the senile monad of a Prospero who will not prosper. The whole problematic of codependency gets eaten by Prospero as the pronouns "You and me" coalesce into the empty sound sense of You-me . . . me-you." As the play ends, you might say that we watch Prospero's theatrical extinction. His last word names a "Caliban" who is no longer even there onstage. For "*in the distance, above the sound of the surf and the chirping of the birds we hear*" different noises now, "snatches *of Caliban's song* . . . Freedom Hi-Day. Freedom Hi-Day!"[21] Thus the offstage, unstaged Caliban-become-sound-effect decouples from Prospero, who searches the dial of his island/radio in vain for anything more than his own voice on its way to a breakdown, a becoming noise or static.[22] We don't get to see the new Caliban. That future remains unimaged. But we are able to listen in on it, the soundtrack to a marooned dead end, as if the play becomes a radio tuning in to a future it does not stage and that Prospero cannot hear.

Waking from the wet death of theatrical revival that we inhabited in *Romeo and Juliet* to *The Tempest*'s shipw/rec/k/ognitions, we tune in to Lamming's radio, to Fanon's book-tattoos, and to Césaire's Master of Ceremonies who rec-ommends that we "*ad lib,*" though "tread water" might be closer to *The Tempest*'s idiom. Accordingly, we drift with its noise and try to listen carefully as the chan-nels change. That's the best way, we think, to approach the "Book" that Prospero throws away, loses, reserves, or shelves, even as it might be drowned. The Master of Ceremonies' instruction to "*ad lib*" invites us all to direct our course "at our pleasure" (*ad libitum*), each of us a sovereign in small, taking liberties, if you like, loitering, siphoning off all those bio/bibliographical effects to our ends. Let the future take care of itself. Let's stay tuned to the noise or noises this island's full of and see what listening very carefully to Prospero's mooted drowning of his book may lead us to discover about the coarticulation of *bios* and *biblion*, of (human) life and its various forms of backing that we sometimes call books.

Oh, but the signal's shifting. There's another voice coming through—sometimes a man's, sometimes a woman's, sometimes perfectly androgynous. It tends to change with the passing of time. Did you miss it? Don't worry, as the "Announcer" says, "'tomorrow, at nine-thirty, you can hear again . . .'" "'Stand by, stand by, we will go ahead in ten seconds from . . .'"

BIBLIOCLASH

Now. A bunch of stuff coming through about elves and spirits and graves and whatnot that we didn't quite make out—we figure it'll repeat in a moment—but here's a bit that makes an odd sort of sense. It's Prospero minus the peccaries and opossums on his way to quitting the island:

> . . . But this rough magic
> I here abjure; and when I have required
> Some heavenly music (which even now I do)
> To work mine end upon their senses that
> This airy charm is for, I'll break my staff,
> Bury it certain fathoms in the earth,
> And deeper than did ever plummet sound
> I'll drown my book. (5.1.50–57)

This passage usually provokes a question about Prospero's character. Why does he give up his magic? What is at stake in the acts of breaking his staff and drowning his book and how should they be understood? Do these actions represent a surrender of control, a return to . . . what? Is Prospero even to be believed? More recently, the passage has provoked a question about the kind of book Prospero says he will drown: is it a magic book?[23] We want to ask a different question: why does Prospero say he is going to "drown" his book? Why does the play go out of its way to differentiate or to introduce a set of yet-to-be-determined differences between burials on land (inhumation) and at sea (drowning). And what does such a constellation of terms have to do with the biopolitical quotient to the play? Inhumation makes a certain amount of sense—it comes freighted with a terrestrial grounding. You can point to where the thing lies buried. You can even exhume the staff to prove a point.[24] But drowning augurs in a stranger fashion. This mode of disposal, if that is what it is, remains clouded by the ooziness of the ocean bed into which, moments after this speech, Alonso will offer to sink if that would save Ferdinand, his son, and Miranda, Prospero's daughter (5.1.150–53).

Curiously, the word *drown* has remained partially submerged to editors and critics of *The Tempest*, periodically bobbing into view but usually slipping back beneath the surface of a reading as it speeds up to find itself becalmed by the linear. Editors of the play tend not to comment on the word choice. Now classic, New Historicist criticism tended to be concerned with the generalized modes of linguistic colonialism it found in the play and possible resistance to such mechanisms. Accordingly, Prospero's putative drowning of his book takes a back seat to the more readily processed book burning that Caliban ventures as his preferred method of prosecuting Prospero's destruction. Caliban's biblioclasm represents Shakespeare's treatment of "the startling encounter between a lettered and an unlettered culture" as is thought to have occurred in moments of contact between Europeans and the indigenous peoples of the Americas.[25] Caliban's warning to "the lower class and presumably illiterate Stephano and Trinculo" reads as canny, prescient, something he has learned the hard way:

Remember
First to possess his books, for without them
He's but a sot, as I am, nor hath not
One spirit to command. They all do hate him
As rootedly as I. Burn but his books. (3.2.90–95)

Stephen Greenblatt identifies a possible source for the attack, the story told by Claude Duret in his *Thresor de l'histoire des langues* (1613) about an encounter from 1607 in which the Hurons "were convinced that we [Europeans] were sorcerers, imposters come to take possession of their country, after having made them perish by our spells, which were shut up in our inkstands, in our books, etc.—inasmuch that we dared not, without hiding ourselves, open a book or write anything."[26] Caliban's imperative that Prospero's books be burnt comes to register then either as an astute attack on Prospero's magico-technological tokens of power or as a sad instance of fetishistic misrecognition in which he misunderstands the efficacy of writing as a technology.[27]

Such a reading remains fairly stable even in more recent criticism that attends to our field's newfound fluency in the matter of the codex. In her essay "Prospero's Book," in which she reads the magic back into Greenblatt's secularizing account of the play, Barbara A. Mowat offers a starkly polarized choice for readers and audiences. "When," she writes, "as in [Peter] Greenaway's film, we see Prospero's books—leather-bound, gorgeous, their pages yielding all the world's mythologies, its temples, its art, its histories—their destruction seems, to lovers of books and admirers of Western civilization, both problematic and poignant. To those who instead share Caliban's view of Prospero, who see Prospero as little more than a tyrant and Western civilization as little more than tyranny, the destruction of the book may be more a matter of celebration. Such a divided response to the play today seems almost inevitable."[28] This poignancy echoes also through the equally richly researched observations in James Kearney's reading of the play, which identifies the topos of the "talking book" as an anchoring trope of the Caliban episode—the "talking book" serving as a kind of "ethnographic shorthand [in the seventeenth and eighteenth centuries] to explain the ways in which the primitive and illiterate misunderstood the all important technology of reading" and writing.[29] Splicing this topos with Claude Lévi-Strauss's famous account of the "writing lesson" he offered to (and was offered by) members of the Nambikwara tribe in Brazil in *Tristes Tropiques*, who responded to his note-taking by miming his gestures and producing wavy lines in place of his script, Kearney reminds readers of Lévi-Strauss's conclusions: "the primary function of written communication is to facilitate slavery."[30] Kearney also aligns Caliban's biblioclasm with class-marked book antagonism in other of Shakespeare's plays, such as the Jack Cade sequence in *Henry VI Part Two* in which Jack and Dick the Butcher embark on what looks like an antiwriting riot set in motion by Dick's memorable lines, "The first thing we do, let's kill all the lawyers."[31] In the end, for Kearney, the play recognizes that "books are both sign and instrument of one man's mastery of another," and its ending moves to relinquish "the illusion of transcendence that authenticates mastery, a story about relinquishing the book."[32] *The Tempest* appears to present us, then, with a choice between a book-burning-bound Caliban, out to destroy his master along with his books, and a bibliophilic Prospero whose magic books condense European humanist book culture with magical booklore and colonial agendas. And depending on who and when we are, we will find ourselves torn between competing identifications, unable, perhaps, to settle into a ready reading or decision about the ending of play.

It's not clear to us, however, that the choice remains so relatively restricted. And it seems crucial to point out that this polarizing reading manifests as the bibliographical form of the same "closure" to the Caliban-Prospero dynamic that we found Lamming and contemporaries attempting to open earlier in this chapter. As poignant as the image of books floating away or of books being burnt or, for that matter, of writing as an index to enslavement may be, this poignancy depends on ignoring or boxing up the interpretive difficulty that attaches to Prospero's stated intention to "drown" his book even as it assumes the transparency or immediate readability of Caliban's imperative that others than himself (Stephano and Trinculo) "burn but his books." The choice, we think, is a false one, of a type with the other ideological lures in the play and works to linearize what remains for us an uncertain parallel that the play orchestrates whereby two mooted acts of possible violence to books, book burning and book drowning, unfold in series, or, more exactly, do not, for both fail to materialize onstage.[33] No books are burned. No books are drowned.

At the heart of the play, then, Prospero and Caliban's stated intentions regarding "books" and an increasingly singularized "book" constitute a moment of what, to adapt further Bruno Latour's term *iconoclash*, we name "biblioclash": several scenes of projected transformations of books (and so of the persons to whom they are attached) that we are at pains to know and understand.[34] For us, this means, emphatically, that Caliban the biblioclast may not be opposed to Prospero the bibliophile. Indeed, given the story Prospero tells Miranda as to how they arrived on the island, his estrangement from the day-to-day government of Milan as he remained "rapt in secret studies" (1.2.77), casts him as bibliomaniac, giving up the management of his state to his brother while he remained in his study or library. In the play, this absorption in books (or devotion to the liberal arts and self-improvement) costs him his dukedom and, in Peter Greenaway's *Prospero's Books* (1991), it costs him his library as well (Alonso's soldiers are shown destroying it). Both he and Caliban remain cathected to "books" or to a "book" in discontinuous and overlapping modes that do not constitute something that we can safely oppose.

In each case, we think that earlier critics of the play have identified key tropes or moments in the archiving/forgetting of scenes of encounter between Europeans and indigenous peoples as they may be said to mark *The Tempest*, but that, following Lamming's caution that leads him to claim the conjoined patronyms of Caliban and Prospero, no single trope—such as that of the "talking book" or the status of a violent book burning as opposed to a gentle book loving—can settle this biblioclash. It's more productive, we think, to endure the uncertainty and to maintain strictly that we are unable, in Latour's terms, to decide whether "the hand[s] at work" burning or drowning are "ready to expose, denounce, debunk, show up, disappoint, disenchant, dispel one's illusions, or let the air out" and so do violence or, "on the contrary . . . elicit, educe, welcome, generate, entertain, maintain, or collect truth and sanctity."[35] Caliban is not exactly "unlettered," even as Prospero and Miranda may judge him not to have taken their "print": he has been "taught . . . language" (1.2.364), which by his own account took the form of "naming" (1.2.337). At issue then, we think, is the question of differential and in some cases "insurgent" literacies of competing, if mismatched, writing machines whose products are not so easily archived as writing worth keeping.[36] Here it's worth recalling also Derrida's response to Lévi-Strauss's "Writing Lesson" in *Of Grammatology* that, contrary to the anthropologist's assumptions, the Nambikwara already had access to "writing" albeit in a different mode than that of Western forms that follow the ratio of the line and the linear.[37] Moreover, such "pluri-dimensional," symbolic modes of writing (wavy lines, patterns, symbols, forms), moments when language involves itself in and as the physical, already mark and invest a broad range of writing practices in *The Tempest*'s England.[38]

Let's loiter, then, and ad lib a reading of Caliban and Prospero's parallel articulations of the fate of his "books" and "book," hearing in both clashing soundtracks to the play and its ending—the throwing away or projection of Prospero's book, its drowning, rippling through the text via the production of other possible fates, other possible outcomes. So stay tuned for the channel's changing, music coming through this time, of a sort, raucous, drunken singing.

RADIO FREE CALIBAN

Three voices form a trio. They tussle over who shall sing the lead. By the end they take on a dubious drummer whom they agree to follow along with even as they figure he might just be a drum machine. "I shall no more to sea, to sea / Here I shall die ashore" (2.2.42–43) sings Stephano staggering into the play, bottle in hand. Caliban fears that one of Prospero's spirits has come to torment him—and it's funny, Stephano's terrible, terrible singing a torment indeed, a whole new order of noise for the isle to be full of. In comes Trinculo and after a bit of suggestive stage business involving two men under a blanket, the two share their survivor stories. "How didst thou scape? How cam'st thou hither?" asks Stephano. "Swear by this bottle," he continues, "how thou cam'st hither. I escaped upon a butt of sack, which the sailors heaved o'erboard—by this bottle which I made with the bark of a tree with mine own hands since I was cast ashore" (2.2.117–21). Caliban drinks and swears. Trinculo confesses to aquatic avian expertise—"Swum ashore, man, like a duck. I can swim like a duck, I'll be sworn" (2.2.125–26). He drinks, or as Stephano now offers, "kiss[es] the book," the butt of sack he rode ashore requiring the reverence represented by the act of kissing a Bible, the bottle made of bark standing in, with no loss of efficacy, for the butt that's stowed elsewhere. Caliban figures they're space aliens "dropped from heaven" (2.2.135) as "the liquor is not earthly" (2.2.123). And soon he too "kiss[es] the book" with increasing regularity—each "kiss" or "swig" lubricating the musicality of the three.

Caliban swears fealty, says he will "kiss" Stephano's foot (2.2.149), and exits to fetch provisions singing his own song, syncopating his own name:

> No more dams I'll make for fish,
> Nor fetch in firing at requiring,
> Nor scrape trenchering, nor was dish,
>> Ban' ban' Ca-Caliban,
>> Has a new master, get a new man.
> Freedom, high-day, high-day freedom; freedom high-day, freedom. (2.2.176–81)

The three reenter in act 3, scene 2, Caliban's "tongue" "drowned . . . in sack" (3.2.11) and Stephano impervious to drowning at sea for, as he tells us, "I swam 'ere I could recover the shore"—his head drowning already in sack (3.2.12–13). When the butt runs dry and there's no more "book" to "kiss" they shall drink water. They plot murder, rape, and revolution—"Remember / first to possess his book" (3.2.91–92) but find themselves haunted or interrupted by the static interference from Ariel's ventriloquism as he or she adds lines to their script that none of the three can quite person. But, assured by Caliban's offering that the "isle is full of noises" (3.2.135), they exit marching in time to the unseen "taborer" (drummer) that is Ariel. In the event, they reach Prospero's cell but not before Prospero remembers that "the minute of their plot / Is almost come" (4.1.141–42) having apparently "forgot" about it up till now—tuning in, as he did, to the resolution of the marriage plot and the celebratory masque, which he now "voids," summoning Ariel to "meet with Caliban" (4.1.166). Thus dismissed, the "*spirits depart*," exiting perhaps to recostume for their zootropic transformation into "*the shape of dogs and hounds*" that set Caliban, Stephano, and Trinculo "roaring" (4.1.252–54).[39]

This drunken insurrection—a plot that fails, that forgets Caliban's instructions to "burn . . . [Prospero's] books"—plays as low comedy but does so in the complicated, unstable mode of the Jack Cade sequence in *Henry VI Part Two*. In that case, editors have to decide, by their use (or not) of asides on whether to deliver a flat text, a script that makes no show of layering in the ironic distancing that is frequently assumed to be at work in the scenes.[40] Arguably, the same instability inheres to the scenes we have just described, steeped as they are in bibulous bio/bibliographical verbal play. "Books" cohabit with "butts" and makeshift "bottles" crafted from the bark of trees. Stephano swam in sack before he ever risked drowning in water. Now they all drown on land. Moreover, Caliban's marching exit to act 2, scene 2 reads to some as a pseudoidolatrous parody of the presentation of "the English Bible" to Elizabeth I at her coronation, a bible that she kissed, writing her own sovereign claims into the text of Biblical authority in quasi-sacramental fashion. Likewise, the bearing of the bottle recalls the carrying of "the monstrance at Corpus Christi."[41] Liquid allegiances coalesce in and around the butt of sack that finds itself dispensed via the "backing" of a bottle fashioned out of bark—and Caliban takes this "celestial" liquor as the "profit" of this new encounter, to reprise the technical humanist term he hurls back at Prospero and Miranda back in act 1, scene 2, when he reminds them that he has learned to curse (1.2.364).

So what then should we make of Caliban's urgent reminder to Stephano and Trinculo first to "possess" and then "burn" Prospero's books? Caliban's lines posit an unhappy, exploitative set of labor conditions underwritten by Prospero's books. Take them away, he says, and Prospero will become but "a sot" (silly person, drunk) "as I am." He'll have "not / One spirit to command" for they "all do hate him / As rootedly as I" (3.2.90–95). Burn his books, therefore, and all "Ye elves of hills, brooks, standing lakes and groves, / And ye that on the sands with printless foot / Do chase the ebbing Neptune" (5.1.33–35), all those "demi-puppets" (5.1.36) and "sleepers" "waked" by their "graves" (5.1.48–49) upon whom Prospero calls in act 5, scene 1 when, getting in touch with his inner Medea, whose lines from Ovid's *Metamorphoses* he adapts, will fail to show up, depart, play their own tunes, make their own noise.[42] Drunk on sack and the possibility of a different script than the one to which he's used but unable to picture a future other than as the negation of his present conditions—"No more dams I'll make for fish, / Nor fetch in firing at requiring, / Nor scrape trenchering, nor was dish" (2.2.176–78)—Caliban's book burning will have the effect of a leveling, rendering both Prospero and him as "sots," drunks, idiots, both conditioned by books, be they figured now as "butts" or "bottles." Burn the book and the "spirits" will fail to show up. Burn the book and we all shall be revealed as prosaically "wet," bodily forms, rendered variously high or variously traumatized by our uptaking of different orders of information (the script or spell in a book, the "sack" or "celestial spirit" in a butt or a bottle).

If the topos of the "talking book" does underwrite the constant reference to and failure of books to appear as such in *The Tempest* (they are never *there* but nevertheless we hear them) then here, Caliban's book-burning venture might be understood to effect a liberation (of all sorts or "sots") from their function as the wetware to media platforms. All those invisible mediators whose feet leave no prints in the sand for their effects are rendered as variously enrapturing or tormenting aesthetic effects (pinches, noise, music) shall find themselves suddenly "let go." All the *voces* in the topos of the *voces paginarum* (literally "the voices of the pages") shall find themselves lip-synching to their own lines, voices without script to follow, going quiet or bellowing new songs. The talking book has become now a radio on which every turn of the dial finds the air alive with competing voices or stunned into a dead silence.

As Roger Chartier reminds, the *voces paginarum* "usually referred to the elimination of voice and ear in favor of silent reading" but also "to books that could read themselves aloud" as well as the relaying of the voices of the dead.[43] For him, at certain historical moments, the trope is indexed to the victory of small-format books that can disappear into a pocket, giving the user access to information on the go (much as today a smart phone renders the user "smart"). But the ideality of a book that reads itself remains predicated on the embedded presence of so many different forms of wetware—the print shop capable of making small-format books, or in its origins, the monks mouthing words while following a text as a mnemonic exercise or as part of their function as the ears, hands, and heads that funded the writing device that was a Medieval *scriptorium*.[44] Caliban's book burning figures an attempt to rewrite the biopolitical quotient to a particular media platform—the magic-technical resources figured as Prospero's books, a relay that has allowed Prospero to control the airwaves as well as the waves themselves. Possession of Prospero's books followed by their burning figures a mode of archival violence, an attack on an archive whose ash or remainder will reveal the "sottishness" or animate "wetness" of all concerned. Caliban's action marks an order of writing that aims to intervene in a writing machine whose infrastructure eludes him and to whom it manifests only in privileged sites or nodes—Prospero's books—that are reserved, set apart, and to which he has no access other than via an invasion or a theft.

In "The Book to Come," Derrida elaborates on the status of the book or *biblion* as backing, the material support or guarantee that, in purely physical terms, permits portability and linearity and enables a manuscript or a person to travel into the hands of readers, to find a slot or niche in the physical, ideological, and semiotic world of its today. For *biblion* we may also read *person*, the "book" now the backing of a particular way of configuring an identity, a mode of citizenship, belonging, and the privileges they afford. As Derrida observes, "the Greek word *biblion* . . . has not always meant 'book' or even 'work'"; instead *biblion* could designate a support for "writing" "(so derived from *biblios*, which in Greek names the internal bark of the papyrus and thus of paper, like the Latin word *liber*, which first designated the living part of the bark before it meant 'book')." "*Biblion*," he continues, "would only mean 'writing paper,' and not book, nor oeuvre or opus, only the substance of a particular support—bark. But *biblion* can also, by metonymy, mean any writing support, tablets for instance or even letters: post."[45] The extension of *biblion* as book represents the development of one particular metonymy that equates the backing of writing, the underpinning of writing by a physical substance with the figure of the "book," collating, if you like, writing and book, text and material support, and linearizing the *biblion* as book. For Derrida, the "book to come" signals not something new so much as something held in abeyance by the repetition and so adoption of one particular metonymy. This repetition makes a world indexed to a particular order of library or archive. And yet, as Caliban's orchestration of a mass labor revolt or general strike of all Prospero's wetware indicates and his syncopating rearticulation of his name in his song or march—"Ban, Ban, Ca-caliban / Has a new master, get a new man" (2.2.179–80)—confirms, there remain other infraworlds, other forms of writing, inhering within the order provided by the book.

Indeed, we may go further and suggest that if by his refusal to take Prospero's impression or "print of goodness," Caliban becomes an order of self-predicating "filth," something close to Giorgio Agamben's category of "bare life," then such a status seems predicated on his resistance to a particular infrastructure of the book, to one mode of archiving, to one infrastructure for producing papery persons or variously imprinted persons, to use the play's own idiom.[46] And further, the putative book burning signals also that where one bureaucratic state filing system (Prospero's island) might derive satisfaction and closure from positing such non-persons as "paperless" and so without an authorizing archive or bibliographical backing, still other forms of self-crafted bio/bibliopolitical backing—via butts and bottles and the bark of trees—remains possible, thinkable.[47]

REPAIR

Of course, the same gestures of leveling and universalizing conditions become the governing moves of the play itself as it moves to closure.[48] Evidence of Prospero's own incipient self-identified "sottishness" appears quickly after the mooted drowning of his book and the scenes of recognition and repair in act 5, where the play moves to closure. Prospero plans, he says, to "retire me to my Milan, where / Every third thought shall be my grave" (5.1.311–12), but the text doesn't allow his bones to rest long. Promising a full narration of the circumstances that have led to this ending, he asks all to "draw near," and the cast exits. There follows an epilogue "spoken by Prospero." He asks to be sent off, to disembark with the "gentle breath" of the audience to fill his sails, as if he were a boat, set free, as if he were a spirit like Ariel, whom he set free only a few lines earlier. Lacking "spirits" now to help, we assume perhaps that his book has been drowned, for it has not been burned, and so it's up to us, the wetware of the theater to fill his sails with the "breath" of our applause. The moment is complicated, however, at least in the First Folio (1623) by the fact that the "EPILOGVE" occupies a strange para-textual space on the final page, on which, transferred from the beginning of the play, appears a list of the "Names of the Actors" and, bleeding through from the verso part of the sheet, part of the title and text of *The Two Gentlemen of Verona*.

The editors of the Arden edition speculate that this list was probably compiled by the scrivener Ralph Crane, and the descriptive terms to the "Names of the Actors" may reflect his knowledge of contemporary stage practice and perhaps, too, his personal assessment of the characters performed at the time.[49] But the effect, in part, is to render Prospero as phantasm, a revenant, who comes back as the play's speaking function, the voice to its pages. Whoever speaks under the name "Prospero" in the epilogue exercises a weak sovereignty over the play, and this sovereignty manifests in stagings or readings of the play that retro-project his presence into act 1, scene 1, disclosing the guiding hand that controls the storm. The epilogue serves then as a kind of guarantee or placeholder for the drowning of a book and the burial of a staff that fail to appear even as they serve also as a remainder or conservation of the voice that Prospero now should be felt to lack. The play ends, if you like, by sorting or separating voices from books, *bios* from *biblion*, actors from roles, just as Caliban attempts but strategically fails to complete or to authorize the separation. As the final lines of the epilogue adduce, if we wish to be "pardoned" from our crimes, then we needs must grant Prospero our "indulgence" (18–19), a word that oscillates between figuring a friendly favor and a piece of paper that, once upon a time, remitted the sins of a good Catholic in return for a donation to the Church.

Caliban's book possession turned book burning figures a radical redrawing or leveling of the bio/bibliographical infrastructure to the play—a utopian mode of negation that might manifest as a cessation of happening, the opening of the island radio to the risk of dead air, unscripted or differently scripted noise, all its inhabitants variously sottish or "wet." But so also the play's own ending, by delivering on a voluntary book drowning that does not take place but whose effects it figures, decoupling thereby *bios* from *biblion*, or seeming to do so, disappears the possibility or even the desire to ask Caliban's questions, for Prospero's self-demotion remains predicated on our recruitment to his embarking. The lines, after and before all, were "spoken by Prospero."

The work the epilogue accomplishes, this sorting or separating out of "persons" from paper, defines the moves in act 5 toward a program of generalized repair and reversal. The ship that was wrecked shall not have been, and we will shortly reembark, homeward bound. Moments before this renunciation of "rough magic," Prospero instructs Ariel to "release" (5.1.30) Alonso, Antonio, Sebastian, and Gonzalo from where he left them in act 3, scene 3. "All," as Ariel reports, are "prisoners, sir." "They cannot budge," he adds, "till your release" (5.1.9–10). Ariel inquires as to Prospero's mood and tells him that his "charm so strongly works 'em / That, if you now beheld them, your affections / Would become tender" (5.1.17–19). Or so Ariel thinks: "Mine would, sir, were I human" (5.1.20). Taking Ariel's inhuman compassion as a mirror, Prospero decides that "They being penitent / The sole drift of my purpose doth extend" (5.1.28–29). And so he decides that "My charms I'll break; their senses I'll restore; / and they shall be themselves" (5.1.31–32).

Ariel exits just before the soliloquy. Prospero *"traces a circle"* and speaks. The circle will mark the zone of recognition within which Alonso, Antonio, Sebastian, and Gonzalo are brought out of their distraction and back to the selves they will take up by Prospero's leave. They *"enter the circle and stand charmed."* Prospero observes them; greets them each according to their role in his exile; forgives them; and, on his way to "discas[ing]" himself (5.1.85) sends the still invisible Ariel to fetch the mariners who have been sleeping the whole while "under the hatches" (5.1.99). Prospero brings Ferdinand back from the dead, troping Alonso's "irreparable . . . loss" (5.1.140) with the "dear loss" (5.1.146) that he feels in the marriage of Miranda. The dramatic irony kicks into high gear as he allows Alonso to misunderstand this "loss" and so to wish that, were the two children "living both in Naples / The king and queen there" (5.1.149–50), he should lie "mudded in that oozy bed / Where my son lies" (5.1.150–51). Then comes the big reveal—Ferdinand and Miranda playing chess—as Alonso discovers that he's won the proverbial biopolitical jackpot: he's regained not just a son but a daughter also, and with that a reunited state. The "wonder" Miranda expresses finds itself variously generalized, as, for example, in the oddness that Alonso remarks that "I / Must ask my child forgiveness" (197–98). Alonso notes the strangeness of Ferdinand's reading of what has happened to him—that by marrying Miranda and finding a "second life" from her and a "second father" in Prospero, Ferdinand reverses the genealogical cast to biological reproduction and so re/fathers Alonso (5.1.194–96). The scene, as we said, figures a generalized repair or *re/père*, to "discase" the intralingual pun on which Shakespeare trades in several of his sonnets.[50]

Gonzalo, a bit like Father Lawrence, notes that he's "inly wept" in hopes of such an event (5.1.200). Hands are given and joined. The Boatswain returns—Gonzalo gets to reprise his comment from act 1, scene 1 that "if a gallows were on land / This fellow could not drown" (5.1.217–18)! Ariel gets successive pats on the head for a job well done; Caliban, Stephano, and Trinculo wander in and are not "pinched to death" (5.1.276)—and everyone else goes off to Prospero's cell to hear the full story, returning thereafter, we suppose to Milan and Naples. So it all ends rather well!

We rehearse the ending that unfolds upon Prospero's mooted drowning of his book in order to demonstrate the economy at work. The book shall be drowned, but the play systematically denies drowning to the living. The leveling or revelation of sottishness that Caliban orchestrates figures here as a systematic sorting of persons from books, a biopolitical salvage operation predicated on a bibliographical disposal. Ferdinand did not drown; Alonso's stated desire that in order to have their children return he would sink in the ooze functions precisely because he did not and will not have to; the Boatswain's now lamely funny marking for dry death, on land, becomes a bit of gallows humor that's now lightly as opposed to luridly funny. Such an ending marks more, we think, than an instance of generic recoding or tragedy taming as the play decides to end as comedy—with marriage and social reproduction.[51] The book shall be drowned. The living shall live. Thus *bios* decouples from *biblion* (or appears to do so). It's worth remarking, however, the way this return, this inversion of the shipwreck or catastrophe of act 1, scene 1 proceeds by Prospero's considered decision to allow all to live, to continue living, the play now become an exercise in reproductive health and biopolitical management, a husbanding of resources. Prospero's reserving of judgment on Antonio and Sebastian—his marking of them as less than "friends" only by an aside to remind them that "were I so minded, / I could pluck his highness' frown upon you / and justify you traitors" (5.1.127–28) confirms, if you like, the biopolitical underwriting of the play's ending and Prospero's return to Milan. If the island figures a state of exception, a place within which literally anything could happen according to the whim of the sovereign, then Prospero's sovereignty operates still on the condition and possibility of an overwhelming violence but will unfold in and by the play's closure as the "power [instead] to 'make' live and 'let' die."[52]

Such moments of radical repair or rebooting tend, of course, to disorient those of us naturalized into familiar or normalized circuits of family or individual belonging. The articulation of persons not merely as resources but as vectors to be managed in order to "establish a sort homeostasis, and compensate for variations within . . . [a] general population and its aleatory field" such that "the biological processes of man-as-species" may be "regularized" as opposed to "managed" makes for an enlivening spectacle.[53] No wonder they are all a bit beside themselves, overcome, prone to mood swings, violence, glee, and bliss—their ignorance is suspended between the two poles, life and death. The characters' moods swing accordingly, recalling the boozy metaphysical shrugs of Trinculo and Stephano earlier in the play. Okay. So it goes. May as well be happy. Such an ending enables us to hear Miranda's famous lines—"Oh brave new world / That has such people in it" (5.1.183–84) as a literal remarking of the making up of persons with which the play ends.[54] Look who we all will be now. Who would have thought it? Is this for real or is this recognition just another shipwreck in the making? But don't worry, Prospero will explain everything. Cue the voice. Set the play to audio, as we're all, all of us, hooked. Just like Alonso, we "long / To hear the story of your life, which must / Take the ear strangely" (5.1.312–14). As always Prospero says he will "deliver all / And promise you calm seas, auspicious gales" (5.1.314–15). He obliges. The play defaults to Prospero's voice, the only voice that seems by the end to matter even as everyone settles into what seems like conversation.

Shall we ever tire of his repetitions? The weather shall be lovely. Here comes that voice again. Let's listen very carefully and ask what it is about the drowning or putative drowning of a book that enables such a programming of the relations between *bios* and *biblion* and that installs a biopolitical fix, rendering Prospero sovereign narrator and weatherman.

SOUNDINGS

> . . . But this rough magic
> I here abjure; and when I have required
> Some heavenly music (which even now I do)
> To work mine end upon their senses that
> This airy charm is for, I'll break my staff,
> Bury it certain fathoms in the earth,
> And deeper than did ever plummet sound
> I'll drown my book. (5.1.50–57)

Projecting forward into a future that no longer requires such sonic effects as "heavenly music" to "work" his "end upon their senses," that "end," we suppose, at an end, Prospero says that he shall break his staff and drown his book. His language gestures forward but fails properly to close on an image. The lineaments of an image take shape but then dissolve. The staff shall be broken, but its burial "certain fathoms in the earth," sea terms (*fathom* designates a unit of six feet and was and is used most usually of sea depths) momentarily coding the land, loses focus.[55] How deep shall the staff go? The act of decision, the strongly agentive act of breaking, falls prey to an uncertain inhumation, a burial that even as it locates the staff's fragments specifically in a certain spot remains uncertainly deep, the word *fathom* rendering the land watery.

Likewise, the book shall drown "deeper than did ever plummet sound," the sonic returning now as the technical term for measuring depth or finding bottom with a lead weight.[56] The agentively strong specificity of the act of drowning (go on, throw a stone, feel the projective force of your arm, picture the stone entering the water) loses itself in the impossible cast to the depth. To drown a book comes to constitute a permanent condition of the book, a continuous drowning that vanquishes forever the tactile specificity of the hand holding the line attached to the lead weight that never hits bottom, that never therefore feels the line slacken, the friction on the hands (as opposed to the ears) cease. Before it even happens, the decision to drown the book finds itself transformed into a permanent condition of waiting, a gerundive conditionality of living on, dying on, as the book keeps on drowning. No more noises then; no more sonic effects that we can person with the wetware that is Ariel, elves, demi-puppets, and so on—they have vanished, which is not to say that they have departed. No more rustling pages, mouthing words—instead a mind's eye image of a silent, sinking book.

Here, it seems worth recalling that Prospero's distinction between inhumation and drowning remains muddied by the way the phrase "deeper than did ever plummet sound" echoes three words Alonso uses when speaking of the drowning of his son, Ferdinand: "Therefore my son i'th'ooze is bedded, and / I'll seek him deeper than ever plummet sounded, / And with him lie there mudded" (3.3.100–102). Alonso's first, soul-destroying voicing of this intention follows hard on the "winds" or "billows" or "organpipe" that he says sung the name "Prosper" in his ears (3.3.95–102). Prospero's repetition of the three words Alonso used to describe the burial of Ferdinand's corpse ("deeper," "plummet," and "sounded") creates something like static interference in the distinction between burying his staff and drowning his book. The biological metaphor that attaches to or derives from Ferdinand, even if all humans resort to clay or earth, does not quite translate to either staff or book. Ferdinand's corpse is structurally parallel to Prospero's book, but it seems mistaken to conclude that Prospero's book will not be buried because its drowning is opposed to the burial of Prospero's staff. Instead the image and the repetitions create the aura of a sinking or gradual enfolding in an oozy medium. If drowning the book is not a burial at sea, we may think of this third kind of disposal as a marination, since characters always mistakenly think others have drowned and marination signifies something on the order of a cryonic storage, of the momentary disconnection and idling of an unknowing order of wetware.

In Prospero's lines the future seems marked by a set of uncertainties that prevent the generation of complete images. The word *sound* compensates; it takes on a vibratory heft that resonates across them and their levels of sense, condensing the auditory and the tactile. The vibratory effects of the "heavenly" noise named "music" by human, or more properly, Prospero's ears, cohabits, then, with the silent sounding of a depth—drowning figuring here as a passing beyond the range of hearing and seeing, accessible only by a kind of blind hearing or deaf seeing that corresponds very closely to what Lamming seeks to capture in the range of strange vocal effects he attributes to the play as island radio. This splicing of the tactile and the auditory, the musicality of certain orders of noise taking on an efficacy in the pursuit of "ends," enters into a strange relation with the vanishing of the book, whose fate lies beyond the reach of Prospero's language, other than his inability to render the image. It begins to feel that we might mistake the whole tenor of the lines—there is no loss here, no regret—perhaps drowning the book proffers a gleeful solution, a casting off that will recuperate Prospero in successive futures, as Lamming recognizes, as his cast abroad comes back as successive broadcasts.

If the play ends by deploying a register of bibliographical disposal and biopolitical repair, separating out *bios* from *biblion*, burning, it must be said, makes a lot more immediate sense. The image generates easily. The symbolism works— "usually books, like witches, were burned," observes Haig Bosmajian. "Since fire was the power that could cleanse the farms and communities of their witches," he continues, "moles, vermin, disease, and pestilence, and since heretical, blasphemous infections, plagues, and poisons could be destroyed through book burnings, the cleansing, purifying, dreadful, magical fire was also ignited to rid the land of seditious and impure obscene works."[57] There is the ash, however, evidence of the madness and the violence of the archive fever, the arson at work. Likewise, burial, however deep, however many fathoms down, comes with the possibility of exhumation and retrieval—the coming back of the thing that's buried. The word *drown*, however, projects the book into an inhuman realm and "calls forth a submarine world where eerie transformations take place, beyond the reach of the human."[58] The conditions of such an act of casting forth or off will produce no ash, no burial site—merely the moment of contact, the "printless" spot where the book hits the waters and the waters close. What happens thereafter, of course, remains to be seen—will the book float, will it sink, will it wash ashore and be taken as some long-lost message in a bottle, a bottle such as the one Stephano crafted out of bark?

Although there is no way to trace a direct connection, the only other instance of book drowning we have been able to trace comes from the feverish account of book disposal found in the story of Saint James the More (or Greater) in the *Golden Legend*, the thirteenth-century compilation of saints' lives by Jacobus de Voragine, which was "Englished" by William Caxton in 1483. The drowning occurs as the resolution to Saint James's encounter with "an enchanter named Hermogenes" (born of Hermes) who had sent his follower Philetus "to prove [Saint James's] . . . preaching false."[59] Such was the plan, but Saint James wows Philetus with several miracles and sends him back to Hermogenes to tell him that he's the real deal and that they should both convert and becomes his disciples. Understandably, Hermogenes doesn't take the "good news" too well. He petrifies Philetus with his enchantments. But the now immobile Philetus manages to send his child (or servant) to Saint James who sends him his "sudary or keverchief" (napkin/handkerchief) to tell him that "'our Lord redresseth them that be hurt, and unbindeth them that be enmeshed;' and as soon as he said so, and touched the sudary, he was unbound and loosed from all the enchanting of Hermogenes."

Hermogenes gets really angry now, calls many devils, and commands them to bring Saint James and Philetus to him so he can be revenged upon them. But Saint James forces the devils to do his bidding instead, and they bring Hermogenes to him with his hands bound. The devils ask Saint James to give them Hermogenes, but he refuses to do so, letting him go his own way instead. Understandably, Hermogenes is now totally confused and so Saint James explains that it's "not to our discipline that any be converted against his will." Hermogenes figures the devils will try to catch up with him when Saint James is gone and asks for a token of his power. So Saint James gives him his staff for protection and then Hermogenes gathers up "all his books of his false craft and enchanting for to be burnt." But "because that the odour of the burning might do evil or harm to some fools," Saint James "made them to be cast into the sea." And after "he had cast his books into the sea [Hermogenes] returned, and holding his feet said: 'O thou deliverer of souls, receive me penitent, and him that hath sustained till now missaying of thee.' And then began he to be perfect in the dread of God our Lord, so that many virtues were done by him afterward."

While there is much to comment upon in the story of Philetus's and Hermogenes's conversions, what's most striking to us is the way the story attends to the efficacy and counterefficacy of different magics, those that are authored by diabolical aid as opposed to belief in the Christian god. Hermogenes, who personifies and treats in one portmanteau name a divinity of magical apprentices, possesses a series of books that enable his "false craft and enchanting," which in the story take the form of his immobilization of Philetus and devil summoning. The first act is countered at a distance merely by a postal delivery of Saint James's napkin or handkerchief, Philetus already, by his returning with the wrong message, his postman. When the devils beset Saint James, they find themselves hopelessly mismatched and are immediately inducted as his factors. Finding himself the victim of a superior efficacy, Hermogenes is confused but initially unrepentant until Saint James lends him his staff, at which point he embarks on a self-appointed book burning against which Saint James intervenes. Beyond the ash that remains, Saint James fears that something of the "false craft" shall be conserved and disseminated by the "odour" of the smoke and that it may do harm to the foolish or impressionable. Better then to "cast them into the sea" in what reads as an act of dilution and disposal but also storage without hope of retrieval.

Throw them into the sea, cast them forth, and you will have demonstrated the desire to convert, to bear the technological tokens of our writing machine, and so you will find yourself among us. But let's not burn your books—oh, no, that would be dangerous; it would produce various ashen and vaporous remainders that might infect still others. If burning cleanses but does not completely erase, offering the diabolical program still other modes of backing, drowning figures as at once a nonspecifying dilution and a hyperspecific decision on the part of Hermogenes, who, it must be said, has until now found himself confused for much of the story. The book disposal stands in direct relation to the production of a susceptible subject, a willing convert, who has undergone some form of *askesis* or voluntary detachment from one mode of media-technical apparatus in preparation for his reattachment to another, superior model. Witness the virtuous makeover to which the story then testifies.[60] So runs the plot of this bio/bibliographical conversion narrative.

On the face of it, then, the figure of a book drowning manifests as an act of disposal and storage allied to what seems an impossible retrieval. The waves close. The books sink and vanish from view. But the books remain. They continue to exist as books, but in static mode. Arguably, following Saint James's logic, we could keep dumping books upon books in the sea and it would make no matter—just add them to the wrecks that sink into the ooze. The sea comes to function then as a limitless container or receptacle, a closed archive or library of banned books. It swallows all impressions but does not erase them. Instead it conserves and confirms their existence even as it fails to make them available for reading. In the case of *The Tempest*, the sea receives a book that we will never read, that was never accessed in a mode that manifests as reading in the course of the play. The book's "throwing away," in Lamming's terms, becomes a prerequisite for its own self or auto-audition.

Beyond the figure of Hermogenes, the structure of disposal we read in Prospero's lines resonates also with one particular practice of removing writing in the period: the practice of whitewashing walls in Tudor and Stuart houses. Juliet Fleming reads the whitewashed wall, a wall perhaps bearing successive layers of wash with various occasional inscriptions, designs, and "wavy lines," sandwiched between them, as a historically specific instance of a "writing apparatus that fulfilled the functions of [unlimited] receptivity and retention" that Sigmund Freud sought to metaphorize in his "A Note Upon the Mystic Writing Pad."[61] "To 'wash' a wall," "in the period," writes Fleming, "is to clean it not by removing what was on it, but by covering it with a fresh surface—whitewash." "Crucially," she adds, "beneath the new surface and whatever contents it may acquire, the original writing remains" and may still, with sufficient expenditure of time, care, energy and resources, be recovered.[62] And for Fleming the whitewashed wall "'represents' . . . consciousness as the reactivation of memories and perceptions that have been stored within writing."[63] Drowning a book, in the sense we develop it, corresponds closely to the infinitely receptive and retentive model of walls that retain their successive layers of inscription even as they no longer show them. The sea fulfills these functions, removing not merely two-dimensional lines of script or images from view but whole books.

That said, the extreme instances we have identified in Prospero's uncertainly stated intention to "drown my book" and Hermogenes's voluntary execution of an order from Saint James push this "representation" beyond its limits. Drowning figures a total loss, a throwing forth or forward that turns a wash into a flood in the case of Hermogenes, who disposes of one mode of telephonic efficacy because he has switched providers, gone over to a broader, more comprehensive network. Accordingly, the older network is engulfed but not erased. It remains, finds itself archived, but the effects it once generated are superseded. For Prospero, the act remains harder to read, offering either a similar act of disposal or perhaps a solution to a problem of local particularity. Does the act of drowning come as an inspired solution to a problem or as a renunciation, or as something else? How to leave the island, to cast off, but to retain the efficacy that his book provides? Does Prospero, in other words, repudiate Medea's invocation of spirits in these lines or does he outdo her? Are we witnesses to the closing down and cancellation of a network of sonic effects or the inundation of the world by a static-free infrastructure that no longer plays as noise?[64]

Nevertheless, in both instances, the word *drown* might be heard to register a flooding or inundation of a surface that obliterates its ability to take impressions or to retrieve layers that lie beneath—less a whitewash than a washout, or what, in the language of limning or miniature making in the period, resonates in terms of all that can go wrong in the application of paint to parchment. Color, instructs Nicholas Hilliard, chief miniaturist to Elizabeth I, should be applied "flowing," but you must avoid flooding your parchment card.[65] The movement required of the hand in limning is challenging because it is qualitatively different from that of "Oyle worke, distemper or washing" in which the color is "driven with the flat of the pensel [brush]."[66] The word *flow* designates a specific rate of application that will cover but not blemish or overwhelm a surface as opposed to the filling in of surface imperfections implied by the word *wash*. Get the rate of flow wrong, misjudge the consistency of your color, overload your "pensel," and you may drown your parchment, rendering it unusable.

To "drown" in this sense deterritorializes whitewashing from its everyday scenes of use and posits a flooding out of sense that saturates the medium, the "wash," perhaps even coming to figure as a mobile medium itself, but one that renders anything it subsumes unreadable even as it continues to be *there*. To "drown" then takes on a relation to a general archiving or storing up of successive orders of media and their effects, subsuming their efficacy under the sign of "noise" and music in the play, auditory effects coming to signify as a privileged, and, in the context of the theater, media-specific, sensory mode that registers the fact of a book (not) being read. What Lamming represents as an island radio, then, activates what we might describe as the archival function that attaches to the word *drown* in the play—a strange mode of archiving, mind you, storage predicated on irretrievability, living on as a mode of blocked access.

UNDERWATER ARCHIVE

So we're sunk. A wave just claimed our radio or book, or whatever the *thing* is. The flood's upon us. And we've hit rock bottom—or rather, we're sinking in the ooze. You see we jumped in after the book, just as Alonso says that he will do in order first to follow Ferdinand (3.3.100–102) and then that he would have done in order to retrieve supracouple Ferdinand and Miranda (5.1.150–52). What else is a father to do when his son dies? Thank goodness the play reverses his putative suicide and repairs the two, father and son.

In our case, though, the book drowning seems to have altered the composition of the sea, unhinged what seemed like a stable set of relations between burning, drowning and burial, and the elements (earth, fire, wind, water). We find ourselves in an altered relation to what it means to store something, to store a book, to put it back on its shelf. The play's sorting of *bios* from *biblion*, denying drowning to the living but assigning it instead to a book, makes everyone, as we saw, feel w/oozy. But it also lowers the temperature on the question of the archive and the ability of a hyperattention to questions of media to solve as opposed to replay problems—of sense, of sovereignty, of collectivity. If you find yourself getting feverish, closing in on this or that bibliographical key, relax; the play has already poured a long dose of cold water in your lap. And so, rather than salvage an emphatically singular book, we sink down into the ooze, where we find a generalized question concerning what it means to archive something, to retain it but in this instance to take no impression or to forget something crucial in the impressing. No *survivance*, as Derrida phrases it in the second epigraph to this chapter, no living on without drowning, without loss by and as retrieval.

If in *Archive Fever*, book burning remains the privileged way of representing archival loss—the books we will never know if Freud has burned and the "ash" the secret of every archive—then *The Tempest's* book drowning renders the distinction between preservation and destruction, inscription and erasure, unreadable, but in a purely productive if discontinuous sense.[67] Inscription, of course, *and* erasure; preserve and destroy. Archiving becomes indistinguishable thereby from remainderless destruction of the order we investigated in nuclear mode in our first chapter—the very condition of living on, of living at all. This indistinction gains the name "anarchivity," a word Derrida coins to mean "the violence of the archive itself, *as archive, as archival violence.*"[68] The play names such a condition, which it locates at the unfathomable bottom to the sea, "the ooze" into which Alonso twice thinks he'll settle: the first time, to reunite with his son, the second time round, in exchange for getting Ferdinand and Miranda back. And this "ooze" or slime or scene of slow decay but also of coming into life is also a scene of bio/biblioprocessing, the parceling out of bio/bibliographical forms such as *The Tempest* imagines as it first de- and then rezones the distinctions between persons, animals, spirits, the living, and the dead.

But as we have seen such distinctions prove reversible, even as they remain fixed, kept in place by specific bio/bibliographical forms that endure. At the end of the play or by the end of the play, death by drowning, so it appears, suits only a book. The rest of us live into or on into a "dry death" such as Gonzalo wished for in act 1—"I would fain die a dry death" (1.1.67–68). Yet Ariel collapses this distinction when, appearing at the illusory banquet of act 3, scene 3, dressed as a harpy, he or she equates hanging with drowning. Alonso, Antonio, and Sebastian are greeted with these words: "I have made you mad; / And even with such-like valour men hang and drown / Their proper selves" (3.3.59–60), essentially undoing Gonzalo's earlier staking of his hope on the fact that the Boatswain "hath no drowning mark upon him—his complexion is perfect gallows" (1.1.28–29). The state reserves the right to drown you—storage without retrieval. Dig deeper and distinctions will muddy. The ooze lies beneath. Even the driest of dry deaths turns wet as bodies enter into a becoming soil or earth and we drown in the stomachs of worms.

SURFACING

Up top we know, as Lamming tells us, divers still "loiter, bribing the sea to release its Dead for an interview with the living."[69] And so we look up from below and see what's rising. *The Tempest* ends with a sorting or separating out of *bios* from *biblion*, but by that gesture it almost demands that the book that was (not) drowned be retrieved and that that retrieval anchor all manner of variously papered sonic effects or scripts become persons. When we look up from the ooze below, we see so many books, veritable libraries that divers salvage, floating above us—the sea less a library than some ph/fantasmatic print-on-demand operation whose products ignite a fever when they come topside. The book, we know, may be a grimoire. But beyond or beside such singular non/identifications, Prospero's book multiplies. Whole libraries it seems were sunk off the shores of the island. Almost as though the "bark" Prospero and Miranda were "hurried . . . aboard" (1.2.145), that "rotten carcass of a butt" (1.2.46) actually went down, as Prospero thinks was intended by his usurpers—Stephano's "butt" and "bottle" of sack coming back, before they are named, in maritime mode. All the books, then, that Gonzalo "furnished" (1.2.166) him with from his library—Gonzalo making a selection, pick those most "loved" (used?)—drown also, vaguely taken by the currents, washing up here, there, nowhere, where the divers await them.

Out of the blue, in a section on "alchemical colour," in *Chroma: A Book of Colour*, filmmaker Derek Jarman announces, "these were the books that Prospero brought to the island: 'The Pimander and Orphic Hymns, Plotinus on the soul—*The Book of Life* (Ficino). *Conclusiones* (Pico della Mirandola). Paracelsus, Roger Bacon. *The Secret of Secrets*, a best-seller in the Middle Ages, Agrippa's *Occult Philosophy* and Dee's *Hieroglyph Monad. Shadow of Ideas* (1592) by Bruno who was burnt for heresy in 1600 in the Campo de' Fiori, Rome."[70] More famously Peter Greenaway decides, "There are twenty-four books that Gonazalo hastily threw into Prospero's boat as he was pushed out to sea to begin his exile."[71] Why not? It's precisely in the nature of such wholesale losses to animate the various wetwares Prospero lets go at the end of the play, leading us to re/back voices we hear as books. Such is the reason Lamming cautions us that the noises of the isle are still there but now naturalized as the infrastructure of broadcast radio in the case of the 1950s Britain he visits.

Such salvage operations are diverting and work their own kind of magic. In Poul Anderson's fantasy novel, *A Midsummer Tempest* (1974), we discover that "Duke Prospero did not really bear away his book to the middle sea, above abysses. He feared there'd be a risk of theft en route."[72] And so our hero Rupert dives down in an improvised bathysphere, raises the book, and uses it to put pay to the awful monster that besets the conjoined worlds of *The Tempest, A Midsummer Night's Dream* (1593–95), and earth. Oberon and Titania act as librarians or custodians at the end of the novel, taking the book back to their forest for safekeeping. The book was not "drowned" then. It can be retrieved, even if it may not exactly be "read." Instead, it may only be summoned in order to generate a certain unfathomable efficacy or agency in your present—be it to vanquish a monster or to sponsor a reading you wish to establish as historical. So, of course, the drowned book become toy or minor machine describes a circle, salvaged in order to be redrowned; available for successive nonreadings.

Sometimes, surfacing the book occasions more complicated questions regarding what the fate of a drowned book may be, what happens to a book in the sea, how it got there, how it moves, how long it lasts, why it comes back now, and what it has to say at a particular moment. Some 15 or so years after *The Tempest*, for example, on June 23, 1626, it so happened that "a Codfish being brought to the Fish-Market of Cambridge and cut up as usually others are for sale" yielded something wondrous and, depending on how you were oriented to such things, miraculous.[73] "In the depth of the mawe of the fish was found wrapped in a piece of canvase, a book in *decimo sexto*, containing three treatises bound up in one," which are reprinted soon thereafter, prefaced by images of the fish, a short foray into the emerging field if ichthyology and a thorough working through and over of the possible veracity of what the book names the "Book-Fish." The treatises that the fish carried in its mouth, and that had returned from their uncertain fate in the sea, were attributed to English reformer John Frith, who was martyred in 1533. And within the world of 1620s Cambridge and the changing fates of religion and political affairs at the Caroline court, the appearance of a talking fish who spat out a series of untimely or only too timely treatises that held within them a critical appraisal of issues still alive and kicking seems, as Alexandra Walsham puts it rather wittily, reprising G. R. Elton but in a more thoroughly fishy context, "a piece of piscatorial politics."[74]

What remains striking about the prefatory materials to the reprinted treatises, though, is the description they yield of the quasi-forensic parsing of oddities that emerged from the sea in the period. Bywords for such chance or providential appearances include "accident," "wonder," "marvel, "and miracle," indicating the potential for revealing noise effects to orchestrate signs of the righteous or wrongful conduct of the world and state. Indeed, as the anonymous author of the volume cautions, "all miracles are marvellous things, but all marvellous things are not miracles" (11). It pays to keep your "*Miranda*" straight from your "*miraculas.*"[75] And so, plucked by chance from a scene of fish buying, the "Booke . . . being much soyled and defaced, and coured ouer with a kinde of slime & Congealed matter" (9) was taken to Daniel Boys, a bookbinder, who "carefully washed"(10) the "leaves." The books it contains are identified, which provokes a series of further questions, not least of which includes why it might be that a fish, the creature chosen to illustrate the Latin proverb, "'*Tam matus quam piscis*, as dumb as a fish" should suddenly become so vocal (4)?

Given the Christian associations to the sign of the fish, its appearance as backing to a set of lost books of topical importance seemed both convenient and miraculous. In effect, this hybrid book-fish or fish-book comes to serve as an instance of Lamming's radio, constituting a writing machine that restores lost things, that speaks with the inhuman cast to Providence, and that does so, as it were, in the person of "nobody." Prospero's book or its like comes back, then, but when it does, it returns as a strange, hybrid, zoo/bio/bibliographical entity that fishifies the rhetorical complexity of *prosopopoeia* (the giving of faces or voices to things).

Figure 4.1 depicts the fish and its contents—though it has been cut open so that the book may be properly revealed, having migrated from its mouth to its belly.

Inquiring further into the circumstances that might have led to such a strange reappearance of these books, the author of the treatise writes that "it seemeth most probable that vpon some wrack this booke lying (perhaps manie years) in the pocket of some man, that was cast away, was swallowed by the Cod, and that it lay for a good space of time in the fishes belly. For the booke was much consumed by lying there, the leather couer being melted and dissolued and much of the edges of the leaues abated and consumed, and the rest very thin and brittle

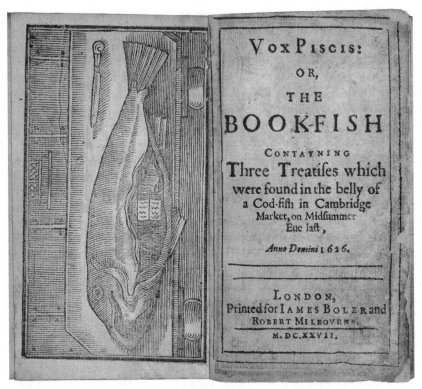

Figure 4.1 Title page to *Vox Piscis: or The Book Fish Contayning Three Treatises Which Were Found in the Belly of a Cod-Fish in Cambridge Market on Midsummer Eve Last, Anno Domini 1626* (London 1627) STC 11395 copy 3. By Permission of the Folger Shakespeare Library.

hauing beene deepe parboiled by the heat of the fishes mawe" (13–14). The scenario narrativizes the condition of the "book" whose condition might best be described as "cooked"—not drowned so much as "parboiled" in the oven that is a fish's belly. But no virtue has been gleaned from this nondigestion. The cod in question has not faired too well either, being very underweight from having its mouth blocked and so unlikely to fetch a good price at market. The fish itself seems to have "been cast into a surfeit or consumption" (14). It takes no "profit" from the encounter. Instead it becomes a mode of conveyance, a condition by which the book that was lost goes mobile once more.

When the *Vox Piscis* announces the identity of the treatises, prefacing them with a prayer to preserve its readers from storms and shipwreck, it presents the following rhetorical question, hoping that by reading it, by decoupling the fish from the contents of its mouth, severing bibliography from ichthyology, we can "fish out the reason why these treatises should bee so strangely preserued in a living dumbe speaking library in the sea" (17). The metaphorical transcoding offered by the *vox piscis* offers an almost irresistible set of rhetorical resources, as here comes through in the almost involuntary or winking invitation to "fish [the truth] out." Aside from the difficulty posed in separating the book-fish from its scene of emergence and the political or ideological work it may or may not have done in 1620s Cambridge, the lesson we reel in from this ill-fated cod lies in the strange status of a fish that becomes backing to a book. For what order of entity or wetware is this book-fish, upon whose death the revelation of the treatises it stores depends? What strange paratextual creature has it become? Did this cod feed on human flesh, taking the canvass package from a man's pocket? If it did, it found that it could not eat this new food, let alone "read" or digest it. Instead, the book, by its newfound mobility, by the fact of its storage in a mouth that cannot speak its lines nor eat their backing, consumes the fish.

The library of the sea yields up its secrets only in a divided and dividing manner. Such books as fish keep in their mouths, mouths that may not serve as the *voces* to its pages, remain strictly unreadable—becoming so only when pried forth and the fish tossed in the garbage or back to sea. The pages of the book represented in the mouth of the cod have been unwrapped, but such writing that appears there remains unreadable. In the illustration, the pages of the book host that same order of wavy lines that the Nambikwara produced for Lévi-Strauss. These lines both resist and await or gesture towards a linearization that will both reveal and reduce their sense. The *Vox Piscis* serves, if you like, as an occasion for depicting the underwater archive we have identified as the ooze into which Prospero's book may or may not sink. The images it offers establish the involution of media required to render up the aquatic survivals as they surface. Here, the retrieval is premised on a transspecies, bio/zoo-media specificity that trades on the things fish can and cannot say, rendering this historical cod, if there was indeed such a cod, "a living dumbe speaking library in the sea" (17). And such a hybrid zoo/bibliographical creature serves as an emblem for the kinds of effects generated in order to imagine the afterlife of Prospero's book after it has sunk—images that re/splice the play's own zoo/bio/biblio/processes.

All sort of images taking shape now. The surface above us becomes a multiplex that represents back to us the partial, folded bio/bibliographical forms that recombine what *The Tempest*, by its ending, parts. Books and such rain down around us now sprung from Julie Taymor's *Tempest* (2010) and Peter Greenaway's *Prospero's Books* (1991) both of which explore the figure of book drowning in their own peculiar fashion.

PROSPERO'S BOOK . . . S

In Peter Greenaway's *Prospero's Books*, Prospero drowns his book, breaks his staff, and throws it in after the book. The title of the film is complicated, however, for it has a double referent to a book or shooting script of the film as well as to the film itself. In different ways, both the book and the film are unreadable: the film engages in a radical fetishism of the book in macro- and microdimensions, as if the film were made for an audience of book historians who had gone off their lithium and turned hardcore bibliomaniacs alert to subtle differences between filmed books and print books. Small differences that do not consistently differentiate books or parts of books are introduced above and below the surface, inside the frame and outside it, and through open and closed books, inversion, reversal,

Figure 4.2   Drowning the book in Julie Taymor's *The Tempest* (2010) and Peter Greenaway's *Prospero's Books* (1991).

doublings, pairings, sequence and serialization, and numerous books that are often unnumbered.[76] The shooting script's odd temporality, coming both before and after the film, its status as source text and as film paratext, makes it impossible to read the one as the source of the other. The shooting script may be said to archive the film, but if it does, it does so badly for the two fail to synch up. They are radically discontinuous, decoupled media—each, we might say, drowns the other. Indeed, it might be safest to say that in the film and the book, Prospero's book . . . s just keep on drowning. Drowning becomes, in effect, the preferred, engulfing mode of book use, the film migrating the biblioclash we located in the play into the multimedia circuits constituted by its doubled reference to a book and to a film.

In the film, some books float on top of other books that have yet to sink. Some books are flotation devices, while others sink; one book sinks intact, while the pages of another are torn and disintegrating; sometimes pages from one of Prospero's inventoried and filmed books are superimposed over a "material" book with its pages open (See Figures 4.3, 4.4, 4.5). Some of the books float on the surface while others are shot from below the surface. Some shots show the entire book that has been thrown in the sea; others show a page or a detail of a page. They are destroyed not only through drowning, however, but also by fire, sometimes by spontaneous combustion, and by acid. The pages of the Folio are framed above a large book at the bottom of the screen floating on the surface of water. Drowning and burning books merge in this sequence. Yet the drowning sequence stops short of supplying an inventory of the books, as does the shooting script.

Indeed, the narrative sequence of books being destroyed is interrupted by the last inventory taking of Prospero's books, arguably the most wild and unreadable of all in that it presents two conventional, bound books made of paper, one

Figure 4.3   Bibliocide I: Montage of opening the book as destroying the book in Peter Greenaway's *Prospero's Books* (1991).

Figure 4.4   Bibliocide II: Montage of book destruction as burning, drowning, liquefying, disfiguration, and mutilation in Peter Greenaway's *Prospero's Books* (1991).

printed and the other handwritten, that appear in forms they were never published. The last book is divided into two books: *A Book of Thirty-Five Plays* and a manuscript of "A Play Called "The TEMPEST."

"There are thirty five plays in the book and room for one more," the narrator says; "nineteen pages have been left for its inclusion right at the front of the book, just after the preface" as the camera shows the First Folio page with the poem titled "To the Reader" (See Figure 4.6). The second of the two books then

Figure 4.5   Bibliocide III: Prospero's library burns; Ariel's handprints on Prospero's manuscript; Caliban's book-burning fantasy in Peter Greenaway's *Prospero's Books* (1991).

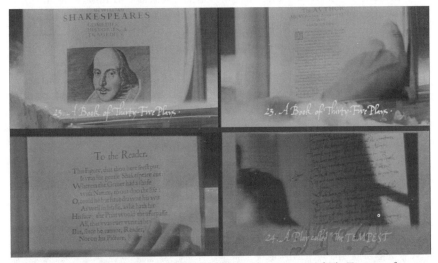

Figure 4.6   Shakespeare's First Folio (1623) and Prospero's manuscript of *The Tempest* surface and are preserved in Peter Greenaway's *Prospero's Books* (1991).

appears as the narrator says, "And this is the thirty-sixth play, *The Tempest.*" Though these books are recognizable, what the shooting script calls "Prospero / Shakespeare's" books cannot be placed either in the narrative sequence of book destruction or in an isolated, inventoried book.[77] If *The Tempest* has been preserved, it has not yet been published. And, strictly speaking, neither has the First Folio as it appears in the film. Both books are not only props but also fac/faux/similes of books that do not exist. Though separately bound, the two materially distinct books are destined to be integrated into one book, itself a collection of books. Yet these two books can never be integrated as such since the First Folio will never have been published without *The Tempest* (its place is already marked despite the pages being blank). Moreover, they cannot be integrated in terms of authorship. The Folio has the initials "W.S" printed on the cover, but neither Prospero's name nor Shakespeare's appears on the cover or the title page of the *Tempest* manuscript. Hence Prospero's book is irreducibly heterogeneous to Shakespeare's *Tempest*; Prospero's unsigned manuscript cannot be added to Shakespeare's, contained within it as a ghostwritten text. To be sure, *The Tempest* is imagined as something like a supplement to the Folio, but it is recovered only as a fantasy text that never existed in that form and that perhaps resembles the lost manuscript of the play. The last shall be first, we might say, but this prophetic destiny is destined, as it were, only because we know the last already was and was not there, the first from the beginning, the First Folio losing, before and after all, its handwritten sources. Such a voiding or looping of citation and practices of signing or countersigning a work are thematized throughout the film as quotations from the play, having become lines in the film, migrate between voice and image, morphing as they do so (see Figure 4.7).

When the narrative sequence resumes after the last two books are inventoried, the already complicated distinction between destroying books and archiving them is further complicated by the manner in which they are preserved. The boundary between publication and unpublished materials comes under the most intense pressure. Caliban, though unnamed in the film, is said to have rescued these two books even though he had earlier rather urged that they be burned.[78] However, we see Caliban surface, take the two books, and then dive back under water rather than take them on to shore. We may wonder if Caliban didn't drown them once again. Some divers that loiter might have still other motives than Lamming suggests.

Figure 4.7   Self-citation gone awry in Peter Greenaway's *Prospero's Books* (1991).

READING UNDERWATER

In Julie Taymor's Miranda-centered *The Tempest* (2011), Prospera breaks her staff and throws it into the sea (see Figure 4.2), and then the film cuts to the end title sequence as the epilogue is sung by Beth Gibbons, accompanied by her British band Portishead (see Figure 4.9).[79] Books begin to drop through the water, slowly falling down the screen. This ending speaks back very deliberately to the opening title sequence, known as an integrated title sequence because the title of the film does not precede it but is part of a prologue. Here Taymor meshes the title sequence seamlessly with a prologue about Miranda. After three-page production credits, the last including "Miranda Films," Taymor begins the film with a single, long take of a close-up of a sand castle that starts to dissolve as rain begins. The camera remains stationary as the title, reduced to "Tempest" appears in glittery capital letters and then fades out (See Figure 4.8).

The camera slowly dollies back to reveal a hand holding the melting castle and then pulls back further to reveal that the hand is Miranda's. After this single take integrating Miranda and the title, the film cuts to the shipwreck from her point of view. In Taymor's Miranda-centric film, the shots of the shipwreck are intercut with shots of Miranda running at full speed in a state of alarm. Prospera is still raging when Miranda first addresses her.

Here Taymor fills in a phantom ellipsis regarding the beginning of the play by placing Miranda where she is not and motivating her alarm about the fate of people who were on board the ship she has just seen wrecked. Only in the end title sequence does Taymor reclaim "The Tempest" as the film's title. The first end title is "Directed by Julie Taymor" followed by "Adapted from the play by William Shakespeare," the referent of the play's full title still missing, an ellipsis most viewers will silently fill in, of course. At the end of the above-the-line credits, "The Tempest" is followed by "A Julie Taymor Film." Is Julie Taymor's film a *Tempest* or *The Tempest*? Or is there a difference? In any case, the division between the partial title and the full title divides the film from itself and then spectralizes the film by adding an ellipsis and then filling it in. Taymor

Figure 4.8   Opening title sequence of Julie Taymor's *The Tempest* (2010).

also integrates the end title sequence by reassigning the epilogue to a voice-over female singer. In the book *The Tempest*, published as a companion piece to the film, Taymor says she originally cut Prospero's epilogue from the film script but ended up restoring it:

> The film's last image of Prospera on the ocean cliff, her back to the camera, tossing her magic staff to the dark rocks below, and the staff's subsequent shattering, is the ending. But when all was cut and timed and scored and mixed, the rhythm of the end of the film felt truncated, incomplete. I asked Elliott [Goldenthal] to take these last great words [the epilogue] and set them to music for the seven-minute-long end-title sequence. And to that haunting female vocal, sung by Beth Gibbons. The credits rolled and we drowned the books of Prospera in the deep dark sea.[80]

Taymor's account of drowning the books is exceedingly brief, perhaps because she out-sourced it, as directors customarily do, in this case to Kyle Cooper, and does not, in our view, do it justice. We think the end title sequence deserves sustained critical attention even if most viewers do not watch end title sequences, leaving the theater or ejecting the DVD or Blu-ray disc before the film ends.

The integrated epilogue creates a strange order of sonic effect—we listen to the decontextualized epilogue, not delivered by a character while reading the credits, and we wait until the credits are nearly finished to discover that the singer is Beth Gibbons. The books that float by are unreadable (see Figure 4.9).

The scene of drowning becomes a paratextual space, then, on which the film writes its credits. The film takes the script as its writing surface, drowning the play in its own paratext. The fish eats the book. The *vox* or *voces*, eat the pages. But the books do not just sink. They undergo some further kind of transformation—the water animating them. The slowness with which they fall and the way the pages of many of them open may remind some viewers of jellyfish. Moreover, they appear to breathe, letting off streams of bubbles, and it is not clear that they die.

The seven-minute-long epilogue, or coda, as Taymor calls it, unfolds as a single take: the camera is submerged under water and, as the credits roll, we

Figure 4.9a, b, c, and d   End title sequence of Julie Taymor's *The Tempest* (2010).

watch Prospera's books, not her book, fall serially and slowly through the ocean entering from the top of the shot and exiting from the bottom. Tiny air bubbles the size of bubbles a scuba diver would exhale from an diving tank pour out of each book, as if it were a bio/biblios, still alive and yet also a machine (Figure 4.9a). An air tank has also been placed below the shot and intermittently emits even more bubbles that float up around the books, as if the books we no longer see were exhaling. Drowning produces a bio/bibliographical remainder in the form of the bubble that is yet to rise to the surface and disappear into air, thin air. The epilogue continues in the end title sequence after the books have "drowned" and the credits below the line (text on an all-black background) scroll down just after the final credits. The sung epilogue ends just as the copyright credit appears.

This much of the film's end title sequence is conventional. Films made since the 1960s with two-part end title sequences typically end with a declaration of the copyright date and copyright holder. Taymor's *Tempest* follows this convention, at least partly. After the below-the-line credits begin, just after the final credits "The Tempest" and "a Julie Taymor film," books continue to fall, although less frequently (Figure 4.9b). Halfway through these titles, books stop falling altogether. However, Cooper adds an ending after the ending. He shows one last book, the largest by far of any we saw drown, after the below-the-line credits end with the copyright.[81] None of the books has a title or an author, and Prospera is never shown throwing any of the books in the ocean. This last book offers a condensed moment of biblioclash, however, in that it is the only book that is not intact. The temporality of its destruction is unclear: apparently someone had already torn out some pages, but that person or someone else then reinserted them. Some torn pages from the book have drifted off, others are falling out of it, and others remain reinserted. This book also stands apart from the others in that it is accompanied by a sound like wind blowing, a final moment of impossible audio in which the drowned book is blown off, so to speak. The book as a book, this large-scale book, is metonymic, we might say, of the drowned book as the sending off of the play, or in this case, the film, after it has already been seen off. Still emitting air bubbles, its unexpected last-minute return amounts to a reprieve: returning after the destruction of books appeared to have finished. The book is not yet dead, not unbound and yet not quite rebounding.

The DVD and Blu-ray menus are designed in a way that may invite further reflection on *The Tempest* as a drowned book. Shots from the film are superimposed over the end title sequence shot of underwater, with bubbles rising and books falling, as if everything were occurring underwater. Some actors appear to be breathing underwater (Figure 4.9d). The images simply circulate while you make your selection, set up the audio, pick a language or opt out, and sneak a peek at things to come. In the tie-in screenplay book, the last two pages show a still taken from the film's closing credit sequence of a book opening up after it has been plunged into the water with the production and cast credits superimposed over the left-hand page. In a paratextual space usually left blank—namely, the inside back cover and facing page, the film credits for the director and actors are printed just to the left of an "uncredited" book falling though water, little bubbles surrounding it. The book of the film thus showcases a book displaying neither title nor author while simultaneously recording Taymor as the film's "author" (asserted via her writer, director, and producer multiple credits here in combination with the "Julie Taymor Adapted from the Play by William Shakespeare" authorial designation on the volume's front cover). The interesting double move in which Taymor claims a kind of hybrid authorship, crediting Shakespeare as her source, appears and disappears as one turns the page and then, presumably, closes the book. That's as much as we can fathom.

"THOU ART INCLINED TO SLEEP"

Yawn! Sorry. But we've come over all sort of sleepy now. The books are still raining down above us, but the ooze is just too lovely. Wherever, whatever it was, we landed, book, radio, island, play, it seems to have gone dead or perhaps the sounds and images have just multiplied beyond the point that we can recognize them. Taymor and Greenaway's films will no doubt provide the dream images for the sleep that is coming, a sleep that wakes to or understands *The Tempest* as a moment of bio/biblio/processing. We're fighting it—but this ooziness is so inviting. We thought we heard someone say that ""'is a good dullness" (1.2.185). The voice whispers that it's a gift—and knows "thou canst not choose" (1.2.186). It aims to save us from all our questions and so now we watch from below as we find ourselves lulled to rest, our ignorance suspended, much like Miranda's in act 1, scene 2 when we meet her for the first time uncertain whether the storm is real or not (wonder or miracle or murder?). The play recruits us all, spectators to an event whose eventfulness we may not judge, read to us from a book we cannot read and yet in which we drown.[82]

CHAPTER 5

ANONYMOUS / ANONY/MESS

> What happens when social science tries to describe things that are complex, diffuse,
> and messy[?] . . . The answer, I will argue, is that it tends to make a mess of it.
> —John Law, *After Method: Mess in Social Science Research*[1]

> Arthur had jammed himself against the door to the cubicle, trying to hold it closed,
> but it was ill fitting. Tiny furry little hands were squeezing themselves through the
> cracks, their fingers were ink-stained; tiny voices chattered insanely.
> Arthur looked up.
> "Ford!" he said, "there's an infinite number of monkeys outside who want to talk
> to us about this script for Hamlet they've worked out."
> —Douglas Adams, *The Hitchhiker's Guide to the Galaxy*[2]

So we're awake. Feeling very refreshed, we must say (all that sea air). Never
slept so soundly. Can't fathom it. Ready, in fact, to take on something that thus
far we have avoided: the question of authorship, of who or what it was that is said
to have written all those plays and poems attributed to "William Shakespeare."
The candidates, you may remember, run as follows: William Shakespeare, the
actor turned writer from Stratford-upon-Avon; Francis Bacon, the writer, sci-
entist, philosopher, and statesman; Edward de Vere, the Seventeenth Earl of
Oxford, who has proved the most popular alternative candidate to Shakespeare
since the 1920s. Then, of course, there are the outliers, the multiplied host of
collaborators (Thomas Middleton, John Fletcher, and so on) as well as the other
variously textual remains that now augment the contents of the First Folio and
complicate matters further, such as the lost play, *Cardenio*, which was performed
apparently by the King's Men in 1613 and may, in some shape or form, find itself
archived (or not) in Lewis Theobald's *Double Falsehood, or The Distrest Lovers*
(1728).[3]

Of course, in the case of *Cardenio*, things are a bit of a mess. No manuscript.
No print record. No play. But still, the compulsion to return what goes or went
missing (even if it did not) to its supposed source proves overwhelming. Such is
the force to the bio/bibliographical yoking of texts and persons that the proper
name become author or author function fixes in place, organizing, so to speak,
successive relays in our archives, libraries, and imaginary realms. Such is the

compulsion to bear witness, to serve as archon to the impression, the traces, the archive that the First Folio (1623) as "monument" and money/mint represents, to recall Ben Jonson's lines from his memorial to Shakespeare as bio/bibliographical entity.[4] But that question of witnessing, of finding oneself recruited and so caught up in a massy, messy ongoing transubstantiation of the bio/bibliographical proves exhausting. There's just too much to do, too much to consider, too much still "out there" to be found—when we have the technology. Must the whole world, finally, bear witness, in Jonson's sense, for Shakespeare to live on?

John Milton's anonymous and untitled dedicatory poem "On Shakespeare" that appears in the Second Folio (1632) addresses this need, or the lack of a need, for a witness to Shakespeare's name. Answering the question as to why Shakespeare's lack of a pyramid for a tomb or "Star ypointing *pyramid*" to house "his honour'd bones" poses no problem, Milton restates the opening line of the poem as a problem of witnessing before proceeding to spend the rest of the poem answering it:

> What needst thou such weak witnes of thy Name?
> Thou in our wonder and astonishment
> Hast built thy self a live-long Monument.
> For whilst to th' shame of slow-endeavouring art,
> Thy easie numbers flow, and that each heart
> Hath from the leaves of thy unvalu'd Book,
> Those Delphick lines with deep impression took,
> Then thou our fancy of it self bereaving,
> Dost make us Marble with too much conceaving;
> And so Sepulcher'd in such pomp dost lie,
> That Kings for such a Tomb would wish to die.[5]

Shakespeare does not need the weak witness of a "pyramid" for his "name" not only because of his "fame" but because the Folio is his tomb. Yet Shakespeare's name is not self-evident; Shakespeare still needs a witness; or, his own witness (the Folio) recruits them. Milton posits a closed circuit in which the "live-long Monument" sustains itself by the "flow" of "easie numbers" (poems, poetic lines) that impress each reader. These "numbers" migrate from the "leaves" of the book to the minds and bodies of his readers as we come to serve as the substrate or backing, the wetware, to Shakespeare.

But these readers are not all that different from pyramids. Our excessive receptiveness ("too much conceaving") makes the reader an archive, a storage unit in which the Folio is "sephulcher'd" as its deep impressions become as unreadable as the lines of his unvalued book. The impressions we take have the effect of killing off our "fancy" or imaginative powers. And so we become "marble," tomb-like, immobile. The referent of "sepulchered" is slightly unmoored, referring to what—the circuit that the Folio forms between readers and numbers? Milton's anonymous sonnet implies that reading the Second Folio will not exactly constitute a witnessing of Shakespeare's name since the reading or impression taking petrifies the witness. We become, if you like, a living tomb—but as we do so we may not share Shakespeare's sepulcher. We will die. And no one will remember. Milton portrays the reader of his poem as just another petrified, nameless remainder exteriorized by the book rather than a subject who interiorizes and maintains it. The Folio, then, becomes a crypt that encrypts its reader. As if responding to Heminge's and Condell's dedicatory poem to the First Folio, Milton glosses the meaning of reading Shakespeare "againe and againe." The problem here is not—as far as we are, or Milton is, concerned—the death of the author or that writing is always posthumous. It is instead twofold: both that the proper name of the author needs a witness and that any witness, any reader who witnesses, ends up thereby anonymous, and so becomes incapable of testifying. Witnessing then becomes a universal condition, a permanent present, being without event. You can begin to understand the rather nasty or double-edged cast to Milton's final thought that, if kings could get such a tomb, they would willingly die. The mode of sovereignty Milton imagines the text/tomb having recruits all who touch it in a mindless chorus that recites the proper name.

Want to stop? To do so you will need to posit another Shakespeare, to un/ Shakespeare "Shakespeare," by denying the necessary, formalizing link between the historical William Shakespeare (*bios*) and the bibliographical corpus of the First or Second Folio. Posit the Earl of Oxford, Francis Bacon, or an "an infinite number of monkeys" as the author and you reshelve "Shakespeare" elsewhere, reconstituting an entire infrastructure. Oh what a massy mess!

In this chapter, we approach these questions—this conflict over what might be described as the quasi-Eucharistic or sacramental function of "William Shakespeare" as a relay that couples a historical person to a series of texts by way of a proper name—throughout Roland Emmerich's *Anonymous* (2011). Now most, if not all, Shakespeare scholars may think that this film is just so wrong, so pernicious, so just plain tacky that it is not worth mentioning, much less discussing. In a way, we agree. The film is a mess. Yes, it is really a mess, even as it is not quite a miss, and much less than a Mass. We assume that very few of you reading this chapter have seen the film, so we've watched it for you, so you wouldn't have to, or perhaps to induce you to watch it anyway, against your better judgment. You see, we think *Anonymous* does something very interesting with anonymity, and the ways in which it does that something badly make the film especially interesting and worth critical scrutiny.

Anonymous, as you may or may not recall, weaves a story of apparent conspiracy. "Our Shakespeare," "our Shakespeare," intones Derek Jacobi in the Broadway play with which the film begins, "Not a single manuscript of any kind has ever been found written in Shakespeare's own hand," and yet he remains, as do his plays, testimony to the heights of human expression. Jacobi proposes to tell another more interesting story—about monarchs, nations, violence, and intrigue. We segue to London in and around 1599. Elizabeth I is old. Essex plots his regime change (or regime conservation if you favor Tudors over Stuarts). The Earl of Southampton takes his friend and mentor the Earl of Oxford to the public theater, which is promptly closed on order of the evil Cecils (senior and junior). Afterward, as he referees a consolatory game of tennis between Southampton and Essex, Oxford asks how many people go to a single performance. Two thousand or so is Southampton's reply. Oxford does the math and registering the thought of reaching ten thousand souls all "listening to the words of one man," tells Essex, "that's power"—more power than words. So Oxford writes a play, recruits Ben Jonson to stand as his cipher, in a perverse reversal of patronage, and his plays take to the stage, sponsoring Essex for King and subjecting the Cecils to a good trouncing in caricature. Along the way, we learn that Oxford wrote the epilogue to *A Midsummer Night's Dream* (1593–95) and played Robin Goodfellow (Puck) as a boy for an appreciative Elizabeth I, or "Bess" as she becomes. The two become lovers and produce a child, a son, who we later discover to be the incestuous product, in fact, of their union, as Oxford is himself Elizabeth's son. (We said it was a mess).

By accident, and then increasingly by sleight of hand combined with drunken self-interest, William Shakespeare, then an actor, takes the stage as the author of all the plays and poems that Oxford writes. Shakespeare basks in the glory, the fame, and the money. He gets a coat of arms. He builds the Globe. He gets laid. All the while, the building of the Shakespeare monument / money/mint unfolds against an uncertainly chronological montage of the plays, which synch up to significant moments in Oxford's life—such as his rash murder of a servant or spy who hides behind a curtain in his chambers where he has been writing. Then a foster child to the Cecil family, Oxford's crime is concealed—but comes out onstage in Hamlet's murder of Polonius, only this Polonius, so it seems, is recognizable by all and sundry as Sir Robert Cecil. Plots thicken. Elizabeth gets older still. James VI of Scotland covets the Tudor throne. Essex revolts and fails; Oxford dies, leaving Ben Jonson as his literary executor and sole witness to his authorship. Pursued to the Globe by Cecil's men as they search for Oxford's manuscripts, Jonson sets off some fireworks that burn the theater down. Do the manuscripts survive? We're not exactly sure. The film ends showing us Jonson recover what appears to be a bundle of scorched but readable papers bearing the title "Julius Caesar," but it's not clear what else remains.

What's curious, we think, about the film is the way it repeatedly refuses to bear witness to Oxford's authorship even when showing him holding a quill, dipping it in ink, and writing words. Like the monkeys that beset Arthur Dent in *The Hitchhiker's Guide to the Galaxy*, Oxford's fingers may be "ink stained," but the act of writing remains tensely off camera, offstage, in the other room. In *Anonymous*, anonymity is not merely, like pseudonymity, a subset of onymity (name bearing), a clandestine or secret truth; anonymity is something else, a mess of writing that lacks not only a signature but also an "I" witness. Anonymous authorship is not reducible to a hidden proper name, nor is it just a mask behind which a unified agency operates strategically within a network that lacks any kind of unconscious or media-related interference or static. The film sponsors Oxford as the writer of the plays in what appears to count as a full-on Bardoclasm, but then the film repeatedly refuses to bear witness to the fact of that writing. The hand that holds the quill that would break the icon, reveal it to be an idol, unfolds its fist, lets the quill that would figuratively "cut" go slack in its grip, and turns into what in our previous two chapters we named a "Bardoclash," an uncertain, unreadable fitting or retarding of our relations to Shakespeare.[6] We attend to Emmerich's film, then, in order to ask what happens to the archive, the witness, and the bio/bib-liographical codes governing attribution and authorship studies when the word *anonymous* becomes both a title and a proper name.

While "Anonymous" is readily personed by the film—when informed that there is a new play in London, Queen Elizabeth remarks, "Anonymous? I love his verse"—the film's successive refusals to connect person to page treats anonymity as a governing condition or state into which texts or an archive may fall. Deriv-ing from the Greek *anonymos*, the word *anonymous* enters English as an adjective that accords very much with the second sense in which the film deploys the term, voiding or complicating thereby the nominalization of the word into the clandestine proper name "Oxford."[7] Where the film proceeds and delivers on an alternative Oxfordian renaming of Shakespeare and reattribution of the plays, it ruins its own act of naming, withholds a sufficient witness, in Milton's sense, and leaves the archive a massy, messy morass of paper and ash.

SIGNATURE SECRETIONS

To begin, it is important to understand what kind of a film *Anonymous* actually is. It has been widely mistaken for a conspiracy thriller.[8] But if *Anonymous* were a genuine conspiracy film, the title wouldn't be *Anonymous*. The title would name or refer to a person such as Edward de Vere, or his title, the Earl of Oxford. Emm-erich could easily have adopted a variation of titles of Oxfordian books modeled on *The Da Vinci Code* such as Jonathan Bond's *The De Vere Code* (2009), Virginia M. Fellows's *The Shakespeare Code* (2006) and *The Shakespeare Secret* (2007), or precursors like Graham Phillips's book titled *The Shakespeare Conspiracy* (1994) and an Oxfordian film of the same title directed by Michael Peer and narrated by Sir Derek Jacobi.[9] Obviously, Emmerich chose not to do so.[10] Unlike generic con-spiracy thriller films such as *The Da Vinci Code* (2004), *Anonymous* presents no mystery to be solved. It remains always perfectly clear that the Earl of Oxford, not Shakespeare, wrote Shakespeare's plays. There is no detective figure in the film, and nothing like detective work gets done. There is no Oxford Code, no Oxford-ian version of the Fibonacci sequence or Sir Francis Bacon's bilateral cipher, no tomb, no gravestone, not even an unmarked grave (a scene of Oxford's funeral was cut from the film but is included as a deleted scene on the DVD).[11]

In our view, *Anonymous* is a disaster film, a disastrous disaster film, not a con-spiracy thriller. If we regard *Anonymous* from an auteurist perspective, we can place it without much difficulty in line with earlier of Emmerich's science fiction, disas-ter blockbusters such as *Stargate* (1994), *Independence Day* (1996), *The Day after Tomorrow* (2004), *10,000 B.C.* (2008), and *2012* (2009). Although *Anonymous* might seem, on the face of it, to differ radically from these earlier sci-fi films, you might almost predict that Emmerich would make *Anonymous* since most of these earlier films in many ways concern the archive and its destruction.[12]*Anonymous* makes a critical advance on these films not only by turning the archive into a mess. It's a mess from which all attempts to derive a Mass, a relay by which to suture *bios* to bibliography, will fail, generating only a succession of partial, spec-tral, presences. Indeed, the film might be said to embark on an auto-archiving in ways that make it a catastrophic mess. We will not attempt to decide whether the film is, among other options, a brilliantly and finely executed mess designed to succeed at failing or just a messily executed mess that fails, fails again, fails worse. Please make your call.

NOT WHODUNIT BUT WHO/WROTE/IT?

Anonymous uses the disaster film genre to figure anonymity as an archive, thereby scrambling the generic and forensic codes both of Shakespeare attribution studies and of the authorship debate. In our view, *Anonymous* indirectly puts deconstructive pressure on some uncritically held assumptions that both Stratfordians and Oxfordians share about anonymous authorship, writing and other media, testimony, and the archive and that are funded by the genres of detective fiction and the conspiracy thriller. In the preface to *Contested Will: Who Wrote Shakespeare*, for example, the confirmed Stratfordian James Shapiro remarks, "Much of what has been written about the authorship of Shakespeare's plays follows the contours of a detective story, which is not all that surprising, since the authorship question and the 'whodunit' emerged at the same historical moment. Like all good detective fiction, the Shakespeare mystery can be solved only by determining what evidence is credible, retracing steps, and avoiding false leads. My own account in what follows is no different."[13] In the passage, Shapiro does our work for us by showing, albeit indirectly, that Oxfordians and Stratfordians differ only on the narrow issue of who the real author is. They share the exact same set of assumptions about the right way to reach that conclusion, a way that also deconstructs the distinction between legal detection and detective fiction. Any account of authorship in Shakespeare's case will necessarily be one story among others.

Critically unexamined binary oppositions between biography and autobiography, biography and bibliography, forgery and authentic text, history and fiction, secret and revelation, criminal and creator, all may gradually be seen to self-deconstruct in that the author is already positioned as a criminal even before his or her work is discovered to have been forged. The seemingly central question of attribution studies—namely, "Who wrote it?"—bypasses more fundamental ontological and epistemological questions about authorship: "who" is the subject of the writing? (Does the subject have an unconscious? Is that unconscious already hardwired, a mystic writing iPad?) And what kinds of "writing" bear the marks of a graphic unconscious? (Where does one draw the line between writing and drawing? Is writing reducible to alphabets, ideograms, hieroglyphs, and so on? Can cryptonyms be written in nongraphic forms?) Hence attribution studies takes for granted that reading is limited without establishing what the limits of reading are.

Thus, despite their sometimes vociferously stated differences, Stratfordians and Oxfordians agree on just about everything about the plays apart from the proper name of the author who wrote them: both sides agree that everything by either author is archived, that everything is readable, and that everything is to be read in relation to rules of evidence as established in detective fiction. For Stratfordians and Oxfordians alike, the archive is fully operational, without what

Derrida calls "anarchivity," "the violence of the archive itself, *as archive, as archival violence*," the radical destruction of the archive and the remains of what can never be archived, the ash of the archive.[14] We maintain that *Anonymous* is a radically "anarchivic" film in that it figures the archive as a total mess, as a set of texts that are always already finished and stored manuscripts in a library and yet that have also always already been destroyed—both fully present and available and yet always unavailable, always going up in smoke before your eyes, leaving you with nothing but a bunch of ash. Emmerich's disaster film turns anonymity into a graphic mess that cannot be cleaned up by viewers: at a number of points, it is not necessarily clear what may be recognized as a crux and even a cryptonym, as a graphic mark, nor is it always clear where the film's paratexts draw a line dividing writing from drawing. What we will call various kinds of "overwriting" in *Anonymous* and its paratexts spill out in a surplus of writings, writing in overplus, writing that blots, scratches out, or stets items rather than accretes, sorts, and stores them in an economical, easily accessible, rational order. Under the heading of the archive, we put the related issues of media, data storage, inscription and preservation, erasure and destruction, the signature, testimony, and witnessing. The results may, as Milton warns, prove petrifying.

MESS THIS MANUSCRIPT AROUND: IN THE NAME OF THE TITLE

We may begin to grasp concretely how *Anonymous* scrambles the generic and forensic codes of attribution and authorship studies by attending to the film's confusion of the referent of the title, film or play. The opening title sequence conspicuously shows only the film's title, not the stars and the director as opening title sequences typically do. Roland Emmerich's name appears only at the end of the film in the second-to-last shot. The last shot scrolls the rest of the credits.

The opening title sequence also makes the referent of the film's title momentarily uncertain. The title first appears on a theater marquee we see shortly after Derek Jacobi hastily gets out of a New York City taxi, presumably near Times Square (Figure 5.1a). (Perhaps in a humble fashion the film does not say if the theater is on 42nd Street or somewhere off-Broadway or perhaps even off-off-Broadway.) The exterior shot of the theater marquee then fades to black while leaving the same white letters in place (Figure 5.1b). This dissolve may produce at least momentary semantic confusion for some viewers. Is *Anonymous* the title of a play and the title of a film? An adaptation of an off-Broadway play you've never heard of before and wonder if you missed? In addition to this momentary confusion, some viewers may notice that the title on the marquee is a digitally produced special effect. The letters have a kind of spectral effect, the referent having been effectively blacked out in a way that is similar to black and white splotches on the film poster. Derek Jacobi's familiar face, which refers back also to his Chorus in Kenneth Branagh's *Henry V* (1989) (Figure 5.1c and d) both calms and enervates the effect further. Perhaps even more anarchivically, "Anonymous" becomes something like a proper name.

Figure 5.1a, b, c, and d   Opening title sequence of Roland Emmerich's *Anonymous* (2011) and Derek Jacobi as Chorus in Kenneth Branagh's *Henry V* (1989).

The anarchivity of the title sequence is writ large in *Anonymous* as a whole. The film's narrative is structured by a paradoxical archive structured by two polar opposites: on the one hand, the archive is fully intact; on the other, the archive is also destroyed. This opposition between the complete, preserved archive and its apocalyptic destruction is neatly captured by two sets of archival scenes in the film: the first, de Vere's library and wonder cabinet where nearly all, or apparently all, his plays have been written and stored; the second, Ben Jonson's rediscovery, near end of the film, of the singed manuscripts intact, not the more apparently opposite scene near the beginning of the film that shows these manuscripts apparently burning up along with the Globe theater, an inference strengthened when Jonson shortly thereafter, while being tortured, tells Queen Elizabeth's chief adviser Robert Cecil that the manuscripts all burned.

We will examine the library scene first (Figure 5.2). Jonson visits de Vere after Shakespeare claims, after a wildly popular production of *Henry V*, that he is "anonymous." Oxford takes several manuscripts down before settling on *Romeo and Juliet* and handing it to Jonson.

The plays de Vere gives to Jonson and in a later scene gives to Shakespeare to perform onstage have already been written. When deciding which play to give Jonson, he pulls several notebooks off the shelves of a bookcase, opening each in turn to reveal a manuscript contained inside it. The title of each play de Vere holds and examines is shown in close-up. The anarchivity of de Vere's archive is figured by the mess that fills out the mise-en-scène. To be sure, de Vere's manuscripts, like the writings on his desk and rolled up in bowls, form an apparently highly disorganized archive; de Vere may nevertheless have organized it, in the fashion of many practicing academic scholars, in a way that only he knows. The limits of the archive's anarchivic disorganization are not clear, however. The mess of papers testifies to the continual availability of the plays, of all the plays, even perhaps *Cardenio*, but only in the form of such a mess or morass of papers. We never get an index of the plays or anything approaching an inventory, only

Figure 5.2   Edward de Vere, Earl of Oxford's archive in Roland Emmerich's *Anonymous* (2011).

a later montage of *Julius Caesar*, *Romeo and Juliet*, *Macbeth*, and the manuscript of a play he does not take down from the shelf—namely, *Hamlet*. The film does not bother to establish whether *Hamlet* has already been written or was written after this scene. *Richard II*, the play revived for a special performance on the eve of the Essex Revolt in 1599, turns into a staging of Richard III that permits the lampooning of Richard Cecil in the form of the hunchbacked Richard III. Knowledge of the plays unfolds literally and figuratively as a given.

To make things more confusing, de Vere does not use a coherent filing system. The manuscripts are enclosed in identical leather folders, none of which is labeled. After quickly glancing at the title pages, de Vere throws the discarded manuscripts on a desk behind him instead of reshelving them, and it is not clear he has a backup copy of the *Romeo and Juliet* manuscript he hands over to Jonson. We can't tell if the order of the plays de Vere pulls off the shelf is also the order in which de Vere composed, nor can we tell if de Vere was searching for *Romeo and Juliet* from the start or settles upon it after looking at the other manuscripts and discarding them one by one as unsuitable for performance. Nevertheless, the remnants of de Vere's filing system are shown in two scenes, one in which de Vere, on his deathbed, is shown writing *King Lear*. As he closes the leather folder over a text we cannot read, a little piece of paper with the words "King Lear" written on it is visible slipped into the manuscript like a Post-it note. The same kind of note appears when Jonson finds the manuscripts in the burned-down Globe theater. Jonson places a detached piece of paper with the words "Henry V" on top of the singed manuscript, as if the title were not only a filing label but something akin to a bandage or skin graft covering up the burns on the title page of the manuscript of *Henry V* (see Figure 5.3d).

We take both poles of the opposition the film draws between complete and completed archive and its anarchivic deconstruction to be so unstable that the opposition self-deconstructs, or remains under construction. De Vere's messy space we call, perhaps messily, an archival library approaches a paradoxical state: it appears to be complete, the manuscripts collected and shelved, written perhaps when he was a boy, given that he already at that point had written *A Midsummer*

Night's Dream, or written perhaps before he was even born, given the incestuous emptying out of lines of filiation and reproduction in the play. The anarchivic force driving these questions about the archive emerges also in the titles of plays. Just before de Vere examines the manuscript of *Romeo and Juliet*, the camera cuts to Jonson peering over de Vere's manuscripts and dropping on the title page of *Twelfth Night*. The shot is parallel to the close-up shots of the title pages of the manuscripts, making it seem to be one of a series and hence comparable to the completed manuscripts of which we also see only the title page. Has *Twelfth Night* been written? Or is yet to be written? If it is in progress, is it any further than the title page? (We will return to the writing on this particular page.)

The opposite number of the archival library scene is not, as one might reasonably expect, the anarchivic destruction of de Vere's manuscripts the viewer is initially meant to think were burned along with the Globe theater but Jonson's recovery of the manuscripts, an event we see in the second narrative frame of the film; the most anarchivic scene is paradoxically the one in which Jonson recovers intact the de Vere manuscripts he'd stored in a fireworks box he emptied out while hiding underneath the stage of the Globe theater while evading Cecil's guards (Figure 5.3).

Jonson opens the box, the contents reflecting light from the inside of the lid on Jonson's face, as is he were looking at a computer screen, or perhaps as if he were opening the ark recovered by the Nazi archaeologist at the end of *Raiders of the Lost Ark* (Figure 5.3a). On top of Oxford's singed but intact manuscripts Jonson finds *Henry V*.

The recovery of the manuscripts leads to the immediate reanimation of *Henry V*, the first play we see performed in the film in the form of a montage, albeit that the Prologue's voice rather than music provides the continuity between shots (Figure 5.3b and c). The extinguished fire in the globe catches flame in the words "O for a muse of fire." As when we first see the play, the Chorus is speaking the first lines of the prologue *Henry V*, dressed just as he was before; the newly crowned King James watches the play being performed at court and engages Robert Cecil

Figure 5.3a, b, c, and d   Ben Jonson retrieves the archive in Roland Emmerich's *Anonymous* (2011)—or does he?

in a conversation about theater as the Chorus continues in voice-over to recite the prologue sotto voce, including a shot of Shakespeare backstage watching James watching *Henry V.* While this montage sequence effectively reanimates de Vere by repeating the "same" play, it is somewhat confusing. The shot of the Chorus appears initially to be a shot of him in the Globe; only after we see King James do we realize that the Chorus is performing on a royal stage. Furthermore, the montage leaves some holes in the totally recovered archive unfilled. We are left to wonder, for example, how Jonson or someone else—the printer, perhaps?—lost the manuscripts, especially since de Vere personally gave them to Jonson and told him to watch over them. Moreover, Jonson's reliability is put into question by Robert Cecil's mistaken conclusion that Jonson "speaks the truth" when saying the manuscripts were burned. Since Jonson immediately goes to the theater in search of the manuscripts, he must have been lying, however. And Jonson only creates further problems in witnessing their recovery. The Prologue had pointed out in the first narrative frame that Shakespeare left no manuscripts behind. Yet since there are no manuscripts for any of the plays and poems in the Shakespeare canon, we may wonder how and why these manuscripts went missing. So the archive winks in and out of being, in and out of the shot. Both there and not there, a given to be assumed but not fully screened. It figures as pure potentiality that nevertheless constitutes a done deal, to be linked to successive proper names as indexed at one time or another to a historical person.

But the film then messes this structure up further in two distinct ways that we shall describe. It amps up the radical anarchivity of the condition of anonymous authorship in scenes that figure the archive in thematic and generic ways, as more or less messy kinds of writing that we saw in the messy library scene above. These figures include the proper name and the title, with respect to the medium of paper, the circulation of handwritten manuscripts and published works, and the medium of stage performance, witnessing, wills, and legacies. These archival figures appear in the film's representations of Oxford composing, reciting works, signing his work. But beyond such thematic and generic involutions, the linear plotting of the film disturbs any timeline on which we could clearly and easily place the events as the film narrates them. Excessive formal repetitions constitute a specific kind of messy anarchivity, an anarchivity that disrupts the capacity of *Anonymous* itself to serve as an archive of de Vere's authorship. If, for Derrida, the archive is oriented to the future, not to the past, to a set of operations for disseminating the past in various presents, *Anonymous* atomizes our sense of linear time. Furthermore, it uses flashbacks in ways that disrupt the coherence of all grammatical tenses. The linear narrative the film tells, or tries to tell, in nonlinear fashion through the use of flashbacks, is constantly disoriented by cinematically incoherent shifts in time. While certain kinds of formal repetitions in *Anonymous*—the two narrative frames that bookend the film and the same shot used to begin flashbacks that different characters have—may be characterized as obsessive, they never attain a signature effect that would authorize them as properly meaningful. They are not compulsively repetitive—in Freud's words, neither fully "*Fort*" nor "*Da*"—and so they end up proving to be neither here nor there, just gone.[15]

Shakespeare Unsigned

We proceed with our focus on thematic archival figures of what we take to be the fully paradoxical and self-deconstructing, messy anarchivity of anonymous authorship in *Anonymous*, an anarchivity that reaches through storage spaces like de Vere's library or Jonson's fireworks box to the paratexts in the film, such as the titles of de Vere's unsigned manuscripts, the titles of posters and playbills, media, names, signatures, and so on. While the posters for *Twelfth Night*, *Romeo and Juliet*, *Hamlet*, and *Macbeth* all include the name "William Shakespeare," no other work in *Anonymous* bearing a title we recognize as Shakespeare's bears any signature whatsoever. Similarly, neither the title page nor the cover of the published *Venus and Adonis* bear Shakespeare's name, even though Oxford tells Shakespeare in the scene immediately preceding the scenes of the printing of the poem, Shakespeare reading, and two ladies in waiting reading it aloud, he, Shakespeare, has "had a poem published today." When Shakespeare reveals to the crowd that he is "Anonymous," Shakespeare also reveals his own anonymity with respect to publication. The props he holds are an ink quill and a prompt book; we never see a book with his name on it. The book cover of *Venus and Adonis* is not shown and cannot be seen until the scene ends with one of two ladies in waiting caught reading it aloud by Elizabeth handing it over to her. Sometimes paratextual information drops out. When the older Elizabeth talks to the younger Cecil about "Anonymous" writing *Venus and Adonis* for her in a later scene, the book's title is seen in middistance at first, then gradually falls out of the frame as the shots of Elizabeth holding it become tighter and tighter close-ups.

Anonymous goes consistently from showing texts authored by de Vere with no name on them to texts not authored by Shakespeare with his name on them. Shakespeare's name may appear on posters, but not on books.

Scenes involving names in manuscripts prove even more dizzying than names on printed texts. Manuscripts screened are virtually illegible. Consider scenes involving a signature (Figure 5.4).

Figure 5.4a, b, c, and d   Shakespeare's signatures in John's Madden's *Shakespeare in Love* (1998) and Roland Emmerich's *Anonymous* (2011).

Anonymous includes a scene in which Oxford does write a signature on a piece of paper. However, the name he signs is not his own (Figure 5.4c). As if intending to recall the opening title sequence of *Shakespeare in Love*, Oxford signs Shakespeare's name on a blank page. The title "Shakespeare in Love" appears on the screen in red ink as if invisibly handwritten, moving from left to right (Figure 5.4a and b). The title of the film appears over a close-up of Shakespeare (Joseph Fiennes) continued to cover the second of two pages with his signatures, each time using different abbreviations for "William," many of them crossed out. The shot with the title *Shakespeare in Love* ends when Shakespeare writes "Will Shakespeare."

As if taking up where *Shakespeare in Love* left off, *Anonymous* shows Oxford writing "Will Shakespeare" after he's had a visit from Ben Jonson (Figure 5.4c). Oxford's wife enters as Jonson leaves him, and Oxford, still writing, holds out his hand as if to say "please wait just a second, I've almost finished." The next shot shows him rewriting his signature as "William Shake-Speare," finishing by carefully inserting a hyphen between "Shake" and "Speare" (Figure 5.4d). Oxford's invention is not a forgery (Oxford is not copying Shakespeare's signature, and apparently Shakespeare can't sign his own name). It is never shown on the title page of any of Oxford's works (they are all unsigned, as we have seen). And Shakespeare's last name is deformed, its syllables separated into words and thereby turned into a pun.

Beyond its function within the scene, the shot of Oxford putting the hyphen between "Shake" and "Speare" might be read as an animated emblem for the recursiveness of the film's narrative structure: Oxford finishes his "signature," by going back from the last "e" at the end to the middle and writing the hyphen from left to right. Furthermore, Oxford finishes not with a letter but with a punctuation mark, dividing up into words that stop short of the wordplay Oxfordians find in Shakespeare's name, or supposed pseudonym ("Shake" becomes a verb and "speare" becomes a noun).[16] Yet no scene in the film stands as its master emblem since it can be shown to repeat in some way an earlier scene or anticipate its repetition in a later scene.

Another emblem of authorship might be the shot of the title page of *Twelfth Night*, on Oxford's desk furtively spied by Jonson as Oxford takes down finished plays from his library shelf. This page shows *Twelfth Night* written near the top and crossed out with a single, continuous strike-through, followed by *What You Will* in smaller size below, and *Twelfth Night* at the bottom written exactly as it is crossed out near the top of the page. The page, which is only momentarily visible when viewed, as the film plays 24 frames a second (or its digital equivalent), renders it a genetic critic's fantasy come true. Unlike an animated signature or a palimpsest, the page is a record and archive that shows in transparent, linear fashion, from top to bottom, left to right, the history of Oxford's revisions. Yet, like Oxford finishing with a hyphen, the revised text loops back from bottom to top: Oxford apparently changed his mind and went back to his original title. Moreover, the revised title page leaves the title and subtitle in reverse order: *What You Will* is the title, *Twelfth Night* the subtitle. If Oxford got around to retitling it (the poster for the play shows "Twelfth Night," but not "Or What You Will"), then we might say that *Anonymous* has no will to archive, or, put somewhat differently, has a will to will-lessness.

DRAWING THE LINE

Anonymous seems wedded then to an economy of diminishing returns that erases authorship and makes writing in general anonymous. Rather than revealing a particular author, we may notice that *Anonymous* also subjects the opposition between the true author named de Vere and the fake author named Shakespeare to anarchivic deconstruction. When it comes to signing one's name, Shakespeare is just as anonymous as de Vere. The film refuses to stick to its (historically unfounded) distinction between illiterate actors and literate dramatists. (Shakespeare wants the play role of Romeo, but Jonson tells him "Keep off the stage. Writers do not have time to act.") Although Emmerich portrays Shakespeare as an opportunist and blackmailer, even strongly implying that he murdered Marlowe, the film slightly hedges its bets when it comes to the question of whether Shakespeare can write at all. After Shakespeare puts in an appearance at the Mermaid Tavern feeling very proud at being able to show his theatrical colleagues the design and motto for his newly bought coat of arms, Jonson testily translates "non sanz droict" as "Not without right" and thinks he can expose Shakespeare as an illiterate, a supposed dramatist who is unable to write even a single letter or even a mark like an "X" as his signature. Jonson first suggests that Shakespeare write *e* then *i*,—"it's a straight line"—but Jonson thereby exceeds the limits of alphabetic writing and crosses over into drawing; moreover, Jonson gives Shakespeare a quill but not ink even though the film has many scenes with ink, paper, and quills. "No ink," says Shakespeare, off the apparent hook, and shoves the paper and quill Jonson has handed him back at Jonson, and walks out, thereby answering the Prologue's (Derek Jacobi) rather rhetorical questions about Shakespeare's illiteracy in the affirmative.

The same kind of thematic erasure of the proper name is repeated elsewhere in the film a number of times. Oxford's "Shake-Speare" signature, or forged signature, or drawing of a signature, or wordplay, is only the icon or emblem of a more general erasure. Instead of a crime scene investigation, the film presents us with anarchivic texts that have unidentifiable authors. One scene showing Oxford finishing writing the manuscript of *Richard III* makes it perfectly clear that Oxford wrote it. Oxford does not finish the play in a conventional manner, however. The last word he writes before turning the manuscript over is *Amen*, not *Finis*. Even scenes in which we see Jonson and Oxford writing, what they are writing or have written is often illegible. For example, Oxford's second flashback includes a scene of him as a young man writing, which begins after he's just had sex with a lady-in-waiting named "Bess." As in the film poster, Oxford and his writing are consistently obscured: we don't see who is having sex, nor do we see the man writing in the next two shots, one of him from behind follows before the film crosscuts close-ups of a lady-in-waiting sitting on the bed talking to Oxford, who is writing at his desk. When we finally do see that it is Oxford writing, we cannot make out what he is writing.

Examples of erasure can be easily multiplied. In the economy of evidence and analysis that governs literary criticism, to provide more examples would generally be counterproductive since a law of diminishing returns, or less is more, would mean that more examples would be redundant. But given the mess that is *Anonymous*, and given the way we take its replaying of the question of authorship and the function of anonymity within the medium of film, we want to give a few more examples of the archive's anarchivity in order to demonstrate as precisely as possible the film's own anarchivic economy of diminishing returns. In an earlier scene that pointedly recalls the scene in *Hamlet* when Hamlet murders Polonius, Oxford kills a man hiding behind a tapestry who had been spying on Oxford's writings and spilled ink on part of a manuscript page after purloining a few pages. The film renders the legible parts of the paper with spilled ink unreadable by shooting the page upside down. As the spy dies, he comes out from behind the curtain and lets the pages he has stolen fall on the ground. But we never see or learn what they are or if his theft of those pages in particular has any significance.

One of the more enigmatic scenes of writing occurs on de Vere's deathbed. After a long shot of him writing, the film cuts to a close-up of what he has been writing. All we see, however, is de Vere make a very short line next to a word, a mark that bears no resemblance either to an alphabet or to numbers. The shadow cast over the page makes it impossible to read even when played on a Blu-ray. The film cuts almost immediately to de Vere folding a leather cover over the text. Similar problems appear when other writing desks are shot in close-up and playwrights are shown writing in close-up. For example, a letter sealed with wax has been filed upside down in Cecil's writing desk.

In an almost parallel close-up shot, Jonson's hand crumples up sheets of paper on which he has crossed out nearly every line of a page of a new (untitled) play he has been writing and tosses them away in frustration. Even when Jonson presents Henslowe with a completed manuscript he hopes the Lord Chamberlain's Men will perform, he does not mention the title or summarize the plot, nor does the manuscript cover have a title or name on it. Shakespeare does not blot a line since he can't write one, but everyone who can write in *Anonymous* crosses out more lines than not.

Again along very similar lines, other major characters refuse to sign documents. Robert Cecil tells the apparently demented, aged Elizabeth seen sucking on the index finger of her right hand, "I have brought you something to sign, your majesty. It's the 'Act of Succession'" and then commands her to "sign." She first reads the document in a close-up, points to her name, "Elizabeth Rex" written in conspicuously large letters and extravagantly surrounded by numerous calligraphic flourishes. The film then cuts to a reaction shot of Cecil, pointing to James's name in the same position and same size lower down the document, shot in a parallel close-up. Rather than sign, Elizabeth grabs the parchment document out of Cecil's hands and flings it at the camera. The film then cuts to a helicopter shot of her funeral, thereby suggesting that Elizabeth did and did not sign off. Instead of showing characters signing documents, *Anonymous* includes a number of sequences of fingers pointlessly pointing at names or words become displaced, ephemeral, de-iconized manicules.[17] The shots of Elizabeth pointing at her name and James's name recall similar shots of Shakespeare pointing at each of the words *"Non sanz droict,"* and of the two posters for *Hamlet* in which we see a hand pointing an index finger at a the words "The Lord Chamberlain" in the poster on the right. Rather than giving a signature, the film highlights Elizabeth's finger: after sucking on it, she points first to her name and then, two shots later, points to James VI's name, in somewhat less fancy handwriting, before throwing the parchment toward the camera in a final act of defiance. (The title of the document, "Act of Succession," is almost buried under "Elizabeth Rex," set off to the left in smaller size below the name.) In these ways, among others, *Anonymous* refuses to attach signatures to texts and the titles of literary works to the proper names of authors. The result seems a strategic projection of anonymity throughout the archive, an anony/mess.

Such effects are magnified and complicated further by the film's paratexts. In addition to the erasure of the proper name in the trailer and poster we discussed above, additional paratexts of *Anonymous* extend the anarchivity of anonymity to include the disrupting boundaries between writing and drawing. Consider the theater lobby poster for *Anonymous*: the same image with slightly different text is used on the cover of the DVD, Blu-ray, and pictorial moviebook, *Anonymous: William Shakespeare Revealed* (2011), the film trailer, and the DVD and Blu-ray menus.[18]

The poster generates suspense well enough, but without making any reference to Oxford (Figure 5.5a). The title of the film presumably answers the question "Was Shakespeare a Fraud?" Since the man in the image has turned his back to us, we cannot determine who the man holding the quill, presumably "Anonymous," the real author, is supposed to be. Instead, the quill that does not write, that stands aloft like some further, dysfunctional manicule or index, seems to have discharged its ink on the image itself, though the ink appears to have coalesced into the inky figure of the man who holds the quill. As we have begun to see,

Figure 5.5a, b, and c   Poster and trailer for Roland Emmerich's *Anonymous* (2011).

Anonymous makes the paratextual link between author and writing unreadable in a surprising number of different ways. Here, the writing that does and does not occur in the film returns or precedes as a mode of "plus-size writing." By "plus-size writing" we mean not only that some writing covers over other writing but that it figures a graphic surplus that extends beyond alphabetic writing. The black ink splashed on the white background is clearly not text at all. The missing ink from Shakespeare's quill in the scene in which he does not write his name comes back or precedes it.

Yet the poster also puts into question the boundary between writing and painting. It is not even clear whether the medium is ink or paint (Figure 5.5a and b). Are the black splotches a kind of figurative writing meant to be read even if they do not form letters? Are they a kind of blotting done by the man holding the quill? The lobby poster literally stages a graphic image, an ink blot test. Who do you hallucinate in the archive? How do you transubstantiate this mess into a Mass? But the interpretive density and confusion enabled by the poster's lack of parergonal closure may perhaps best be registered in the way the reader of the poster implicitly occupies the same position as would the implied person who splashed the man in the poster with white ink. To read the image is to deface it, to write or paint over it figuratively, to create a new surface that blanks out the connection between writer, writing, and signature. What is the condition of this unreadability? Plus-size writings, none of which override the others and that together do not form a palimpsest in the film's baroque hall of broken mirrors.

Taken together, the graphic design of the *Anonymous* poster, the film trailer, and the design of the DVD animated menu constitute an example the film's archiving of its own procedures. The trailer for *Anonymous* effectively animates the poster's graphic design. Shots from the film are intercut with shots of text that begin with black ink splashing on a white background in slow motion as a loud percussive "swoosh" sound effect that matches the image of ink splashes on the screen.

The shot of ink after Essex is beheaded suggests that what looked like ink is now Essex's spurting blood. The medium is fluid. As in all trailers, the text is anonymous. But writing remains anonymous through the trailer: in the first shots, close-ups show the hand of someone writing. Later shots of Oxford do not show him writing. Nor do we see anyone else we can match to the close-up shot of a handwriting on paper on a desk. Such then are the epitexts, as Gerard Genette calls them, to *Anonymous*. DVD and Blu-rays usually have animated menu loops, and *Anonymous* is no exception. The menu loop develops the graphic design of the poster and trailer. A line of black ink spreads into pools that show part of a shot from the film in black and white before it turns into color. In this case, the line is easy to follow even though, as in all menu loops, the images constitute an abstract montage of shots from the film. Each splash of ink becomes progressively recognizable, usually obscuring a face or a manuscript. The DVD extra titled "Who Is the Real William Shakespeare?" recuts the first four shots of the trailer, inserting a few additional shots between them, before showing the title written in the same style of splashed ink that appears in the film's other paratexts we have examined thus far. It goes further than they do, however, in suggesting that the line from one point to another has no logic to it and leads nowhere, literally taking the viewer in an endless circle.[19]

FLASH FLOOD

Such looping or circling figures also in the film's use of flashbacks, which do not quite round on themselves, disturb narrative coherence and make history something not reducible to a clear linear narrative. Many films, not just films in remote historical periods, begin and end with flashbacks in bookend fashion: *Double Indemnity* (dir. Billy Wilder, 1944), *Sunset Boulevard* (dir. Billy Wilder, 1950), and *D.O.A.* (dir. Rudolph Maté, 1950) are well-known examples (*Lost Weekend* ends by repeating the first shot of the film in reverse.) Flashbacks in Hollywood films typically have the main character narrate the events, usually in voice-over, to help the audience understand how the film transitions in and out of it.[20]*Anonymous* is exceptional, however, in the number of flashbacks it uses. Hollywood narrative films and contemporary narrative films that follow their conventions typically have one flashback sequence involving one character. *Anonymous* has four sequences, and they involve four different characters. Moreover, each flashback is shot in very similar fashion: each begins with a close-up of the person having the flashback as words spoken by someone in voice-over are repeated and given an echo effect to indicate that the person on the screen is tuning out the diegetic present. According to Hollywood narrative conventions, a flashback should return to where it began; logically, if we begin with an older Elizabeth, we should return to the older Elizabeth to complete the sequence. But we don't. In fact, none of the flashback sequences return to where they began. In the case of Elizabeth watching *A Midsummer Night's Dream*, an extradiegetic parallel between the actresses playing the older and younger Elizabeth, Vanessa and Joley Redgrave, may provide some viewers a sense of continuity: Vanessa Redgrave is Joley Redgrave's mother. Instead of returning to the present at the end of flashback "forty years earlier," the film cuts abruptly to an entirely new plot development, the time and place of which we have to infer.

Some flashbacks are even more disorienting in being internally incoherent. After Jonson tells Shakespeare he can't play Romeo, we cut to a performance of *Romeo and Juliet* with the leads performing the holy palmer's sonnet during the Capulet ball scene. Skipping ahead, the film cuts to Oxford in close-up, sitting in the balcony and watching the performance. His flashback begins as we hear Romeo "I ne'er saw beauty 'til this night" and ends as the film cuts to a high-angle shot of the young Elizabeth dancing with the young Oxford at a ball presumably being held in her honor. The flashback seems to be intentionally confusing as *Romeo and Juliet* disappears entirely. Elizabeth first compares Oxford to Henry V and then to Puck, the role he actually plays in the performance she sees as a young woman (when Oxford is nine years old). But that happened in a completely different flashback the older Elizabeth had.

Jonson's flashback during his interrogation is incoherent in another respect. It flashes forward "precursively," as it were, to an event we will see again later in the film but shot very differently. Jonson's flashbacks transition to two unspecified moments in the past: the flashback consists of five shots, the first two of which briefly show an audience laughing in a theater and the last three and longer shots show Shakespeare taking a bow. *Anonymous* never makes clear what role Shakespeare played in the play the audience is applauding, what the play was, or when it was performed. As if inverting the conventions of a conspiracy thriller like Oliver Stone's *J.F.K.* (1991), in which mourning John F. Kennedy takes the form of finding his true assassins, *Anonymous* does not focus on one character, in this case Oxford; rather, the film clarifies, by proceeding obliquely, the condition of mourning an author whose name cannot be named—namely, that the narrative not be reducible to a biopic, that the story not be a biography of one character or his or her bio/bibliography.[21]

What is in many respects a simple linear narrative that *Anonymous* tells gets regularly derailed due to the film's excessive recursiveness, its almost virtuoso display of different semiotic orders to establish parallels through repetition and the use of different thresholds of legibility in repetition. The shot of Shakespeare watching James watch *Henry V* at court repeats almost exactly an earlier shot of Oxford watching Elizabeth watching *A Midsummer Night's Dream* at court. In addition to employing very similar shots to set up flashbacks and formal repetitions of the same shots with different characters, *Anonymous* deconstructs its two narrative frames. As do many historical films and biopics, *Anonymous* uses a narrative frame with Derek Jacobi playing the "Prologue" in the beginning and end of the film. The ending recalls the beginning in order to provide narrative closure. In *Anonymous*, formal repetitions recall not just one earlier moment but also a network of relays between earlier moments that also recall other moments. There are two narrative frames in *Anonymous*, the second concerning Ben Jonson and the fate of de Vere's manuscripts, but both the beginning and the ending of this frame bleed into the narrative of film itself, confusing events that happened in the past with events that are happening in the present.

THE COLLECT CALL

So how should we understand the mess that anonymous locates in and as its archive—an archive that it screens, so to speak, that it constitutes as its cinematic object? In a lively essay about variations on anonymity in modern and early modern culture, Kate Tunstall introduces the telephone book to illustrate a distinction between authored and unauthored books:

> The name of the author is a crucial element in today's publishing world: the reader expects to see it on the book cover; it is key to the publisher's marketing strategy; and indeed what the author is hoping for in publishing his work is to make, precisely, his name. Or at least, that is the case for most books. We would not, for instance, consider the phone book to be anonymous. It may be full of names but the fact that it bears no authorial name on its cover does not make it anonymous, and that is because it does not so much lack an authorial name as raise no expectations that there might be one to publish or, consequently to withhold. Thinking about anonymity thus provides a new way of approaching Foucault's question

"Qu'est-ce qu'un auteur?" The phone book does not have an author, and so, like the blank wall, it is not so much anonymous as, we might say, "un-authored."[22]

Extending our analysis of *Hamlet's* telephone, we want to put Tunstall's distinction between authored and unauthored books under deconstructive pressure: anonymity does indeed have a telephonic structure, but that structure is not reducible to a proper name and the lack of a proper name; rather, the anonymous telephonic relay network provokes the question "Who's there?" ("Is anyone, in fact, there?") and divides what otherwise may be presumed to be the indivisibility of authorship (who is writing?), and with it any notion of attributing an indivisible piece of writing to an indivisible writer via an indivisible medium.

In an unusually long footnote in *The Post Card*, Derrida recounts the story of a collect call that indirectly makes clear an archival problem related to this kind of telephonic network having to do with name of the caller, a caller who may be dead.[23] The call was placed by a "Martini" Heidegger. It's a call Derrida decides not to accept:

> And Freud has plugged into the answering machine of the *Philebus* or the *Symposium*. The American operator interrupts and scrambles: Freud is not paying enough, is not putting enough quarters into the machine. The great symposium, right, the gag on Europe, Eros in generalized telephonic relation. The demon calls, Socrates picks up, wait here's Freud . . . and the demon speaks to Freud, directly, from the beyond, like his ghost which says to him "wait," *hold on*, come back with your spool, don't hang up, here's Heidegger. Myself I tender Heidegger to the pupil: hold on, take, understand, and me along with it, and me first, you too (wait a minute, on "to tender"—what one does, tenders, when one says "hold on," there is the thought of the "*reichen*," "to porrect," *porringer* that translators on Heidegger's French switchboard say—"and here I take it as porridge"—on "to tender," therefore, to send, to destine, *schicken*, etc. *Zeit und Sein* [*Time and Being*] . . . will have had the power of (knowing) (thinking) plugging everything back in, to think plugging everything back in, all the (a)ways of making one's (a)way, every possible *Weg* [way], before the Being and time that there is (*es gibt*) on what there is to give.[24]

Derrida notes the date and time of the collect call from the "ghost or Geist of Martin."[25] He got the "*collect call*" from the United States, he says, "from Martin (she says Martine or Martini) Heidegger." Of course, if it were Heidegger on the line, he would have been calling from beyond the grave.

Derrida confronts the problem of being his sole witness, of proving that he actually got this call. He knows he "will be suspected of making it all up since it is too good to be true." "But what can I do?" Derrida continues, claiming, within a book in which he pointedly dares others to "prove it," that there are witnesses:

> It is true, rigorously, from start to finish, the date, the content, etc. Heidegger's name was already written after "Freud," in the letter that I am in the course of transcribing on the typewriter. This is true, and moreover demonstrable, if one wishes to take the time of inquiring: there are witnesses and a postal archive of the thing. I call upon these witnesses (these waystations between Heidegger and myself) to

make themselves known. All this must not lead you to believe that no telephonic communication links me to Heidegger's ghost, as no more than one other. On the contrary, the network of my hookups, you have the proof of it here, is on the burdensome side, and more than one switchboard is necessary in order to digest the overload.[26]

Derrida's account of witnesses clearly does not jive with the legal understanding of witnesses in large part because of uncertainty both about the proper name of the caller and about whether the caller is alive or dead. It's not clear whether he has received a call or a crank call. Did the American telephone operator mispronounce the name of the caller who was waiting on the other end of the line and presumably listening to the conversation between the operator and Derrida? Does the fact that Derrida was transcribing Heidegger's name matter? In Derrida's terms, the condition of anonymity is something like this order of collect call. It's spectral. You never know who's on the line, who's waiting for you, whether the call is serious or a crank. Even as we write, if you have caller ID on your telephone or cell phone, you may read the words "caller," "unknown caller," or "name withheld" when checking to see who is calling you. And what Derrida calls the archive authenticating the call, the impossibility of proving that he really is not making it all up, is always in need of management, the archive taking a medial form of posting, of written records of calls made and received. If the caller is a phantom referent, the phantom is also anonymous, only plausibly identifiable.

WEAK WITNESS

To our account of anonymity as telephonic, we wish to add that onymous authorship depends—without knowing it—on a weak notion of witnessing. The author's proper name, whether a handwritten signature or typewritten, always implicitly serves as a witness, as if the name were testifying to the fact that a person with a given proper name is without question the author of a given text. In *Demeure: Fiction and Testimony*, Derrida complicates an understanding of witnessing that opposes both live to recorded testimony and fiction to testimony. Derrida maintains that the law necessarily proceeds on the assumption that testimony is given by a witness who is a fully present living person. "For to testify," Derrida writes,

> the witness must be present at the stand himself, without technical interposition. In law, the testimonial tends, without being able to succeed in this altogether, to exclude all technical agency. One cannot send a cassette to testify in one's place. One must be present, raise one's hand, speak in the first person and in the present, and one must do this to testify to a present, to an indivisible moment, that is at a certain point to a moment assembled at the tip of an instantaneousness that must resist division. If that to which I testify is divisible, at that moment it is no longer reliable, it no longer has the value of truth, reliability, or verifiability that it claims absolutely. [27]

Even if Shakespeare could testify at a trial about his authorship, his word would be just that, his word, his side of the story. And since he cannot testify, there is no getting around detective fiction when examining his authorship or de Vere's now. All attempts to settle this particular score must somehow navigate the mess that is the authorship question.

WITLESS

How then should we process the mess that is *Anonymous*? It is tempting to offer it up as some order of cinematic *Trauerspiel* (mourning play). The film's doubly nested narrative frames, multiple flashbacks, and baroque mirrorings make who or what is being mourned impossible to identify. Accordingly, the film could be salvaged as an explicit ruination of allegory, an emptying out of the codes of authorship as they fund its anonymous morass.[28] The film itself makes mourning a maudlin affair. There is no mor/gu/e, no remainder even of a storage container. Nothing like stone is rolled back by de Vere's acolytes; there are no memorials, only images destined for successive audiences that film might be said, following Milton, to petrify. The soundtrack, derived from Chinese action films such as *Ashes of Time* (dir. Wong Kar Wai, 1994), *Crouching Tiger, Hidden Dragon* (dir. Ang Lee, 1994), *Hero* (dir. Yimous Zhang, 2004), and *The House of Flying Daggers* (dir. Yimous Zhang, 2004) turns *Anonymous* into an unconvincing male weepie.

In the second narrative frame, Jacobi makes it impossible to mourn de Vere because Jacobi does not name him. As the Prologue, Jacobi first provides an epilogue of sorts, telling us what happened to various characters in the film: "Robert Cecil remained the most powerful man in the Court of King James. And in 1623 [Jonson] wrote the dedication to the collected works of the man we call William Shakespeare." Shakespeare is named, and mention is made of him even though we saw him just minutes earlier watching King James watching *Henry V*. But "William Shakespeare" then becomes something other than a proper name. More surprisingly, even de Vere's name cannot be spoken; he is only the referent of "the man we call William Shakespeare." The Prologue gives something of a non-eulogy for Oxford, to whom Jacobi refers ambiguously as "our poet," in which he apparently alludes to lines from *Henry V*'s Saint Crispian's Day speech and John Milton's sonnet "On Shakespear," and that happens, as we saw earlier, to address Shakespeare's name: "And so . . . though our story is finished, our poet's is not. For his monument is ever-living, made not of stone, but of verse, and it shall be remembered . . . as long as words are made of breath and breath of life." But whose breath and whose life? Does Jacobi refer to the eventalizing fact of a performance, a performance albeit captured on film—the breath an effect of the soundtrack? The film remains hostage to the terms that Milton sets forth in the sonnet with which we began—if it was Milton, of course, for the sonnet appeared anonymously if not anony/messily. The film blocks any possible mourning of de Vere by rerouting lines supposed to be his through allusions to lines we recognize only because they are famously Shakespeare's. The authorship controversy becomes, if you like, an indistinguishable mess and Mass. No Shakespeare means no de Vere, as Shakespeare served, so it seems, as his wetware—wetware mistak-enly supposed to be the origin of the texts and, like it or not, their conduit, in our successive presents.

Beyond lines of dialogue that may or may not strike the ear strangely, Jacobi as Prologue serves as a ghost witness. According to the film's paratext Jacobi is playing a character called "the Prologue," but in the film seems to be playing himself as well, as if he were reciting lines from a script but also speaking them in his own name. Unlike all parties in the Shakespeare authorship debate who back one candidate or another by his or her proper name, Jacobi divides the presum-ably pseudonymous author de Vere from himself, as if de Vere's name could only be uttered as a pseudonym. If the Prologue witnesses Oxford's authorship, he doesn't really name names. Jacobi does not present the viewer with anything remotely like evidence, much less proof. And any witnessing Jacobi might be said to provide is compromised by the fact that he too is anonymous in the film; his witnessing would thus remain extradiegetic since his name appears only in the end credits. So Jacobi plays an anonymous witness, an unnamed "Prologue," even as you may or may not recognize him as the inimitable "Derek Jacobi" or, for that matter, as the Chorus in Kenneth Branagh's *Henry V* (Figure 5.1c and d). In another case of plus-sizing, Jacobi overwrites Jonson's two diegetic eulogies in the film, the first delivered to Oxford's wife after Oxford dies and the second delivered to Cecil in the immediately following scene just before Cecil releases Jonson from jail.

No archon of the de Vere archive then in *Anonymous*. No witnesses. Guards, yes, but Cecil's guards, committed to destroying the manuscripts. De Vere's archive may never be witnessed not only because it is never published but also because it cannot even be spoken aloud *as such*. You can wink; you can "know"; you can let your eyes and ears and mind wander as you're petrified by the "easie numbers" as they work upon you, but you remain a weak and, sometimes, witless witness.

Jacobi's and the film's last audible words run as follows, reprising both Jon-son's dedication to the First Folio and Milton's sonnet in the second: "So, though our story is finished, our poet's is not. For his monument is ever-living, made not of stone but of verse. And it shall be remembered as long as words are made of breath, and breath of life." Shakespeare's, by which the Prologue means de Vere's, lines live on only for as long as they are spoken. The conversion from words to breath to life ventures a media-specific, or more properly biologically specific, set of conditions for the continued efficacy of verse as monument. The future of the de Vere archive is therefore medium specific and yet has a lifespan that has nothing to do with the material supports of the archive or the lifespan of a text but the possible future extinction of the human species, or more precisely, the extinction of "life." No requirement is made that the mouths that speak the verse be human. Jacobi is thus a witness in a way that is quite different from Jonson; he does not survive the death of anyone, nor does he guarantee the preservation of the archive through publication. The survival of the de Vere crypt depends on the survival of a witness, but the witness can only survive in *Anonymous* as a revenant, an anarchivic force that recalls by crossing wires, that is already hung up on and hung up by the archive.

The closing shots of the audience clearing the theater replicate the same issue. The offish-Broadway theater audience shown exiting in the final shot of the film makes up the film's final instance linking anonymity to the absence of witnesses, assuming the viewer bothers to watch the credits roll to the end—as the film already models an uncertain petering out of a performance, a slightly muted audience nonreaction. Shot from behind the stage, Jacobi exits as "A Roland Emmerich film" appears, then the shot dissolves as the curtains close to a shot at the back of the theater orchestra seats, showing the audience quietly leaving the theater as the rest of the credits roll.[29] The audience, of course, just so many convenient extras, is never credited: it's the fate of wetware to remain strictly anonymous. To be sure, some audience members in the theater can be heard talking as they leave. But their voices are so soft that one cannot hear what they are saying. Murmur and rumor live, but as the noise or spectral response to the play we have not seen, remain unable to read, because in its place we have seen the film. Moreover, the end credits, the purpose of which is to align proper names to the actors and crew, may be read as sort of somber and ephemeral epitaph or roll call of the dead whom the viewer is presumably supposed to mourn. Rather like the folio as tomb that Milton's dedicatory poem posits, *Anonymous* is itself the unnamed crypt for Oxford, a partial, messed-up recruitment of readers become viewers. We may now understand better why *Anonymous* is both a title and a proper name in the film. De Vere can only be considered the true author of Shakespeare's works because those works may only be borne witness to as texts. They may never be proven to have been written by any author, by anyone at all.

The ideal viewer of *Anonymous* remains, apparently, the one who sees everything but who witnesses nothing. The archive remains emphatically complete but unreadable.

WEATHER REPORT

The mess that is *Anonymous* proves instructive, we think, but only if we are prepared to render it precisely as *Anony/mess* and so not to reduce the problems it generates or archives. As we move now to close this book and the paratextual forms of ending beckon (codas, epilogues, afterwords, bibliographies, the index, variously eschatological and moral philosophical modes of recommending that you and yours do this or don't do that), *Anony/mess* gives us pause. What's the worst thing you can do to Shakespeare? Well, there's always something worse than can be imagined, isn't there? But there's also always the comforting, consoling order that comes with return of the paratextual frame, the replacing of books on shelves, returning them to their respective niches, where they sit quietly. Ah, the quiet that comes with a bibliography.

When unreadability looms, writ large on silver screen, in the mind's eye, or by the announcement of a rival (Edward de Vere, Thomas Middleton, Francis Bacon, an infinite number of monkeys), it tends to manifest as a momentary rippling or tearing of bibliographies that quickly settles into a tidy reordering of books onto shelves. The books have new names inscribed on them (or do not) so as to enable the resurrection of different zoo/bio/bibliographies—Edward de Vere, Thomas Middleton, Francis Bacon, if not yet all those monkeys. How then ought the zoo/bio/bibliography to our book look? Should it be arranged by author and title (and species?) and so reinforce the *status quo* of canons and their ideological switchboards by which they re/produce whole worlds or should we leave you with something more "cloudy?"

Clouds (technical, literal, mushroom, etc.) remain keyed to the limits of our perceptual apparatus, to the relation between the visible and the invisible, the phenomenal and nonphenomenal, presenting as a crossroads or crux in our discourses. They demand to be read and yet always exceed the impressions with which they leave us and so remain unreadable. Accordingly, they assume a spectral quality, generating but also traumatizing our sense of futurity. Beyond those soft and billowy or threatening storm clouds that we name "weather" or take as an omen, the word *cloud* refers also, obviously now, to the vast technical relay and agglomeration of terrestrial resources projected as water vapor hanging in the air, liberating your memory and your archival anxieties from the massy weight of external memory devices. This terrestrial grounding seems somehow fitting, for the word *clod* (earth) cohabits with *cloud* in Old and Middle and Early Modern English—the earth just as massy and messy as those shapes that appear in the sky. While the iCloud (or any such device) offers you (some order of) data security and storage gently "pushing" information to all your myriad platforms, that "push" remains premised on a set of terrestrial relays and its wetware. We remain tied to the ground even as our data floats above and around and through us. Our data shall or may live on, but still we shall die.

How else, then, should we leave you than with this closing bio/bibliographical weather report of interpretive problems, cruxes, ellipses, specters, revenants, that we encourage you to expand, the weather "cloudy with a chance of Shakes/appearing"—for the text's "a/live"?

NOTES

CHAPTER 1

1. William Shakespeare, *The First Folio of Shakespeare: The Norton Facsimile*, eds. Charlton Hinman and Peter Blayney (New York: W. W. Norton and Co., 1996), A3r.

2. On survival as a surplus or living on, an "afterlife" lived by others as their lives (and deaths), see Walter Benjamin, "The Task of the Translator," in *The Selected Writings of Walter Benjamin*, vol. 1, ed. Michael W. Jennings, *1913–26* (Cambridge, MA: The Belknap Press of Harvard University Press, 1996), 253–63, and readings of this essay by Paul de Man, "'Conclusions': Walter Benjamin's 'The Task of the Translator,'" *The Resistance to Theory* (Minneapolis: University of Minnesota Press, 1986), 73–105, and by Jacques Derrida, "Des Tours de Babel," in *Psyche*, eds. Peggy Kamuf and Elizabeth Rottenberg (Stanford, CA: Stanford University Press, 2007), 195–225. See also, Jacques Derrida, *The Beast and the Sovereign*, vol. 1, trans. Geoffrey Bennington (Chicago: University of Chicago Press, 2009) and *The Beast and the Sovereign*, vol. 2, trans. Geoffrey Bennington (Chicago: University of Chicago Press, 2011). In the course of these seminars and in particular in the coreading of Daniel Defoe's *Robinson Crusoe* alongside Martin Heidegger's *The Fundamental Concepts of Metaphysics*, the structure of *survivance* comes to comprehend questions of archiving, the archive, and the book. See especially, Derrida, *The Beast and the Sovereign*, vol. 2, 119–46.

3. For a modeling of human users as "wetware" see Richard Doyle, *Wetwares: Experiments in Postvital Living* (Minneapolis: University of Minnesota Press, 2003). For a reading of Shakespeare's sonnets as rhetorical software for readers becomes biocultural "wetware," see Julian Yates, "More Life: Shakespeare's Sonnet Machines," in *ShakesQueer: A Queer Companion to the Works of Shakespeare*, ed. Madhavi Menon (Durham, NC: Duke University Press, 2011), 333–42.

4. For an allied argument that treats the relation of performance studies to theater history as a melancholy misrecognition of their fetish objects, see William N. West's "Replaying Early Modern Performances," in *New Directions in Renaissance Drama and Performance Studies*, ed. Sarah Werner (New York: Palgrave Macmillan, 2010), 30–49. Focusing on the figure of "replaying" as a neutral relation to anteriority, West asks his readers to consider "performance . . . less an event than the management of a rhythm of repetition—a practice of filling an ordinary gesture, word, or phrase with meaning through iteration, spacing, and change" (35).

5. The choice is never between having a "fetish" or not but between competing fetishes, some bad, some good, some too good to be true. See Peter Stallybrass, "Marx's Coat," in *Border Fetishisms: Material Objects in Unstable Spaces*, ed. Patricia Spyer (New York and London: Routledge, 1998), 184. As William Pietz argues, any accusation of "fetish" refers only to an irreconcilable difference between competing systems of value, "The Problem of the Fetish, 1" *Res* 9 (1985): 5–17.

6. For an energetic contribution that enlarges the scope of media specificity to include animal and vegetable remainders, see Joshua Calhoun, "The Word Made Flax: Cheap Bibles, Textual Corruption, and the Poetics of Paper," *PMLA* 126, no. 2 (March 2011): 327–44.

7. See William Sherman, *Used Books: Marking Readers in Renaissance England* (Philadelphia: University of Pennsylvania Press, 2007).

8. All references are to Randall McCleod, "Un 'Editing' Shakespeare," *Sub-Stance* 33, no. 4 (1982): 28–55. Subsequent references appear parenthetically in the text. Strangely McCleod's essay seems to have fallen out of circulation and tends not to appear in bibliographies where one might expect that it should.

9. Zachary Lesser and Peter Stallybrass, "The First Literary *Hamlet* and the Commonplacing of Professional Plays," *Shakespeare Quarterly* 59, no. 4 (Winter 2008): 371–420.

10. See Jacques Derrida, *Archive Fever: A Freudian Impression, trans. Eric Prenowitz* (Chicago: University of Chicago Press, 1996), especially his discussion of the hallucinated "recollection" of the impression as a "real" moment where pen hits paper, where foot touches ground to produce a print: "It is the condition for the uniqueness of the printer-printed, of the impression and the imprint, of the pressure and its trace in that unique *instant*, where they are not yet distinguished from one another" (99).

11. Lesser and Stallybrass, "The First Literary *Hamlet*," 373.

12. Catherine Gallagher and Stephen Greenblatt, *Practicing New Historicism* (Chicago: University of Chicago Press, 2000), 20–48. For a critical analysis of this chapter, see Richard Burt, *Medieval and Early Modern Film and Media* (New York: Palgrave, 2008; rev. 2010), 177–85; 237–47.

13. Michael Bristol, *Big-Time Shakespeare* (New York: Routledge, 1996).

14. Thomas Middleton, *Thomas Middleton: The Collected Works*, eds. Gary Taylor and John Lavagnino (Oxford: Clarendon Press, 2007); Gary Taylor and John Lavagnino, eds., *Thomas Middleton and Early Modern Textual Culture* (Oxford: Clarendon Press, 2007); Gary Taylor and Trish Thomas Henley, eds., *The Oxford Handbook of Thomas Middleton* (Oxford: Oxford University Press, 2012).

15. *Thomas Middleton: The Collected Works*: eds., Gary Taylor and John Lavagnino (Oxford: Clarendon Press, 2007), 25.

16. Ibid.

17. Taylor and Lavagnino, *Thomas Middleton and Early Modern Textual Culture*, 19.

18. Ibid.

19. Taylor and Henley, *The Oxford Handbook of Thomas Middleton*, 1.

20. For a sense of the stakes to choosing Middleton over Shakespeare as an orientation to the past, as it might alter our stories about questions of race, see Gary Taylor, *Buying Whiteness: Race, Culture, and Identity from Columbus to Hip-Hop* (New York: Palgrave, 2005).

21. Terry Eagleton, *Literary Theory: An Introduction*, 2nd ed. (Minneapolis: University of Minnesota Press, 1996), 9. Subsequent references appear parenthetically in the text.

22. Walter Benjamin, "On the Concept of History," in *The Selected Writings of Walter Benjamin* vol. 4, ed. Michael W. Jennings, *1938–40* (Cambridge, MA: The Belknap Press of Harvard University Press, 1996), 389–400.

23. Jacques Derrida, "No Apocalypse, Not Now," *Diacritics* 14, no. 2 (Summer 1984): 27.

24. Ibid., 28.

25. Ibid.

26. Jacques Derrida, *Paper Machine*, trans. Rachel Bowlby (Stanford, CA: Stanford University Press, 2005).

27. Karl Marx, *Grundrisse: The Foundations of Political Economy*, trans. Martin Nicolaus (London: Penguin Classics, 1993), 110–12. "The equation of the incompatible, as Shakespeare nicely defined money" (163) is how Marx invokes Apemantus's address to the gold in 4.3.381–92 of *Timon of Athens*.
28. Ibid., 110–11.
29. Ibid., 111.
30. Ibid.
31. "The Eighteenth Brumaire of Louis Bonaparte," in *The Marx and Engels Reader*, 2nd ed., ed. Robert C. Tucker (New York and London: W. W. Norton and Co, 1978), 595.
32. We allude here to Carl Schmitt's *Theory of the Partisan*, trans. G. L. Ulmen (New York: Telos, 2007), and Jacques Derrida's *The Politics of Friendship*, trans. George Collins (New York: Routledge, 1997).

CHAPTER 2

1. Subsequent references will be to William Shakespeare, *Hamlet*, eds. Ann Thompson and Neil Taylor (London: The Arden Shakespeare, 2006).
2. Subsequent references will be to Avital Ronell, *The Telephone Book: Technology, Schizophrenia, Electric Speech* (Lincoln: University of Nebraska Press, 1989), 2.
3. On *biblion* meaning "niche" and indexing the book to the library, see Jacques Derrida, *Paper Machine*, trans. Rachel Bowlby (Stanford, CA: Stanford University Press, 2005), 4–6.
4. Actors themselves, of course, may be described as "speaking properties." They serve as relays for the vocal and gesture effects we name "character." See Frances Teague, *Shakespeare's Speaking Properties* (Lewisburg: Bucknell University Press, 1991).
5. On the function of writing in the play, see especially, Jonathan Goldberg, "Hamlet's Hand" in *Shakespeare's Hand* (Minneapolis: University of Minnesota Press, 2003), 105–31; Peter Stallybrass, Roger Chartier, J. Franklin Mowery, and Heather Wolfe, "Hamlet's Tables and the Technologies of Writing in Renaissance England," *Shakespeare Quarterly* 55 (2004): 379–419; Robert Weimann, *Author's Pen and Actor's Voice: Playing and Writing in Shakespeare's Theatre* (Cambridge: Cambridge University Press, 2000); Margaret Ferguson, "*Hamlet*: Letters and Spirits," in *Shakespeare and the Question of Theory*, eds. Patricia Parker and Geoffrey Hartman (New York: Methuen, 1985): 292–309; Alan Stewart, *Shakespeare's Letters* (Oxford: Oxford University Press, 2009).
6. Tom Stoppard, *Rosencrantz and Guildenstern Are Dead* (London: The Grove Press, 1994).
7. Jonathan Goldberg, "Hamlet's Hand," 105–31.
8. In the "Epistle Dedicatory" to the book, Dover Wilson recounts, uncannily, his telephonic recruitment to the task of solving *Hamlet*'s cruxes. He reads W. W. Greg's "Hamlet's hallucination," which posits the ghost as hallucination and the dumb show as a moment that reveals Hamlet's true madness, murderous intentions, and mistaking of the manner of his father's murder. Dover Wilson's career unfolds in repsonse to what he perceives as Greg's attack on the linearity of the play, and he describes the way he parcels out the labor of canceling out Greg's reading first into the monumental editing of the text and then the strategic splicing of the text with its performance so as to disambiguate the action. See John Dover Wilson, *What Happens in Hamlet* (Cambridge: Cambridge University Press, 1967), 1–23, and W. W. Greg, "Hamlet's Hallucination," *Modern Language Review* 12, no. 4 (October 1917): 393–426.

9. Stephen Ratcliffe, *Reading the Unseen: (Offstage) Hamlet* (Denver, CO: Counterpath Press, 2009).

10. See Linda Charnes, *Hamlet's Heirs: Shakespeare and the Politics of the New Millennium* (New York: Routledge, 2006).

11. Stephen Greenblatt, *Hamlet in Purgatory* (Princeton, NJ: Princeton University Press, 2002).

12. Terrence Hawkes, *That Shakespearean Rag: Essays on Critical Process* (London and New York: Methuen, 1986), 107–9. Hawkes's essay sponsors a specular redescription of *Hamlet* spliced to a symptomatic reading of Dover Wilson's "Pauline" recruitment. Refusing to positivize his reversal of the play as the "real" *Hamlet*, Hawkes offers readers instead the play's doubleness or self- reversal as an insufficient product. It should be noted, however, that this self-reversing *jouissance* is funded by the absolute legibility of Dover Wilson's ideological position to Hawkes. In effect, the textual density to *Hamlet* is rendered tolerable by the immediate readability of Dover Wilson.

13. Marjorie Garber reads Dover Wilson's tussle with W. W. Greg as a form of "dull revenge," discerning in the compulsive repetition and circulation of roles—"we have fought backwards and forwards over almost every line of [the play scene] as violently as ever Hamlet and Laertes passed at foils"—a basis of reading "literary scholarship and textual editing . . . themselves [as] species of revenge." Marjorie Garber, "A Tale of Three *Hamlets* or Repetition and Revenge," *Shakespeare Quarterly* 61, no. 1 (2010): 44, and Dover Wilson, *What Happens in Hamlet*, 21.

14. See Scott A. Trudell's well-executed "The Mediation of Poesie: Ophelia's Orphic Song," *Shakespeare Quarterly* 63, no. 1 (Spring 2012): 46–76.

15. On ash as a figure of forgetfulness, of the archive as also an anarchiving loss, see Jacques Derrida, *Archive Fever: A Freudian Impression*, trans. Eric Prenowitz (Chicago: University of Chicago Press, 1996), 100–101.

16. Jacques Derrida, "Typewriter Ribbon: Limited Ink (2) (within Such Limits)," in *Material Events: Paul de Man and the Afterlife of Theory*, eds. Tom Cohen, Barbara Cohen, J. Hillis Miller, and Andrzej Warminski (Minneapolis: University of Minnesota Press, 2001), 333–34.

   While readers might expect us to cite Derrida's *Specters of Marx* here, given its treatment of the *Hamlet*, we route the play through Derrida's extended work on the figure of the archive. We go so far as to venture that *Specters of Marx* serves as a reduced treatment of the governing matrix of the play, one, perhaps, keyed to preserving the figure of a messianic futurity that in later Derridean texts receives a very different treatment by way of the figure of the archive and the afterlife. Key texts for us, among others, are *Archive Fever*, trans. Eric Prenowitz (Chicago: University of Chicago Press, 1996); the essays and lectures gathered together as *Paper Machine*, trans. Rachel Bowlby (Stanford, CA: Stanford University Press, 2005); and *The Beast and the Sovereign*, vols. 1 and 2, trans. Geoffrey Bennington (Chicago: University of Chicago Press, 2009 and 2010). We take Derrida's engagement with spectralization and temporality in *Specters of Marx* to constitute a case study of a larger argument in the making about cultural graphology. See *Specters of Marx: The State of the Debt, the Work of Mourning, and the New International*, trans. Peggy Kamuf (New York: Routledge, 2006).

17. Derrida, "Typewriter Ribbon," 334.

18. Accordingly, we remain fascinated by and admiring of the work of sociologist of science Bruno Latour and his modeling of what amounts to a translational poetics that would depathologize concepts of mediation and mimesis but we are cautious with regard to the interpretive certainty or even "archive fever" his model produces when itself translated to media and literary studies. A strategic difference between the likes of Latour and

those of us housed in the humanities resides in the way we find ourselves oriented to our objects of study. Tuned to things past—to the fragments of chains of making long severed, partially interrupted—and so to "actor networks," to use Latour's terms, that have dropped actants as they have added new ones, we are obliged to deal with the objects that result from these dropped connections. It is these texts or traces that we take as our points of departure. Our object remains always the archive of a practice, the remnants of some *thing*, which, by our joining, we re/activate. We must be alive then continuously to the ways the archive, itself an "actor-network" enables certain modes of joining and disables others, makes certain worlds or prospects un/thinkable. In our modeling of "Shakespeare" in this book, and of *Hamlet* in this chapter, we draw on Latour's rich work but seek to do so in a nonsalvific, noncelebratory mode that remains tuned to the stakes of deconstructive reading (and not reading). Convenient points of arrival for first-time readers of Latour might include Bruno Latour, "An Attempt at a Compositionist Manifesto," *New Literary History* 41, no. 3 (Summer 2010): 472–91; *On the Modern Cult of the Factish Gods* (Durham, NC: Duke University Press, 2010); and *Reassembling the Social: An Introduction to Actor-Network Theory* (Oxford: Oxford University Press, 2005). For an attempt to render Latour's relation to Derridean deconstruction by way of the correlation between recipes and play texts as archival objects, see Julian Yates, "Shakespeare's Kitchen Archives," in *Speculative Medievalisms: A Discography*, ed. The Petro-Punk Collective (Brooklyn, NY: Punctum Books, 2013), 179–200.

19. On the spectral qualities of Horatio and for the turn to Horatio as privileged locus of critical interest for critics today, see Christopher Warley, "Specters of Horatio," *English Literary History* 75, no. 4 (Winter 2008): 1023–50.

20. Our modeling *Hamlet* in relation to an infrastructure of *survivance* allies itself with many of the insights we find in Lee Edelman's reading of the play in two overlapping essays: "Hamlet's Wounded Name," in *ShakesQueer: A Queer Companion to the Complete Works of Shakespeare*, ed. Madhavi Menon (Durham, NC: Duke University Press, 2011), 97–105, which excerpts and augments from "Against Survival: Queerness in a Time That's Out of Joint," *Shakespeare Quarterly* 62, no. 2 (Summer 2011): 148–69.

Like Edelman, we read *Hamlet* as a structure that anarchives as it archives, that registers the structure of forgetting that obtains to any act of remembering, drawing on the same sense of the "anarchivic" and "anarchiviolithic" that he locates in Derrida's *Archive Fever* (See Derrida, *Archive Fever*, 11; Edelman, "Against Survival," 155). The question Edelman raises in the last line to his shortened essay and that we take up in this chapter replays Hamlet's "to be or not to be" soliloquy as asking "how [we may] resist survival's archive, its consignation, by becoming what lets the future be and by being what lets [hinders] the future" (Edelman, "Hamlet's Wounded Name," 105). We read the play as already resisting this infrastructure, narrating its effects, and rending itself into a fragmented multimedia archive and its ash.

While we admire Edelman's unfailing critique of what he calls "the secularized messianicity of reproductive futurism" (Edelman, "Hamlet's Wounded Name," 105) and are sympathetic to his unfailing pursuit of a negativity that would decouple the future from its scripting by a past, we think it worth pointing out that his subordination of Derridean deconstruction to a Lacanian account of the Symbolic order tends to present as a desire for "cancellation" in all-out apocalyptic mode (see especially the reading of *Archive Fever* presented in Edelman, "Against Survival"). In presenting the play as multimedia archive, we seek to resist the attempt to derive from what remains, as we think Edelman wishes to do, a stable moral philosophical script, canceling out the play in order to posit a "pedagogy [that could] renounce the sublimation inherent in acts of reading, taking seriously the status of teaching as an impossible profession and assault on meaning, understanding, and value" (Edelman, "Against Survival," 169).

Sympathetic as we are to Edelman's project, we think it is crucial to point out that here it produces a weak sovereignty over the play, leaving Hamlet behind, as it "lets" in the future constituted as a blank that Edelman begins to fill in. Such sovereignty is underwritten further by a reading that chooses Folio over Quarto in deciding on the text of the play, treating the text therefore as essentially stable. The key lines, in both essays, which capture the tenor of the paternal "screwing" to which Hamlet is subject, read as follows: "O God, Horatio, what a wounded name, / Things thus unknown, shall I live behind" (5.2.328–29). "Live behind" captures the temporality of a present hostage to a future that is already canceled out by the repetition of its past. But in Q1 the second line reads "shall I leave behind," which parses Hamlet's predicament slightly differently. We are not out to derail the political import of Edelman's position with textual quibbles (as if we could), but we do think that the textual wobble he avoids here suggests that stitching Derridean deconstruction to Lacanian psychoanalysis may prove counter- (which is to say, all too) productive, sedating the text in order to assert an ownership of "place" that deconstruction will not allow.

As Derrida speculates in *Archive Fever*, returning to the position he ventures in *Of Grammatology*, psychoanalysis would be very different had Freud had email rather than print as his metaphoric substrate. Under such circumstances, we wonder whether the future as such may be thought of outside of its metaphoric media, which leads us to provincialize psychoanalysis as a media-specific model tuned to the writing machines of one order of *survivance*. The challenge remains, we think, to read and write beyond and without and within still other terms. See Derrida, *Archive Fever*, 16–18; and also *Of Grammatology*, trans. Gayatri Chakravorty Spivak (Baltimore and London: Johns Hopkins University Press, 1974), 84–85, where psychoanalysis is offered as a study of the ways in which we are cathected to certain writing instruments. On "reproductive futurism," see also Lee Edelman, *No Future: Queer Theory and the Death Drive* (Durham, NC: Duke University Press, 2004).

21. On the rebranding / business model as a way of metaphorizing issues of sovereignty in the play, see Michael Almereyda's *Hamlet* (2000).

22. On the arbitrary quality of "sovereign violence" or law-making violence, see Walter Benjamin's "Critique of Violence" [1921] in *Walter Benjamin: Selected Writings*, vol. 1, eds. Marcus Bullock and Michael W. Jennings (Cambridge, MA: The Belknap Press of Harvard University Press, 1996), 236–52. See also key readings by Giorgio Agamben, placing Benjamin's essay in conversation with Nazi Jurist Carl Schmitt in *The State of Exception*, trans. Kevin Attell (Chicago: University of Chicago Press, 2003), and *Homo Sacer: Sovereign Power and Bare Life*, trans. Daniel Heller-Roazen (Stanford, CA: Stanford University Press, 1998). See also Jacques Derrida's reading of Benjamin in "Force of Law: The Mystical Foundation of Authority" in *Deconstruction and the Possibility of Justice*, eds. Drucilla Cornell, Michael Rosenfeld, and David Gray Carlson (New York: Routledge, 1992), 3–67. We take the play already to imagine what it means in Agamben's terms to live a "bare life," a becoming "wetware," mediator, or relay to an elaborated infrastructure / media platform that may continue to deploy your voice or body after your death. On the need to imagine such a relation and Agamben's inability to do so, see Derrida, *The Beast and the Sovereign*, vol. 1, 305–34.

23. It is worth recalling that here Ronell follows Jacques Derrida's staging of "the history of life . . . [or] differrance as the history of the *grammè*," which aims to make visible modes of cognition, historical consciousness, and forms of personhood that do not respect the ratio of the line or the linearization of the world that occurs in a phonetic writing system.

The story, as you remember, begins with the observation lethal to any metaphysics of presence that "life" begins with the writing event of "genetic inscription" and "short programmatic chains regulating the behavior of the amoeba or the annelid up to the passage beyond alphabetic writing to the orders of the *logos* and of a certain *homo sapiens.*" Frequently mistaken for something like a maximal entropy formalism with a linguistic bias, deconstruction instead takes as its object a "general" or "generative text," a generalized question of coding. See, Derrida, *Of Grammatology*, 84–85.

24. Ronell's citations are to a translation of the interview that appears as "Only a God Can Save Us Now: An Interview with Martin Heidegger," trans. David Schendler, *Graduate Faculty Philosophical Journal* 6, no. 1 (Winter 1977): 5–27. The original interview in German appeared as "Nür noch ein Gott kann uns retten," *Das Spiegel* (May 31, 1976): 193–219.

25. Jacques Derrida, *The Beast and the Sovereign*, vol. 2, 164.

26. On erasable wax tablets, writing tables, or "table books," see Stallybrass, Chartier, Mowery, and Wolfe, "Hamlet's Tables," 379–419. See also, Roger Chartier, *Inscription and Erasure: Literature and Written Culture from the Eleventh to the Eighteenth Century*, trans. Arthur Goldhammer (Philadelphia: University of Pennsylvania Press, 2007), 22–24.

27. Goldberg and Edelman are particularly astute readers of this scene. Building on Goldberg, Edelman writes, "Hamlet . . . becomes a sort of appendage to this living book, the material substrate of a survival that lives, in more than one sense, in his place. Goldberg evokes this perfectly when he notes that 'Hamlet voices his father's text.'" Edelman, "Hamlet's Wounded Name," 100, and Goldberg, *Shakespeare's Hand*, 45. We agree with this reading but feel no surprise or scandal at Hamlet's recruitment. Being is always hardwired and always technologized; "places" are always constituted parasitically, and no rights of ownership attach to them.

28. See John Dover Wilson, *What Happens in Hamlet*, 52–86, especially in reference to debunking Greg by offering a more perfectly historicized account of ghosts in the period.

29. Jacques Derrida, *Specters of Marx*, 61.

30. Trudell, "The Mediation of Poesie," 61–69.

31. See Harold Jenkins's illuminating appendix to the swearing in William Shakespeare, *Hamlet*, ed. Harold Jenkins (London: The Arden Shakespeare, 1982).

32. On Carl Schmitt's *Hamlet or Hecuba*, see the special issue of *Telos* dedicated to the text edited by Julia Reinhard Lupton, *Telos* 153 (Winter 2010), and also Julia Reinhard Lupton, *Thinking with Shakespeare* (Chicago: University of Chicago Press, 2011).

33. On time effects (past, present, future) as products of a media platform or "actor network," see Bruno Latour, *Aramis: Or the Love of Technology*, trans. Catherine Porter (Cambridge, MA.: Harvard University Press, 1993), 88–89.

34. Derrida, *Archive Fever*, 62–63. See also Maurice Blanchot and Jacques Derrida, *Demeure: Fiction and Testimony*, trans. Elizabeth Rottenberg (Stanford, CA: Stanford University Press, 2000), where Derrida writes, "A witness and a testimony must always be exemplary. They must first be singular, whence the necessity of the instant: I am the only one to have seen this unique thing, the only one to have heard or to have been put in the presence of this or that, at a determinate, indivisible instant" (40). The logical requirement of exemplarity installs the necessity of substitutability within the very irreplaceability of testimony. "The exemplarity of the 'instant,'" explains Derrida, "that which makes it an 'instance,' if you like, is that it is singular *and* universalizable . . . This is the testimonial condition" (41). It is easy, as Derrida notes, to assume that this *techne* refers to the uncertain agencies of "cameras, videos, typewriters, and computers," but "as soon as the sentence is repeatable, that is, from its origin, the instant it is pronounced and

becomes intelligible, thus idealizable, it is already instrumentizable, and thus affected by technology. And virtuality" (42).

35. On the arbitrariness of the decision to take the skull as Yorick's, see, Warley "Specters of Horatio," 1037–38.

36. On the logic of the freeze-frame, see Latour, *On the Modern Cult of the Factish Gods*, 99–123.

37. For an allied reading of the "digital subjectivity" that the play cultivates, see Lowell Gallagher, "*Mise en Abyme*, Narrative Subjectivity, and the Ethics of Mimesis in *Hamlet*: Gertrude Talks," *Genre*: 513–32.

38. Wilson and Greg both note the strangeness of the dumb show in their readings. See also Dieter Mehl, *The Elizabethan Dumb Show: The History of a Dramatic Convention* (London: Methuen, 1965).

39. In *A Politics of the Scene*, Paul Kottman appears to solve the problem of the relation between the dumb show and the *Murder of Gonzago* by privileging the "essential" aspect of "affirmative speech or action . . . for the experience of the theater." Crucially, for his reading, Claudius reacts to the play but not the dumb show because it repeats something that was mimed "with speech." It is that fact of speech that gets Claudius's attention—making the play, not the dumb show, effective. In grander, philosophical terms, following Hannah Arendt, for Kottman, what matters is the fact of speech, here and now, as we're on the scene, making the scene, inducting one another as witnesses to what is being said—even if we are never able to agree on what it was exactly that we heard. For him, such a colloquy defines the "politics of the scene" and remains a site of potentially productive political action, for he asserts the constitutive fact of speaking, of presence, of being "on the scene" as crucial to the "convoking" of a community. It's worth pointing out that, in this model, the argument holds only to the extent that we understand the attribute of speech to be a preverbal or *phatic* guarantee of the human. Such a position, we feel, appealing as it may be, stores up as many problems for itself as it solves, erasing the problem of "noise" or static, of *phone* merely and *logos*, as necessary exclusions to a scene of communication. See Paul Kottman, *A Politics of the Scene* (Stanford, CA: Stanford University Press, 2008), 1–26, 139–65. On the dumb show, see especially 163–65.

40. Greg's commentary remains extraordinarily fine. See Greg, "Hamlet's Hallucination," 393–421.

41. See especially Dover Wilson, *What Happens in Hamlet*, 144–63.

42. For a fine account of how the scene is supposed to go based on a reading of *Hamlet* as embarked on humanist-fueled understanding of theater as quasi-pedagogical reenactment, see William N. West, *Theaters and Encyclopedias in Early Modern Europe* (Cambridge: Cambridge University Press, 2002), 122–28.

43. Carl Schmitt, *Political Theology: Four Chapters on the Concept of Sovereignty*, trans. George Schwab (Chicago: University of Chicago Press, 1985), 85.

44. Here the play reworks what Alan Stewart calls "the oldest letter story in the book"—the story of Bellerophon dispatched with letters naming his death from the *Iliad*. For Stewart's insightful reading of the scene see Alan Stewart, *Shakespeare's Letters* (Oxford: Oxford University Press, 2008), 262, and 261–94 generally.

45. Margreta De Grazia's Hamlet *without Hamlet* stands for us as the superlative critical enactment of the drive *Hamlet 2* stages, exorcizing the "materiality" of the text from all spectrality, if not all spectral editing. On the "x without x" formulation de Grazia uses in her title, see Blanchot and Derrida, *Demeure*, 88–89. Other notable un*Hamlet*ings that supplement and so supplant would include John Updike's prequel *Gertrude and Claudius* (New York: Random House, 2001) and the film *Rosencrantz and Guildenstern Are Undead*, directed by Julian Marsh (2009).

46. The best reading of the film thus far, which attends very carefully to its gender and racial politics and topicality, is Courtney Lehmann's "'Brothers' before Others: The Once and Future Patriarchy in *Hamlet 2*," *Journal of Narrative Theory* 41, no. 3 (Fall 2011): 421–44.

47. *The Works of Thomas Nashe*, reprint, ed. Ronald B. McKerrow (Oxford: Basil Blackwell, 1958), vol. 2, 211. Subsequent references appear parenthetically in the text. Nashe's argument seems to transfer St. Augustine's reformulation of prostitution as sex or desire work in *De Ordine* II.iv to public theater. Understandably, Nashe's defense has received much critical attention. For reasons of space it is not possible to provide a list of all the relevant critical commentaries here. Especially notable however, in our view, is William N. West's discussion of Nashe's faith in humanist conceptions of theater as providing exempla in *Theaters and Encyclopedias in Early Modern Europe*, 117–19, and Paul Yachnin's pointed reading of Nashe contra Philip Stubbes so as to expose their shared sense of the power of theater to affect its audience. Yachnin will, of course, argue that this efficacy was judged to have been misplaced in the 1590s and beyond, hence his modeling of the later theater as "powerless" in *Stage-Wrights: Shakespeare, Jonson, Middleton, and the Making of Theatrical Value* (Philadelphia: University of Pennsylvania Press, 1997), 1–2.

48. John Michael Archer, *Citizen Shakespeare* (New York: Palgrave, 2005), 84.

49. On Shakespeare's "presentation fantasies" and the sonnets as an experiement in creating a "quasi-human" technology of preservation, see Aaron Kunin, "Shakespeare's Preservation Fantasies," *PMLA* 124, no. 1 (2009): 92–106, and for an allied treatment, see Julian Yates, "Shakespeare's Sonnet Machines," in *ShakesQueer: A Queer Companion to the Complete Works of Shakespeare*, ed. Madhavi Menon (Durham, NC: Duke University Press, 2011), 333–42.

50. Working through the secularization of theological forms of predication as they migrate into secular forms of governance, Jacques Lezra argues that the impossible, self-predicating "logic of sovereignty requires [an order of statements,] . . . what we may now call a past contingent: the capacity to make statements of fact or descriptions . . . into propositions susceptible to revision: because it could have happened otherwise, an act or a decision that I now take, or that the group I am part of now takes, can make it have happened otherwise," can revise and revive, in other words, different pasts in and by our present. "The tense form," he observes, "is impossible; the concept, unthinkable." And to embark on the "decoupling of sovereignty from the onto-theology its performance requires, is to invite madness, conflicting stories, the over- and underdetermination of cultural narratives, mere literature." Nashe's defense, we think, unfolds on this ground, albeit in winking mode, offering up theater as one point of enunciation from which what Lezra calls the "modern experience of terror" might issue. See Jacques Lezra, *Wild Materialism: The Ethic of Terror and the Modern Republic* (New York: Fordham University Press, 2010), 109.

51. Richard Doyle, *Wetwares: Experiments in Postvital Living* (Minneapolis: University of Minnesota Press, 2003), 86–87.

52. William Shakespeare, *Romeo and Juliet*, ed. René Weis (Arden Edition Third Series, 2012), 2.2.33–34. Subsequent references appear parenthetically in the text.

CHAPTER 3

1. Jacques Derrida, "Aphorism Countertime," in *Acts of Literature*, ed. Derek Attridge (New York: Routledge, 1992), 433.

2. *The Works of Thomas Nashe*, reprint, ed. Ronald B. McKerrow (Oxford: Basil Blackwell, 1958), vol. 2, 211–12.

3. On the word *mnemotechnical* as an attempt to insist on memory as an extrinsic technology, see Tom Cohen, *Ideology and Inscription: "Cultural Studies" after Benjamin, De Man, and Bakhtin* (Cambridge, UK: Cambridge University Press, 1998), 1–12.

4. William Shakespeare, *Romeo and Juliet*, ed. René Weis (London: Arden Edition Third Series, 2012), 4.3.15. Subsequent references appear parenthetically in the text.

5. Derrida, "Aphorism Countertime," 433.

6. Bruno Latour, *On the Cult of the Modern Factish Gods*, trans. Catherine Porter and Heather MacLean (Durham, NC: Duke University Press, 2010), 68. We take the figure of iconoclash to mark an end to the problem of "fidelity" as it haunts the engagingly maladapted field or counterfield of "Adaptation Studies." Space precludes an exhaustive survey, but key "events" that define this field of inquiry might include the following: Brian McFarlane, *Novel to Film: An Introduction to the Theory of Adaptation* (Oxford: Clarendon Press, 1996); Linda Hutcheon, *A Theory of Adaptation*, 2nd ed. (New York: Routledge, 2012); Thomas Leitch, "Twelve Fallacies in Contemporary Adaptation Theory," *Criticism* 45, no. 2 (2003): 149–71, and *Film Adaptation and Its Discontents: From Gone with the Wind to The Passion of the Christ* (Baltimore: Johns Hopkins University Press, 2007); as well as Simone Murray, *The Adaptation Industry: The Cultural Economy of Contemporary Literary Adaptation* (New York: Routledge, 2012) and "Phantom Adaptations: Eucalyptus, the Adaptation Industry and the Film That Never Was," *Adaptation* 1, no. 1 (2008): 5–23. For an examination of film adaptation in relation to textual editing, see "Hamlet's Hauntographology: Film Philology, Textual Faux-rensics, and Facsimiles," in *A Companion to Literature, Film, and Adaptation*, ed. Deborah Cartmell (Oxford: Blackwell, 2012), 216–40.

7. The term *iconoclash* stands as an image-specific version of what elsewhere Latour names the "factish," an entity that precedes "fact" and "fetish" and from which both derive by a violent act of contestation or breaking. Here Latour builds on a succession of models he has developed by which questions of reference may be weaned off high-temperature arguments about fidelity, distortion, tampering, and interference in favor of an understanding that mimesis remains forward-looking, proactive, and productive of effects that are not moored to an original. For a selection of Latour's examples of structures of reference maintained by a succession of altering mediators taken from the sciences, see *On the Modern Cult of the Factish Gods*, 93–94.

8. Ibid., 72.

9. Bruno Latour, *Aramis: Or the Love of Technology*, trans. Catherine Porter (Cambridge, MA: Harvard University Press, 1993), 119.

10. For Latour's earnest and yet whimsical rewriting of Moses's second commandment— "Thou shall not freeze-frame the graven image," see Latour, *On the Modern Cult of the Factish Gods*, 97, and for a fuller articulation, 99–123.

11. On the violence of decision as the cutting or the creation of an edge, see, in different registers, Michel Serres, *The Natural Contract*, trans., Elizabeth MacArthur and William Paulson (Ann Arbor: University of Michigan Press, 1995), 55, and Jacques Derrida, *The Gift of Death*, trans. David Wills (Chicago: University of Chicago Press, 1992), 53–82.

12. On the epistemic violence of revivals, see Timothy Murray, *Drama / Trauma: Specters of Race and Sexuality in Performance, Video, and Art* (London: Routledge, 1997), 6.

13. Derrida, "Aphorism Countertime," 417.

14. The phrase *equipment for dying* attempts to render the peculiar, reanimating, retro-projected force we find in Kenneth Burke's famous equipmental modeling of literature in "Literature and Equipment for Living," *The Philosophy of Literary Form*, 3rd ed.

(Berkeley: University of California Press, 1973), 293–304. By inclining the equipmental reading toward death and dying, we wish to foreground the way Derrida's model of *survivance* designates nothing phenomenal but instead constitutes "a groundless ground from which are detached, identified, and opposed what we think we can identify under the name of death or dying . . . like death properly so called as opposed to life properly so called." Jacques Derrida, *The Beast and the Sovereign*, vol. 2, eds. Michel Lisse, Marie-Louise Mallet, and Ginette Michaud, trans. Geoffrey Bennington (Chicago: University of Chicago Press, 2011), 131. Like W. B. Worthen, who offers a Burkean modeling of theater as "equipments for living," we are eager to consider "the potential *agency* of drama in the double scenes of page and stage," or for that matter as translated to any media platform, as "equipments for living," but we are cautious as to the way what we call the bio/bibliographical coproduction of lives, deaths, and media events may reroute the apparent efficacy of texts as they are variously performed. See W. B. Worthen, *Drama: Between Poetry and Performance* (Malden, MA: Wiley-Blackwell, 2010), 23. We are grateful to Julia Reinhard Lupton's characteristically perceptive reading for our thinking on this subject. See Julia Reinhard Lupton, "Response to Paul A. Kottman, 'Defying the Stars: Tragic Love as the Struggle for Freedom in *Romeo and Juliet*,'" *Shakespeare Quarterly* 63, no. 1 (Spring 2012): 39–45.

15. Compare the Prince's lines to Juliet's: "For he hath still been tried a holy man" (4.3.29).

16. Jonathan Goldberg, "Romeo and Juliet's Open Rs," in *Shakespeare's Hand* (Minneapolis: University of Minnesota Press, 2003), 272.

17. Dympna Callaghan, ed., "Introduction," in *Romeo and Juliet: Texts and Contexts* (New York: Bedford/St. Martin's Press, 2003), 1. Quoted in Paul A. Kottman, "Defying the Stars: Tragic Love as the Struggle for Freedom in *Romeo and Juliet*," *Shakespeare Quarterly* 63, no. 1 (Spring 2012): 1. For a signal and still inspiring reading of the play as unmooring desire from gender difference and relocating it as a play of substitutions, see Goldberg, "Romeo and Juliet's Open Rs"; on the endurance of the plot and the couple as transcoded into gay, lesbian, and queer registers see, Carla Freccero, "Romeo and Juliet Love Death," in *ShakesQueer: A Queer Companion to the Complete Works of Shakespeare*, ed. Madhavi Menon (Durham, NC: Duke University Press, 2011), 302–8. On the popularity of *Romeo* and *Juliet* for feline littermates in the elaborated world of human-nonhuman animal companion species, see, PetPlace.com, accessed November 9, 2012.

18. Kottman, "Defying the Stars," 1.

19. Derrida, *The Beast and the Sovereign*, vol. 2, 131.

20. Ibid.

21. For a fuller sorting of possible sources and analogues, see the introduction to *Romeo and Juliet*, 32–37.

22. Richard Gottehrer, Robert Feldman, and Jerry Goldstein, "My Boyfriend's Back," performed by the Angels, on *My Boyfriend's Back*, Collectibles, 1963; Dire Straits, "*Romeo and Juliet*," on *Money for Nothing*, Warner Bros., 1988; Lou Reed, "Romeo Had Juliette," on *New York*, Sire Records, 1989; Melissa Etheridge, "No Souvenirs," on *Brave and Crazy*, Island Records 1989; Mark Knopfler, "*Romeo and Juliet*," performed by the Indigo Girls, on *Rites of Passage*, Epic Records, 1992. For a passing yet still compelling treatment of some of these songs see, Freccero, "*Romeo and Juliet*," 304–6, and for her fuller reading of Melissa Etheridge's "No Souvenirs," see Freccero, *Queer / Early / Modern* (Durham, NC: Duke University Press, 2006), 26–28.

23. Catherine Duncan-Jones records this anecdote in *Ungentle Shakespeare*, 282–84, as does René Weis in *Romeo and Juliet*, 57.

24. Paul A. Kottman notes that "in contemporary Verona . . . one finds marble plaques fixed to the city walls . . . with inscriptions of lines, in English, from Shakespeare's play, along with the mythical balcony and tomb of Juliet, and even a street named after Shakespeare—all, in a city where Juliet's balcony receives a constant stream of pilgrims, presented apparently for visitors" and cites for confirmation his correspondence with the Verona Tourism Office. Paul A. Kottman, *A Politics of the Scene* (Stanford, CA: Stanford University Press, 2008), 166, 250.

25. "Ever Fallen in Love (with Someone You Shouldn't've)," written by Pete Shelley, performed by The Buzzcocks, on *Love Bites*, EMI, 1978.

26. Charles Dickens, *The Life and Times of Nicholas Nickleby*, 1838, ed. Paul Schlicke (Oxford: Oxford World's Classics, 2009).

27. See Goldberg, "Romeo and Juliet's Open Rs," and Kottman, "Defying the Stars," 36, 35–37. We take what Julia Reinhard Lupton describes as Kottman's "philosophical dramaturgy" to constitute at times a lyrical, moving reenactment, adaptation, or attempt to rezone the play that depends on a quasi-telephonic summoning of voices in the aid of deactivating the play's bio/bibliographical program. We think that such attempts, much as we admire them, need to factor the bibliographical or media specificity that accompanies the play's biopolitical quotient. See Lupton, "Response to Paul A. Kottman, 'Defying the Stars,'" 39–45.

28. On semiotic chronology, see Mieke Bal, *Lethal Love: Feminist Literary Readings of Biblical Love Stories* (Bloomington: Indiana University Press, 1987), 107–8.

29. "Time does not count," writes Bruno Latour, "time is what is counted. It is not an explanatory variable; it is a dependent variable that needs to be explained." Networks of actants emit varying time effects by the adding and dropping of actants. See Latour, *Aramis*, 88–89.

30. In Latour's terms, we might say that successive orders of media, by adding actants to a chain of mediators, render the previous term causal. By the same gesture newness is an effect of position within the chain of making. It is a precipitate or product and not an input. In different terms, we might say, following Latour's debts to the cybernetic-based models of Michel Serres, that media effects remain always parasitic on one another; they are already presupposed—as we suggested in our reading of *Hamlet* as a telephone book. See Michel Serres, *The Parasite*, trans. Lawrence R. Schehr (Minneapolis: University of Minnesota Press, 2007). For an allied account of the false teleology to media histories, see Lisa Gitelman, *Always Already New: Media, History, and the Data of Culture* (Cambridge, MA: MIT Press, 2008).

31. Derrida, "Aphorism Countertime," 416.

32. Though referring to the literary object, the points made translate to any medium. Derrida writes, "Framed, embedded, bordered, de-bordered, overrun, the smaller becomes metonymically, larger than the larger—that borders and frames it. Such a frame fixes the space and time given, that is, instituted by a convention, a convention which is, by convention, irremovable. But this structure is rather a movement that also overruns and de-borders the coded language of rhetoric, her of metonymy as identifiable figure. For the very identity of figures supposes stable relations between the part and the whole. This relative stabilization always appears possible, to be sure, and it allows for rhetoric and the discourse on rhetoric. But as no natural stability is ever given, as there is only *stabilization in process*, that is, essentially precarious, one must presuppose 'older' structures, let us not say originary structures, but more complicated and more unstable ones. We propose to call them structures, and even to study them as such in literary processes, because they are not necessarily chaotic. Their relative 'anteriority' or their greater complexity does not signify pure disorder," Jacques Derrida, *The Truth in Painting*, trans.

Geoffrey Bennington and Ian Mcleod (Chicago: University of Chicago Press, 1987), 94–95.

33. *Gnomeo and Juliet* (two-disc Blu-Ray/DVD Combo; Touchstone, 2011).

34. On the claim to "universality," see text for *Chacun son cinéma: Une déclaration d'amour au grand écran* (Studio Canal, 2007).

35. On the cin-off, see Richard Burt, "Sh k es e re Cin-Offs beyond Wreckognition: Film Philology, CiNOma, and Abbas Kiarostami's *Where Is My Romeo*," in *Shakespeare Spin-Offs*, ed. Amy Scott-Douglas (New York: Palgrave MacMillan, 2013). In the majority of cin-offs the authors have seen, the film in the film is shown diegetically on a screen that is a prop, in effect, on the set. It is a film within a film, a self-reflexive moment in which film reflects on its medium by framing it. However, there are almost as many cin-offs in which the film cuts to the film in it by showing it without a screen. All the shots in Jean-Luc Godard's *Vivre sa vie (Her Life to Live)* from Dreyer's *Passion of Joan of Arc* take up the entire screen; they are directly cut from Dreyer's film into Godard's film (See Figure 3.3). Godard does the same thing with the 35 mm rushes of Fritz Lang's *Odyssey* in *Contempt* (1963), and so does Alain Resnais with 8 mm rushes shown in *Muriel, or the Time of a Return* (1963). In films like Hitchcock's *Sabotage* (1936), David R. Ellis's *The Final Destination: 3D* (2009), and Quentin Tarantino's *Inglourious Basterds* (2009), the proscenium arch over the movie theater screen image appears in the cin-offs and, more important, the film in the film is shot from a space behind it.

36. On the cin-off as an archival effect tied to the "death" of cinema, see Burt, "Sh k es e re Cin-Offs beyond Wreckognition." For varying accounts of the "death" of celluloid cinema at the hands of digital cinema, see Garret Stewart, *Between Film and Screen: Modernism's Photo Synthesis* (Chicago: University Of Chicago Press, 2000); Philip Rosen, *Change Mummified: Cinema, Historicity, Theory* (Minneapolis: University of Minnesota Press, 2001); Lev Manovich, *The Language of New Media* (Cambridge, MA: MIT Press, 2002); D. N. Rodowick, *The Virtual Life of Film* (Cambridge, MA: Harvard University Press, 2007); Paolo Cherci Usai, *The Death of Cinema: History, Cultural Memory, and the Digital Dark Age* (London: British Film Institute, 2008); and Giovanna Fossati, *From Grain to Pixel: The Archival Life of Film in Transition* (Amsterdam: Amsterdam University Press 2010).

37. *L'Histoire(s) du cinéma* (dir. Jean-Luc Godard 1988–98). See also Jean Luc Godard, Youssef Ishaghpour, and John Howe, *Cinema: The Archaeology of Film and the Memory of a Century* (Amsterdam: Berg Publishers, 2005).

38. As Richard Brody writes, "the Prince's roar, at 1:51, of the line 'All are punished'— departing from Shakespeare's text by repeating the phrase—speaks clearly for Kiarostami: the injustices done to women are done to all. The female spectators' rapt terror at the spectacle reflects their personal implication in its subject, love rendered illicit." See Richard Brody, "Iran, Inside and Out," *The New Yorker*, August 14, 2009, http://www.newyorker.com/online/blogs/movies/2009/08/iran-inside-and-out.html, accessed November 12, 2012.

39. Richard Brody, "Abbas Kiarostami: The Power of Art, the Art of Power," *The New Yorker*, March 11, 2011, http://www.newyorker.com/online/blogs/movies/2011/03/abbas-kiarostami-the-power-of-art.html, accessed, November 12, 2012.

40. Kiarostami used the same device when making his next film, *Shirin* (2008). He added the soundtrack in postproduction.

41. Anselm Haverkamp, "The Error of Mourning," *Yale French Studies* 69 (1985): 246

42. On the book topos, see E. R. Curtius, "The Book as Symbol" in *European Literature and the Latin Middle Ages*, trans. Willard R. Trask (Princeton, NJ: Princeton University Press, 1953), 302–47.

43. On the uncertain ontology of sleep and, in particular, of drug-induced sleep as regards death and the difficulty of judging the difference between the two in the period, especially in reference to *Romeo and Juliet*, see Tanya Pollard, *Drugs and Theater in Early Modern England* (Oxford: Oxford University Press, 2005), 60–65.

44. Jacques Derrida, "Aphorism Countertime," 433.

45. Kottman offers a lyrical reading of the dual suicides as scenes of individuation in a deeply political sense in which both Romeo and Juliet decouple their lives from the human community (Verona) to which they (no longer) belong. Offering "mourning" as the superlative definition of a human community, Romeo and Juliet's "acknowledging the other's death" without "caring for the other's dead body" becomes a "happy" act of singularized coming into being by way of bearing witness to the other (33). "Each succeeds in seeing in the other's deceased body not the calm, cold repose of death—*rigor mortis* or the foul stench of decay—but an individual warmth and vitality of which each has intimate and singular knowledge" (35). See Kottman, "Defying the Stars," 31–36.

46. Jacques Derrida, *The Beast and the Sovereign*, vol. 2, 117.

47. The verb *to cope* condenses a series of possible modes of association ranging from the commercial to the martial, *Oxford English Dictionary* online, s. v. "cope," accessed October 23, 2012: http://www.oed.com/search?searchType=dictionary&q=cope&_search Btn=Search.

48. Kottman makes this point succinctly: "his plan would free Juliet by reconciling her to the Family, letting her be as 'dead to them' as she has always been." Kottman, "Defying the Stars," 31. We differ from Kottman in that where he remains trained on the biopolitical quotient to the two lovers, we see the yoking of the biopolitical to the bibliographical—the coarticulation of Romeo and Juliet and *Romeo and Juliet*. Indeed, it might be said that he is able to save the two, separately, only by forgetting the title, his essay a virtuoso outrunning of the logic of the proper name, a forgetting of the title's conjunctive *and*.

49. Derrida, *The Beast and the Sovereign*, vol. 2, 210–11.

50. On the wedding of the subject to the "will-have-been of future anteriority," see Lauren Berlant, "Slow Death (Sovereignty, Obesity, Lateral Agency)," *Critical Inquiry* 33, no. 4 (2007): 756. Such an ironic orientation to death as the insistence on a hyperpresent quality to an act recalls Lee Edelman's emptying out of reproductive futurity in *No Future: Queer Theory and the Death Drive* (Durham, NC: Duke University Press, 2004).

51. Jacques Derrida, "Paper or Me, You Know . . . (New Speculations on a Luxury of the Poor)" in *Paper Machine*, trans. Rachel Bowlby (Stanford, CA. Stanford University Press, 2005), 41–65.

52. On the conjoined phantasmatic structure and false choice that obtains between cremation and inhumation, see Derrida, *The Beast and the Sovereign*, vol. 2, 147–71.

53. William Shakespeare, *The Tempest*, eds. Virginia Mason Vaughan and Alden T. Vaughan (London: The Arden Shakespeare, Third Series, 2011), 1.1.1. Subsequent references appear parenthetically in the text.

CHAPTER 4

1. George Lamming, *The Pleasures of Exile* (Ann Arbor: The University of Michigan Press, 1992), 14–15.

2. Jacques Derrida, *The Beast and the Sovereign*, vol. 2, eds. Michel Lisse, Marie-Louise Mallet, and Ginette Michaud, trans. Geoffrey Bennington (Chicago: University of Chicago Press, 2011), 131.

3. William Shakespeare, *The Tempest*, eds. Virginia Mason Vaughan and Alden T. Vaughan, rev. Edition (London: The Arden Shakespeare, 2011), 3. 2. 135–44. Subsequent references appear parenthetically in the text.

4. Lamming, *The Pleasures of Exile*, 14–15.

5. Lamming's modeling of radio and the effect of its scheduling of programs anticipates Raymond Williams's discussion of the way broadcast technologies program (or used to program) our orientation to time and work in *Television*. Writing in 1973–74, in reference to a comparative modeling of British and American broadcast television, Williams names this phenomenon "the mobile concept of flow." Raymond Williams, *Television: Technology and Cultural Form*, 1974, ed. Ederyn Williams (London and New York: Routledge, 2003), 77. For a modeling of cultural forms as mediated always by the "rerun," see Derek Kompare, *Rerun Nation: How Repeats Invented American Television* (New York and London: Routledge, 2005).

6. *A Book at Bedtime* is the name of a long-running BBC show that aired on Radio 4. It has now migrated to various media platforms and may be accessed online at http://www .bbc.co.uk/programmes/b006qtlx.

7. Lamming, *The Pleasures of Exile*, 15. In a conversation with Anthony Bogues, between 2006 and 2009, Lamming explicitly rejected Retamar's position that Caliban is caught in something like a "prison house of language." Lamming says that "if you look at *Pleasures [of Exile]* again, there's not a closure with Caliban. Sometimes I think Roberto Retamar was wrong, there was not a closure with Caliban; the Caliban theme was left open." See "The Aesthetics of Decolonisation Conversation between Anthony Bogues and George Lamming," in *The George Lamming Reader: The Aesthetics of Decolonisation*, ed. Anthony Bogues (Kingston, Jamaica: Ian Randle Publishers, 2011), 231. For Retamar's response to the play, see Roberto Fernandéz Retamar, *Caliban and Other Essays*, trans. Edward Baker (Minneapolis: University of Minnesota Press, 1989).

8. Lamming, *The Pleasures of Exile*, 16.

9. Ibid., 15.

10. *Oxford English Dictionary*, accessed December 24, 2012.

11. We remain indebted here to Jonathan Goldberg's revisionist reading of the play and its afterlives in Jonathan Goldberg, *Tempest in the Caribbean* (Minneapolis: University of Minnesota Press, 2004). For his redaction of the pedagogical quotient to the play and his reading of Miranda's lines, see 117–47, 122–25 especially. For a precursor to Goldberg's efforts from the heyday of cultural materialism in the mid 1980s, see Malcolm Evans, *Signifying Nothing: Truth's True Contents in Shakespeare's Texts* (Brighton, UK: The Harvester Press, 1986). Evans casts his reading of Shakespeare as an explicit exercise in a counterpedagogy, and his reading of *The Tempest* trades on the possibly true, possibly fictional experiences of Edward Harrison, "who taught Shakespeare appreciation in Placencia, British Honduras, between 1929 and 1930" (13) as recorded in his diary. Harrison weaves references and an elliptical reading of the play as grand Hegelian plot into his diary, offering *The Tempest* as a still living text that reads differently given his location on an island. The diary, in effect, becomes a possibly fictional bibliographical intervention against the play. On the play as a colonial paradigm to be variously explored and sloughed off, see also Peter Hulme, *Colonial Encounters: Europe and the Native Caribbean, 1492–1797* (London: Methuen, 1986), and Rob Nixon, "Caribbean and African Appropriations of *The Tempest*," *Critical Inquiry* 13 (Spring 1987): 557–78.

12. Michel Foucault, *Society Must Be Defended*, trans. David Macey (New York: Picador, 2003), 255.

13. Jacques Derrida, "Paper or Me, You Know . . . (New Speculations on a Luxury of the Poor)" in *Paper Machine*, trans. Rachel Bowlby (Stanford, CA: Stanford University

Press, 2005), 41–65. And on the biological continuum as so marked, Derrida, *The Animal That Therefore I Am*, trans., David Wills (New York: Fordham University Press, 2008). For a crucial calling of the question on the connection between biopolitics and the "question of the animal," see Cary Wolfe, *Before the Law: Humans and Other Animals in a Biopolitical Frame* (Chicago: University of Chicago Press, 2012).

14. Frantz Fanon, *Black Skin, White Masks*, trans. Charles Lam Markmann (New York: Grove Weidenfeld, 1967), 21–22.

15. On tattooing see Juliet Fleming, *Graffiti and the Writing Arts of Early Modern England* (Philadelphia: University of Pennsylvania Press, 2001), 79–112.

16. Aimé Césaire, *Discourse on Colonialism*, trans. Joan Pinkham (New York: Monthly Review Press, 1972), 46, and *A Tempest*, trans. Richard Miller (New York: Theater Communication Group, 1992), 1.

17. Octave Mannoni, *Prospero and Caliban: The Psychology of Colonization* (Ann Arbor: University of Michigan Press, 1991).

18. Goldberg, *Tempest in the Caribbean*, 133, and also Césaire, *A Tempest*, 11–12.

19. See, for example, Goldberg's approach to the play through its examination by West Indian and feminist writers in "A Different Kind of Creature" (3–37) and "Miranda's Meanings" (117–47) and also the attention to textual cruxes in "Caliban's Woman," 41–114.

20. Césaire, *A Tempest*, 68.

21. Ibid.

22. On the disappearance of Miranda from the play and the accompanying misogyny, homophobia, and hetero-normative blind spots to Césaire's redactions, see Goldberg, *Tempest in the Caribbean*, 131–33.

23. Barbara A. Mowat argues that the book is a grimoire. See Mowat, "Prospero's Book," *Shakespeare Quarterly* 52, no. 1: 1–33. The essay's speculation proves intriguing and productive even as it is made without, it must be said, much by way of definitive evidence.

24. As Michael Taussig puts it, "cemeteries exist to ensure at least the appearance of a direct bond between name and body," Michael Taussig, *Walter Benjamin's Grave* (Chicago: University of Chicago Press, 2006), 25.

25. In his essay "Learning to Curse: Aspects of Linguistic Colonialism in the Sixteenth Century," Stephen Greenblatt attends specifically to *The Tempest* and to Caliban's key lines. See Stephen Greenblatt, *Learning to Curse: Essays on Early Modern Culture*, New Edition (New York: Routledge, 2007), 32–34.

26. Claude Duret, *Thresor de l'histoire des langues . . .* (Cologny, 1613), 935. Quoted in Greenblatt, *Learning to Curse*, 33.

27. On the efficacy of writing technologies as recognized by indigenous groups, see also the introduction to Stephen Greenblatt, *Marvelous Possessions: The Wonder of the New World* (Chicago: University of Chicago Press, 1991), 9–12 especially.

28. Mowat, "Prospero's Book," *Shakespeare Quarterly* 52, no. 1: 32.

29. James Kearney, *The Incarnate Text: Imagining the Book in Reformation England* (Philadelphia: University of Pennsylvania Press, 2009), 196. Kearney derives his model of the "talking book" from Henry Louis Gates's reading of slave narratives in *The Signifying Monkey: A Theory of Afro-American Literary Criticism* (Oxford: Oxford University Press, 1988) and uses the trope to very productive effect in his reading.

30. Claude Lévi-Strauss, *Tristes Tropiques*, trans. John and Doreen Weightman (New York: Atheneum, 1974), 299. Quoted in Kearney, *The Incarnate Text*, 211.

31. William Shakespeare, *Henry VI, Part 2*, ed. Roger Warren (Oxford: Oxford University Press, 2002), 4, 2, 71. Quoted in Kearney, *The Incarnate Text*, 202.

32. Kearney, *The Incarnate Text*, 222–23

33. The other key "ideological lure" in the play would be the allegation of rape made by Prospero and Miranda in act 1, scene 2. On the function of this charge and on Caliban's response see Goldberg, *Tempest in the Caribbean*, 20. Here Goldberg draws on Richard Halpern, "'The Picture of Nobody': White Cannibalism in *The Tempest*," in *The Production of Renaissance Culture*, eds. David Lee Miller, Sharon O'Dair, and Harold Weber (Ithaca, NY: Cornell University Press, 1994): 262–92.

34. Bruno Latour, *On the Modern Cult of the Factish Gods*, trans. Catherine Porter and Heather MacLean (Durham, NC: Duke University Press, 2010), 72. For our earlier adaptation and explication of the term see the previous chapter on *Romeo and Juliet*.

35. Latour, *On the Modern Cult of the Factish Gods*, 72.

36. For readings that suggest the presence of complicated enfoldings of differential literacy in moments of biblioclasm, see Roger Chartier's reading of *Henry VI, part 2*, "Jack Cade, the Skin of a Dead Lamb, and the Hatred for Writing," *Shakespeare Studies* 34, 78–87, and Steven Justice's reading of rebel biblioclasm as highly particularized attacks on certain types of legal documents during the Peasant's Revolt of 1381, *Writing and Rebellion: England in 1381* (Berkeley and Los Angeles: University of California Press, 1994), 13–60, and for "insurgent literacies," 41. For a totally different model of coevolving writing systems that argues for the coevolution of indigenous and colonialist forms, see Max Cohen, *The Networked Wilderness: Communicating in Early New England* (Minneapolis: University of Minnesota Press, 2009).

37. Jacques Derrida, *Of Grammatology*, trans. Gayatri Chakravorty Spivak (Baltimore: Johns Hopkins University Press, 1982), 85–87.

38. For a careful explication of Derrida's response to Lévi-Strauss as it opens up the way modes of assumed linearity are funded by the "pluri-dimensional" in early modern forms of writing (writ large), see Fleming, *Graffiti*, 115–18.

39. On the syncopation of Caliban's self-naming and the vocal soundscape of the play, see Bruce R. Smith, *The Acoustic World of Early Modern England: Attending to the O Factor* (Chicago: University of Chicago Press, 1999), 338.

40. In Roger Warren's Oxford edition, act 4, scene 2 of *Henry VI Part Two*, in which Jack Cade's companions enter into a comic lampooning of him, is rendered as a flat text. Warren walks readers through his decision not to reduce the potential for reading the Cade sequence as disruptive or even self-ironizing carnival, finding the marking of asides an unnecessary editorial intrusion. He cites a performance of the play in 2001 in which "the comments were overt, mocking statements, relished [and heard] by all" *Henry VI Part Two*, 52.

41. Anthony B. Dawson and Paul Yachnin, *The Culture of Playgoing in Shakespeare's England: A Collaborative Debate* (Cambridge, UK: Cambridge University Press), 157.

42. For Medea's lines, see *Ovid's Metamorphoses: The Arthur Golding Translation, 1567*, ed. John Frederick Nims (Philadelphia: Paul Dry Books, 2000), book 7, lines 265–84. For a reading of the play as keyed to Prospero's philosophical or metaphysical education, see Michael Witmore, *Shakespeare's Metaphysics* (London: Continuum, 2008), 90–126.

43. Roger Chartier, *Inscription and Erasure: Literature and Written Culture from the Eleventh to the Eighteenth Century*, trans. Arthur Goldhammer (Philadelphia: University of Pennsylvania Press, 2007), 63.

44. Mary Carruthers, *The Book of Memory: A Study of Memory in Medieval Culture*, 1990, 2nd ed. (Cambridge: Cambridge University Press, 2008), 211.

45. Jacques Derrida, "The Book to Come," *Paper Machine*, trans. Rachel Bowlby (Stanford, CA: Stanford University Press, 2005), 5–6.

46. Giorgio Agamben, *Homo Sacer: Sovereign Power and Bare Life*, trans. Daniel Heller-Roazen (Stanford, CA: Stanford University Press, 1995), 1–12, and throughout.

47. We read recent attempts to imagine alternate endings or alternate polities emerging from the play as allied to this project, even if we see them also as limited or disallowed by the play's move to closure. See, for example, Julia Reinhard Lupton's reading of Caliban's emergent "majority" in Julia Reinhard Lupton, *Thinking with Shakespeare: Essays on Politics and Life* (Chicago: University of Chicago Press, 2011), 187–218.

48. On the play's orchestration by an opening of the question of the universal and the particular in terms of categories of being and "creatureliness," see Julia Reinhard Lupton, "Creature Caliban," *Shakespeare Quarterly* 51, no. 1 (Spring 2000): 1–23.

49. William Shakespeare, *The Tempest*, 127–28.

50. On the availability of the intralingual pun in Shakespeare's sonnets see *Shakespeare's Sonnets*, ed. Stephen Booth (New Haven, CT: Yale University Press, 1977), xi–xii. And for a reading of this inverted genealogy of father and son in "Sonnet 16," see Julian Yates, "More Life: Shakespeare's Sonnet Machines," in *ShakesQueer: A Queer Companion to the Complete Works of Shakespeare*, ed. Madhavi Menon (Durham, NC: Duke University Press, 2011), 323–42.

51. W. H. Auden, *The Dyer's Hand and Other Essays* (New York: Vintage Books, 1990).

52. Foucault, *Society Must Be Defended*, 241. On the state of exception, see Giorgio Agamben, *The State of Exception*, trans. Kevin Attell (Chicago: University of Chicago Press, 2005) and *Homo Sacer*.

53. Foucault, *Society Must Be Defended*, 246–47.

54. The phrase "making up people" comes from Ian Hacking, "Making Up People," in *Reconstructing Individualism: Autonomy, Individuality, and the Self in Western Thought*, eds. Thomas C. Heller, Morton Sosna, and David E. Wellbery (Stanford, CA: Stanford University Press, 1986), 222–36. For an impressive exploration of population modeling in early modern England see David Glimp, *Increase and Multiply: Governing Cultural Reproduction in Early Modern England* (Minneapolis: University of Minnesota Press, 2003).

55. On fathoms and sea terms see, Steve Mentz, *At the Bottom of Shakespeare's Ocean* (London: Continuum, 2009), 8.

56. The word *sound* quite obviously condenses the sonic and the aquatic, *Oxford English Dictionary*, accessed December 29, 2012.

57. Haig Bosmajian, *Burning Books* (Jefferson, NC: McFarland, 2006), 31. Quoted in Bruce R. Smith, "Dot Dot or Dash: A Strange SOS from Prospero's Island" in *Shakespeare without Boundaries: Essays in Honor of Dieter Mehl*, eds. Christa Jansohn, Lena Cowen Orlin, and Stanley Wells (Newark: University of Delaware Press, 2011), 148.

58. Dawson and Yachnin, *The Culture of Playgoing in Shakespeare's England*, 158.

59. *The Golden Legend or Lives of the Saints*, compiled by Jacobus de Voragine, Archbishop of Genoa, 1275, trans. William Caxton, 1483, vol. 4, ed. F. S. Ellis (Temple Classics, 931): 47–49. We are grateful to Katelyn Nicole Mesler for generously bringing this possible source for the book drowning to our attention and also for sharing the section of her dissertation on the Saint James episode. See Katelyn Nicole Mesler, "Legends of Jewish Sorcery: Reputations and Representations in Late Antiquity and Medieval Europe" (PhD diss., Northwestern University, 2012), 230–33. Bruce R. Smith mentions the legend of Saint James in passing in his "Dot Dot or Dash," 147.

60. As Mesler notes in several earlier versions of the legend, Hermogenes is also forced to dispose of various idols "(*idolum; idole*) from which he received prognostications (*divinationes; oracles*)," which in *The Golden Legend* seem to have been absorbed into his books. Mesler, "Legends of Jewish Sorcery," 232.

61. Fleming, *Graffiti*, 74. See also Sigmund Freud, *The Standard Edition of the Complete Works of Sigmund Freud*, trans. James Strachey (London: 1953–73), vol. 29.

62. Fleming, *Graffiti*, 76.

63. Ibid., 78.

64. As Barbara A. Mowat observes, Prospero's invocation of "elves" and "demi-puppets" (5.1.33–54) preserves the challenging vocabulary of Ovid's *Metamorphoses*, whereas Ben Jonson softens the language considerably in his use of the same moment in *The Masque of Queenes* (1609). See Ben Jonson, *The Masque of Queenes, Celebrated from the House of Fame . . . at Whitehall* (London 1609), sigs. C2v–C3r, and Mowat, "Prospero's Book," 29.

65. *Nicholas Hilliard's the Art of Limning*, eds. Arthur Kinney and Linda Bradley Salamon (Boston: Northeastern University Press, 1983), 34. Limning, miniature making, or painting from the life was an intense process and used a highly evolved palette in addition to purpose-made parchment cards about the same size as a playing card.

66. Ibid., 37.

67. In the last paragraph of the postscript to *Archive Fever*, Derrida writes, "We will always wonder what, in this *mal d'archive*, he [Freud] may have burned. We will always wonder, sharing with compassion in this archive fever, what have burned of his secret passions, of his correspondence, or of his 'life.' Burned without limit, without remains, and without knowledge. With no possible response, be it spectral or not, short of or beyond suppression, on the other edge of repression, originary or secondary, without a name, without the least symptom, and without even an ash," Jacques Derrida, *Archive Fever: A Freudian Impression*, trans. Eric Prenowitz (Chicago: University of Chicago Press, 1998), 101. On "ash" as a figure of archival loss, ibid., 100.

68. Ibid., 7.

69. Lamming, *The Pleasures of Exile*, 15.

70. Derek Jarman, *Chroma: A Book of Colour* (Woodstock, NY: The Overlook Press, 1994), 75.

71. Peter Greenaway, *Prospero's Books: A Film of William Shakespeare's The Tempest* (New York: Four Walls Eight Windows, 1991), 17.

72. Poul Anderson, *A Midsummer Tempest* (New York: A Tor Book, 1974), 96.

73. *Vox Piscis: or, The Book Fish Contayning Three Treatises Which Were Found in the Belly of a Cod-Fish in Cambridge Market on Midsummer Eve Last, Anno Domini 1626* (London, 1627), 8. Subsequent references appear parenthetically in the text.

74. Alexandra Walsham, "*Vox Piscis*: Or The Book-Fish: Providence and the Uses of the Reformation Past in Caroline Cambridge," *The English Historical Review* 114, no. 457 (1999): 605, 574–606. Walsham's meticulous reconstruction of the commentary the appearance of the unlikely cod generated paints a portrait of Cambridge at the time, reading the resulting treatise as a political instrumentalization of either the true or fraudulent appearance of the fish. The veracity of the book fish remains beside the point. We are grateful to Steve Mentz both for his wonderful blog, "The Book-Fish," and for directing us to Walsham's essay.

75. On "accident," see Michael Witmore, *Culture of Accidents: Unexpected Knowledge in Early Modern England* (Stanford, CA: Stanford University Press, 2001); on "wonder," see Lorraine J. Daston and Katharine Park, *Wonders and the Order of Nature: 1150–1750* (New York: The MIT Press, 2001).

76. The book titled *Prospero's Books* we take to be an archive of the film that is also a memorial, filled with leftovers that now might be DVD or Blu-ray extras, including the shooting script (what was planned to be shot, not the screenplay), the record of what was shot, as well as an index of Prospero's 25 books with brief descriptions of each preceding the shooting script. If it had been possible for the film to have initially been released on DVD, the book might have been reproduced in the form of extras, including the

shooting script, photos from the sets, Greenaway's sketches, an index of all 25 of Prospero's books, and an account of the Paintbox used to make the books in the film. In other words, the book would have become a DVD paratext.

77. Greenaway, *Prospero's Books*, 164

78. The film follows the shooting script: "The books land together on the water and Caliban surfaces—spurting and spouting water from a long underwater swim—he snatches both books and disappears again under the surface. The water is calm . . . as though it had never been a witness to the destruction of so many books." Greenaway, *Prospero's Books*, 162.

79. Julie Taymor, *The Tempest, Adapted from the Play by William Shakespeare* (New York: Abrams, 2010).

80. Ibid., 21.

81. The end after the end goes back as far as Nicolas Roeg's *Walkabout* (1971) and was an experimental film effect at that time. A deleted scene inexplicably occurs in *Deliver Us from Eva* (dir. Gary Hardwick 2003), a spin-off of *A Taming of the Shrew*, after the end credits.

82. On the play's affiliation with the key trope of philosophical inquiry, that of the disinterested spectator observing a shipwreck, see Hans Blumenberg, *Shipwreck with Spectator: Paradigm for a Metaphor of Existence*, trans. Steven Rendall (Cambridge, MA: MIT Press, 1997), and Mentz, *At the Bottom of Shakespeare's Ocean*, 21. For the key passage in Lucretius designating the trope of gazing out to sea, see *De Rerum Natura*, trans. W. H. D. Rouse, rev. Martin F. Smith (Cambridge, MA: Harvard University Press, 1992), book 2, 1–2.

CHAPTER 5

1. John Law, *After Method: Mess in Social Science Research* (London and New York: Routledge, 2004), 2.

2. Douglas Adams, *The Ultimate Hitchhiker's Guide to the Galaxy* (New York: Ballantine Books, 2002), 59. We should like to thank Noah Yates for insisting that we use this epigraph.

3. The recent Arden edition attributes the play to Shakespeare; William Shakespeare, *Double Falsehood*, ed. Brean Hammond (London: Arden Shakespeare Third Series, 2010).

4. *The First Folio of Shakespeare: The Norton Facsimile*, eds. Charlton Hinman and Peter Blayney (New York: W. W. Norton and Co., 1996), A4r. On archon as witness and necessary to the formation of an archive, see Jacques Derrida, *Archive Fever: A Freudian Impression*, trans. Eric Prenowitz (Chicago: University of Chicago Press, 1998), 2.

5. William Shakespeare, Second Folio (London, 1632). Reprinted in most editions of the complete works of the play. See, for example, *The Riverside Shakespeare* (New York: Houghton Mifflin Company, 1974), 1845.

6. Bruno Latour, *On the Modern Cult of the Factish Gods*, trans., Catherine Porter and Heather MacLean (Durham, NC: Duke University Press, 2010), 72.

7. On the literary history and etymology of *anonymous*, see Anne Ferry, "*Anonymity*: The Literary History of a Word," *New Literary History* 33, no. 2 (Spring 2002): 193–94. See also such studies as Marcy L. North, *The Anonymous Renaissance: Cultures of Discretion in Tudor-Stuart England* (Chicago: University of Chicago Press, 2003), and John Mullan, *Anonymity: A Secret History of English Literature* (Princeton, NJ: Princeton University Press, 2008). On the use of "Anon." as an intervention in the archive, see, of course, Virginia Woolf's famous "Anon who wrote so many poems without signing them, was

often a woman," Virginia Woolf, *A Room of One's Own*, 1929 (San Diego: Harvest Book Company, 1981), 49.

8. "If nothing else, it's the best Elizabethan conspiracy-theory action flick you'll see this fall," a *New Yorker* blogger writes Michael Schulman, "Shakespearean Actors on the Oxfordian Stage," http://www.newyorker.com/online/blogs/culture/2011/10/shakespearean-actors-on-the-oxfordian-theory.html#ixzz208Ey8qNZ, accessed January 11, 2013. Similarly, the *Washington Post* ran a review by Ron Charles titled "*Anonymous* and the Shakespeare Conspiracy Theory That Wouldn't Die," http://www.washington post.com/lifestyle/style/essay-anonymous-and-th...conspiracy-theory-that-wouldnt -die/2011/10/25/gIQAebibPM_story.html, accessed January 11, 2013. See also Dana Stevens, "*Anonymous*: The Problem with This Shakespeare-Conspiracy Movie Is That It Wasn't Dumb Enough," *Slate*, Thursday, October 27, 2011, http://www.slate.com/articles/arts/movies/2011/10/anonymous_reviewed_roland_emmerich_s_shakespeare _conspiracy_ movi.html, accessed January 11, 2013.

9. Jonathan Bond, *The De Vere Code* (Canterbury: Real Press, 2009); Virginia M. Fellows, *The Shakespeare Code* (Bloomington, IN: The 1st Press, 2001) Graham Phillips, *The Shakespeare Conspiracy* (London: Century Books, 1994). There are, obviously, a vast number more titles in this burgeoning genre.

10. *The Shakespeare Conspiracy* (TMW Media Group, 2008).

11. The closest *Anonymous* comes to coding authorship is through repeated shots of two quills arranged in a shape resembling the letter *V* in the foreground or Jonson's hand resting on *Henry V* title with a burn mark that looks initially like the letter *Y* until Jonson puts his hand on the page, making the letter into *V* (which, incidentally, matches the roman numeral V, which on the page is spelled out as "fifth"). Of course, the *V* shape may be a cryptogram. It might mean, assuming it means anything at all, that de Vere was the leader of a group of Renaissance playwrights whose code name is modeled on the computer-hacking group Anonymous that formed in 2003 or perhaps the *V* is an homage to the Guy Fawkes–inspired film *V is for Vendetta* (Warner Bros, 2005)? In any case, we do not get anything in *Anonymous* like "deVere-onica," as it were, a "vere" (true) icon of Oxford's face or even an image of his writings impressed on a shroud after his death. On Saint Veronica, see John P. Leavey and Georges Didi-Huberman, *Confronting Images: Questioning the Ends of a Certain History* (University Park, PA: Pennsylvania State University Press, 2005), 188–99.

12. *2012* is about the building of a postapocalyptic Noah's "Arkive"; a central plot of *The Day after Tomorrow* takes place in the New York Public Library, showing survivors burning books to keep warm; *Stargate* imagines an archive in the form of cave paintings; and *10,000 B.C.* includes a lost, highly developed ancient city. Rather than view Emmerich as an auteur and *Anonymous* his signature film, however, we want to emphasize the singular continuities and discontinuities in Emmerich's productions of films before *Anonymous* and in making *Anonymous*.

13. James Shapiro, *Contested Will: Who Wrote Shakespeare?* (New York: Simon and Schuster, 2010), 4.

14. *Archive Fever: A Freudian Impression*, trans. Eric Prenowitz (Chicago: University of Chicago Press, 1998), 7. For a Derrida-friendly positive legal history of the archive, see Cornelia Vismann, *Files: Law and Media Technology*, trans. Geoffrey Winthrop-Young (Stanford, CA: Stanford University Press, 2008). For a history organized by the printing apparatus, Ann Blair, *Too Much to Know: Managing Scholarly Information before the Modern Age* (New Haven, CT: Yale University Press, 2010). On the archive and data storage, see also Julian Yates, "The Brief Case of Benjamin Walter / Benjamin Walter's

Briefcase: An Invent/Story," *Rhizomes* 20 (Summer 2010), http://www.rhizomes.net/issue20/yates/index.html; "Thomas Middleton's Shelf Life," in *The Middleton Handbook*, eds. Gary Taylor and Trish Henley (Oxford: Oxford University Press, 2012), 16–31; and Richard Burt, "Read after Burning: Delivering Derrida's *Post . . .* Posthumously (with Love, without Such Limits)," *Glossator* (forthcoming); Richard Burt, "Shelf-Life: Biopolitics, the New Media Archive, and 'Paperless' Persons," in *New Formations* 77 (May 2013); Richard Burt, "Putting Your Papers in Order: The Matter of Kierkegaard's Writing Desk, Goethe's Files, and Derrida's Paper Machine, or the Philology and Philosophy of Publishing After Death," *Rhizomes* 20 (Summer 2010), http://www.rhizomes.net/issue20/burt/index.html; and Richard Burt, "Duly Noted or Off the Record? Sovereignty and the Secrecy of the Law in Cinema," in *Secrets of the Law*, ed. Martha Umphrey, Lawrence Douglas, and Austin Sarat (Stanford, CA: Stanford University Press, 2012), 211–56.

15. Sigmund Freud, *Beyond the Pleasure Principle*, in Sigmund Freud, *The Standard Edition of the Complete Works of Sigmund Freud*, trans. James Strachey (London: 1953–73), vol. 18.

16. Anti-Stratfordians regularly play with puns in Shakespeare's name when it is separated into two.

17. A manicule is a small drawing of a hand with an index finger pointing to a portion of text in a book or manuscript. For a brief history of the manicule, see William Sherman, *Used Books* (Philadelphia: University of Pennsylvania Press, 2009), 25-52.

18. The title *Anonymous* runs across the top of the DVD and Blu-ray covers, with the tagline "Truth is the greatest tragedy of all" written in a smaller font size at the bottom; the book, like the poster, puts *Anonymous* across the bottom and adds "William Shakespeare Revealed" in a significantly smaller font size.

19. Gerard Genette, *Paratexts: Thresholds of Interpretation*, trans. Jane E. Levin (Cambridge, UK: Cambridge University Press, 1997); on cinematic paratexts, see also Richard Burt, *Medieval and Early Modern Film and Media*, 2nd ed. (New York: Palgrave Macmillan, 2010).

20. The flashback conventions are quite flexible and may sometimes be broken for a clear purpose. *Citizen Kane* (dir. Orson Welles, 1941) uses a reporter to anchor the flashback of various characters he interviews. In most of *That Obscure Object of Desire* (dir. Luis Bunel, 1977), the main character tells his story episodically in a train coach. *The Edge of the World* (dir. Michael Powell, 1937) ends abruptly with a character's death and does not return to the opening flashback. *Missing* (dir. Costa-Gavras, 1982) also inventively follows the father of a missing child around and cuts to flashbacks.

21. On the conspiracy film genre, see Richard Burt, "Duly Noted or Off the Record? Sovereignty and the Secrecy of the Law in Cinema," in *Secrets of the Law*, ed., Martha Humphrey, Lawrence Douglas, and Austin Sarat (Stanford, CA: Stanford University Press, 2012), 211–56.

22. Kate E. Tunstall, "'You're Either Anonymous or You're Not!': Variations on Anonymity in Modern and Early Modern Culture," *Modern Language Notes* 126 (2011): 671–88.

23. Jacques Derrida, *The Post Card: From Socrates and Beyond*, trans. Alan Bass (Chicago: University of Chicago Press, 1987).

24. Ibid., 31, 21.

25. Ibid., 21.

26. Ibid. Elsewhere, in the body of the "Envois" of The Post Card, "Derrida" twice worries that readers will think he is making his story up, ibid., 63, 217; Derrida also twice demands that someone else "*prove it* / '*prove it*," ibid., 235, 518.

27. Maurice Blanchot and Jacques Derrida, *The Instant of My Death / Demeure: Fiction and Testimony*, trans. Elizabeth Rottenberg (Stanford, CA: Stanford University Press, 2000), 32–33; Jacques Derrida and Bernard Stiegler, *Echographies of Television: Film Interviews* (New York: Polity, 2002), 113–32.

28. Walter Benjamin, *The Origin of the German Tragic Drama*, trans. John Osborne (London: Verso, 1977).

29. Compare the messy dissolve to the last shot of *Anonymous*, in which the candles behind the stage curtains appear suddenly to be in front of the curtains, to the much more neatly edited ending of Roland Emmerich's *Stargate* (1994). After the last shot, the film cuts to black, and the words *The End* in a very large font size appear; in the next shot, cued by a change in music, the credits roll in white type over a black background.

INDEX

Printed in the United States of America